Megastructure

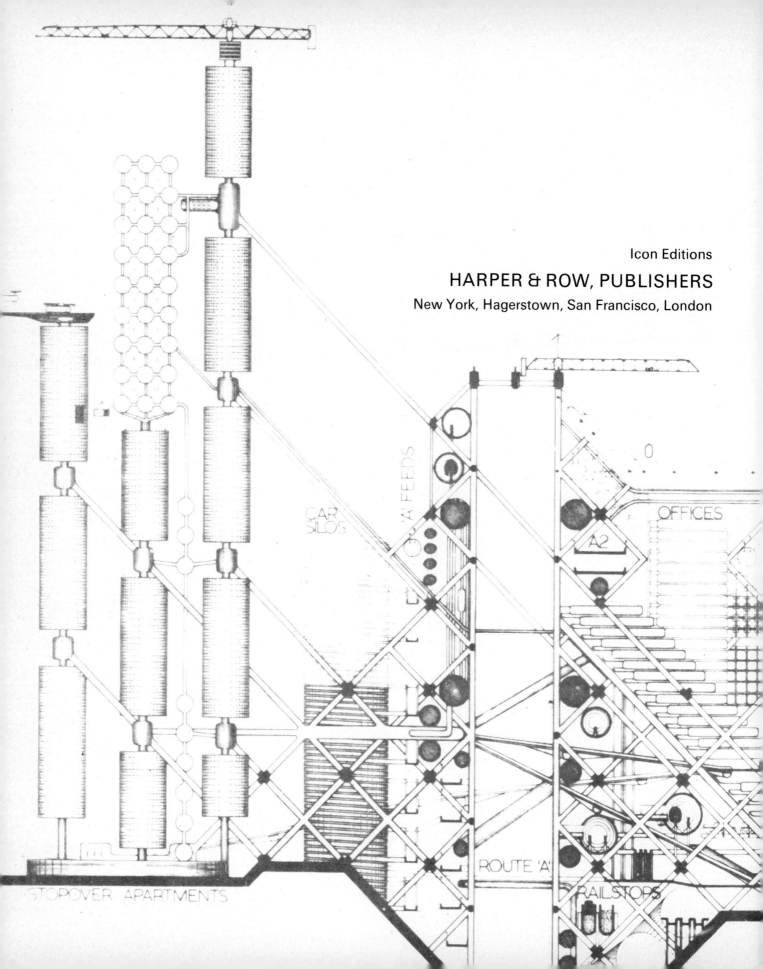

Icon Editions

HARPER & ROW, PUBLISHERS

New York, Hagerstown, San Francisco, London

STOPOVER APARTMENTS

CAR SILOS

'A' FEEDS

A2

OFFICES

ROUTE 'A'

RAILSTOPS

REYNER BANHAM

Megastructure

URBAN FUTURES OF THE RECENT PAST

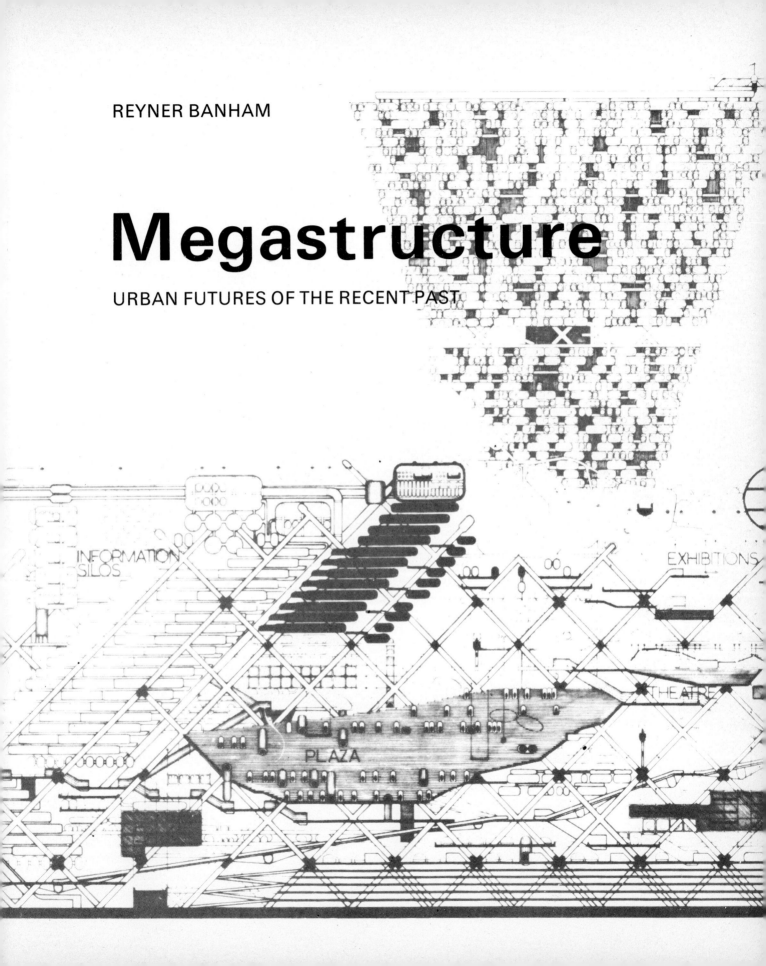

INFORMATION
SILOS

EXHIBITIONS

THEATRE

PLAZA

in memoriam
JOHN VOELCKER

architect and teacher,
who first introduced me to
the idea of megastructure

FIRST US EDITION

ISBN: 0–06–430371–3

LIBRARY OF CONGRESS CATALOG CARD NUMBER:
76–12061

Contents

Acknowledgments

This book is, in all useful aspects, a product of what we used to call 'the great ongoing international megastructure conversation' of the 1960s — a worldwide talk-in with a cast of thousands, to all of whom I am indebted. Such order and rigour as the book's argument presents is largely due to those schools and other institutions that offered me the opportunity to conduct orderly seminars or lectures on megastructures, most notably the Facoltá di Architettura in Naples, Art Net and University College in London, the Pratt Institute in Brooklyn and Columbia University, New York. The following individuals also provided particular insights or information: Ray Affleck, Marcello Angrisani, Peter Blake, Melvin Charney, Peter Cook, Guy Desbarats, Hans Hollein, Henry Liu, Fumihiko Maki, Cesar Pelli and Moshe Safdie. Most of them also, together with Dennis Crompton of Archigram, gave invaluable help in locating illustrations. In spite of their best efforts, however, and those of the publisher's expert staff, some key pictures proved already to have passed over into the limbo of legend — hence the less-than-perfect quality of some of the illustrations in this book (though some were far from perfect even when they were newly collaged or freshly sketched).

1 Introduction:
Dinosaurs of the Modern Movement

Megastructures in their time were all large buildings – but not all large buildings of the time were megastructures. If there is a single large work that marked this distinction, it was the Vertical Assembly Building at Cape Canaveral, Florida (1). Though it contained the largest single room ever built by men – big enough to contain its own weather as well as fully assembled space rockets upright on their transporters – the scholarly query as to whether it was a megastructure always brought the baffled but decisive answer 'No'.

Megastructures, then, were large buildings of a particular kind, though what kind remains difficult to define with neat verbal precision. Where one can be precise, however, is in defining their most general ancestor: Le Corbusier's Fort l'Empereur project from his Algiers plan of 1931. The famous drawing for it (2) shows, in curving and accelerating perspective, the massive sub-structure of an

1 *Vertical Assembly Building, Cape Canaveral, Florida (Urbahn, Roberts, Seeley and Moran, 1966). At an internal volume of 150,000,000 cubic feet the largest building in the world on completion, but not a megastructure because of its singleness of function and image.*

2 *Projet 'A', Fort l'Empereur, Algiers (Le Corbusier, 1931). Recognized as a true ancestor of megastructure because of its seemingly unlimited length and the clear distinction between the main permanent structure and the infill housing adapted to individual needs – note the famous 'Moorish' house in the centre.*

elevated super-highway, built like a giant bookcase of reinforced concrete on the shelves of which the inhabitants have built two-storey houses to suit their own tastes, not necessarily in *le style Corbu*.

The theme was not one to which Le Corbusier notably returned, but it contained the essential elements of the megastructure concept as it was to emerge thirty years later. Visible connections between this prime ancestor and its widely distributed progeny were few, yet the fundamental discrimination between the parts of urban high-density construction persists: on the one hand a massive, even monumental, supporting frame; on the other, various arrangements of habitable containers beyond the control of the architect.

This fundamental discrimination is present in the first two formal definitions of megastructures to be promulgated. Fumihiko Maki's *Investigations in Collective Form* of 1964 defines 'Mega-Structure' (still with its primitive hyphen) as

a large frame in which all the functions of a city or part of a city are housed. It has been made possible by present day technology. In a sense it is a man-made feature of the landscape. It is like the great hill on which Italian towns were built....[1]

Three paragraphs later, in acknowledging the part played by his former master, Kenzo Tange, as one of the immediate ancestors of his own megastructures, he significantly includes Tange's proposal for

a mass-human scale form which includes a Mega-form, and discrete, rapidly-changing functional units which fit within the larger framework.

Four years later Ralph Wilcoxon, planning librarian at the College of Environmental Design, Berkeley, prefaced his invaluable *Megastructure Bibliography* with an introduction including a proposed etymology of the word 'megastructure' and this serviceable four-part definition of megastructure as

not only a structure of great size, but . . . also a structure which is frequently:
1 constructed of modular units;
2 capable of great or even 'unlimited' extension;
3 a structural framework into which smaller structural units (for example, rooms, houses, or small buildings of other sorts) can be built – or even 'plugged-in' or 'clipped-on' after having been prefabricated elsewhere;
4 a structural framework expected to have a useful life much longer than that of the smaller units which it might support.[2]

Now, Wilcoxon's definition already includes a multitude of matters and implications not present in Maki's, but the main weight of his words still lies upon the concept of a permanent and dominating frame containing subordinate and transient accommodations. However overlaid by formalistic obsessions or technological excitements, this discrimination runs right through the whole history of megastructures from their first emergence to their final decadence in the 1970s. For the two decades of its maximum potency it was also, probably, the hinge of a crisis in architectural thinking that may also prove to have been the terminal crisis of 'Modern' architecture as we have known it.

That may sound over-portentous; in the megastructure years it would have sounded unjustifiably disloyal and pessimistic. Yet it is clear that by the 1960s Modern architects had argued themselves into a dilemma from which there was no logical escape, and from which megastructure was only a dubious deliverance: while the architectural profession would not relinquish its distinct 'Modern' claim to responsibility for 'the design of the whole human environment', it had by now been forced to recognize that the homogeneously designed 'total architecture' demanded by such as Walter Gropius would be as dead, as culturally thin, as any other perfect machine.

The claims of urban 'spontaneity' had been canvassed as early as the 1951 meeting of the *Congrès internationaux d'architecture moderne* (CIAM); subsequent movements of the fifties and sixties, notably the rise of Pop art, had emphasized the non-professional contribution to the visual urban fabric. A tide of interest in vernacular architectures, culminating in Bernard Rudofsky's exhibition 'Architecture without Architects' (1964),[3] had also produced an interest in what Maki contemporaneously described as 'group form' — the repetition and agglomeration of seemingly standardized folk-building elements into settlements of conspicuously clear plan or striking silhouette, epitomized by the unavoidable image of Italian hill-towns cited by Maki and practically everyone else at that period.

Like Maki, many megastructuralists saw their task as being the proposal of 'urban structures for the future' — as the Swiss architect Justus Dahinden (see pp. 201–2) named them — in which a modern, high-technology society could construct its own equivalent of spontaneous group form by natural accretion and reconstruction. Even if, in practice (as at 'Habitat', Montreal), the built result was apt to be more like a memorial sculpture to a folk urbanism that was supposed to have happened already but in fact had not, megastructuralists generally and genuinely hoped such processes could take place — but within a framework created by professional architects and reflecting the monumental and aesthetic values of professional architecture. Even that most permissive-seeming of megastructure theorists, the Dutch architect Nicholas Habraken, who was passionate in his demand that citizens should have a 'natural relationship' to an urban fabric they themselves had helped to create, still saw that fabric as being carried in gigantic support structures that snaked across the landscape on the scale of, and in much the same style as, Le Corbusier's Fort l'Empereur project.[4]

Nevertheless, Habraken's ideas differ importantly from Le Corbusier's. The permissiveness of the infilling of the Algiers structure seems to be largely a matter of indifference, as if the master-architect, having secured the grand design for himself, was prepared to let the lower orders shift for themselves over the details. This, assuredly, was the attitude of many megastructuralists, but

Habraken is clearly and deeply concerned that ordinary citizens shall no longer feel alienated from an urban fabric whose creating has been neither their pleasure nor their responsibility: his great support structures are mere frameworks for the do-it-yourself inventiveness of the public's housing instincts. And, in the end, it was a growing belief that these instincts should prevail over the professional values of architecture that left megastructure stranded by the end of the sixties, the few built examples standing isolated in the architectural wilderness like dinosaurs surviving, not from any past epoch, but from a fossil future that was not to be. . . .

Habraken's influence, indeed, worked paradoxically. In 1961, when his book *De Dragers en de Mensen* ('the people and their supports') first appeared, he and most other architects saw *de dragers*, the massive support structures, as proper and natural. By the end of the sixties, when he had become something of a guru among the younger activists, the support structures were unthinkable; only the spontaneous housing was acceptable. Megastructure, deserted by the avant-garde, was left to the despised Establishment as a conventional method for maximizing the returns from urban redevelopment.

Thus the megastructures which were actually completed were more or less guaranteed a bad press and a hostile reception: they had taken so long to build, because of their great size, that the intellectual fashion that had given them birth had passed away before their completion. Nevertheless, the concept of megastructure had been for one hectic decade the dominant progressive concept of architecture and urbanism. It had enjoyed that dominance because it offered to make sense of an architecturally incomprehensible condition in the world's cities, to resolve the conflicts between design and spontaneity, the large and the small, the permanent and the transient.

Like all such dominants, it had tended to sweep up and absorb all other current concepts in its passage: observe the number of concepts like 'modular', 'extensible', 'clip-on', 'plug-in' etc. that are in Wilcoxon's definition but not in Maki's. Observe also a kind of 'dominance of form' as megastructure appropriates all the most forceful formal innovations of the time, from *brut* concrete through tetrahedral space-frames to round-cornered windows and transparent inflatables. Quite often some accidental combination of forms from this fashionable repertoire would lead to the discovery that buildings with quite other intentions were *mégastructures trouvées*: piers, oil-rigs, grain elevators, even Old London Bridge!

Obviously it would be rare to find the complete register of all these forms and concepts present, intentionally or otherwise, in any one building; not even Cumbernauld Town Centre, sometimes called 'the most complete megastructure built', displays them all. The whole register is only seen by viewing megastructural activity globally – and global indeed it was! France, Italy, Japan, Canada, Britain, the USA were extremely active, and Austria, Holland, Germany, Switzerland hardly less so, while Argentina may claim, among other things, to have produced the first megastructure project on which work was actually begun: the aborted design for a new university in Tucumán advanced by Horacio Caminos in 1951.

The most striking question left behind by all this feverish activity must always be: whence came the self-confidence, the sheer nerve, to propose works of such urban complexity and vast scale, culminating in a project by two young British architects (see chapter 9) for a 'Comprehensive City' of one billion souls stretching across the United States from sea to shining sea? The economic explanation, though handy, is too pat to be convincing. Though it is true that these were years when economic indices seemed to have nowhere to go but up – even 1968 was a fat year in Dow Jones territory – and a lot of mad money was going in and out of central city redevelopment, it is still very noticeable that those who built property empires in, say, London (Clore, Hyams, Levy) did not build them out of megastructures.

Clients for megastructures were more likely to be universities, expositions, municipalities, central governments. More strikingly, they were proposed by socialist régimes in eastern Europe – or even Cuba – where the pressures of the market as normally understood do not operate, and fortunes in property are not to be made. Where survivors of the epoch are prepared to speak frankly, most will admit that the self-confidence, not to say arrogance, to propose such works came from within the profession of architecture itself; that architects had talked themselves into the position where they had no option but to propose megastructures if they were to retain any credibility as 'comprehensive designers'. Even if there had been a massive slump around, say, 1965, megastructures would have been offered as the kind of large-scale public works needed 'to get the economy rolling again'. Many megastructuralists did, indeed, make much of the 'urban crisis' of pollution, crime, congestion, dysfunctions of municipal services and the rest of the litany of Nekropolis, yet their projects paradoxically present a physiognomy of manic optimism – everything for the best in the best of all possible megastructures.

To have the nerve to present such 'monumental follies', as Peter Hall was to call them, seemed as natural in the mid-sixties as it must seem astounding today. But it must also, surely, seem intriguing, perhaps even exhilarating. The chapters that follow aim to illuminate as well as chronicle the megastructure movement, and to expose something of the frame of mind in which it was conceived, elaborated and finally abandoned, a whitening skeleton on the dark horizon of our recent architectural past.

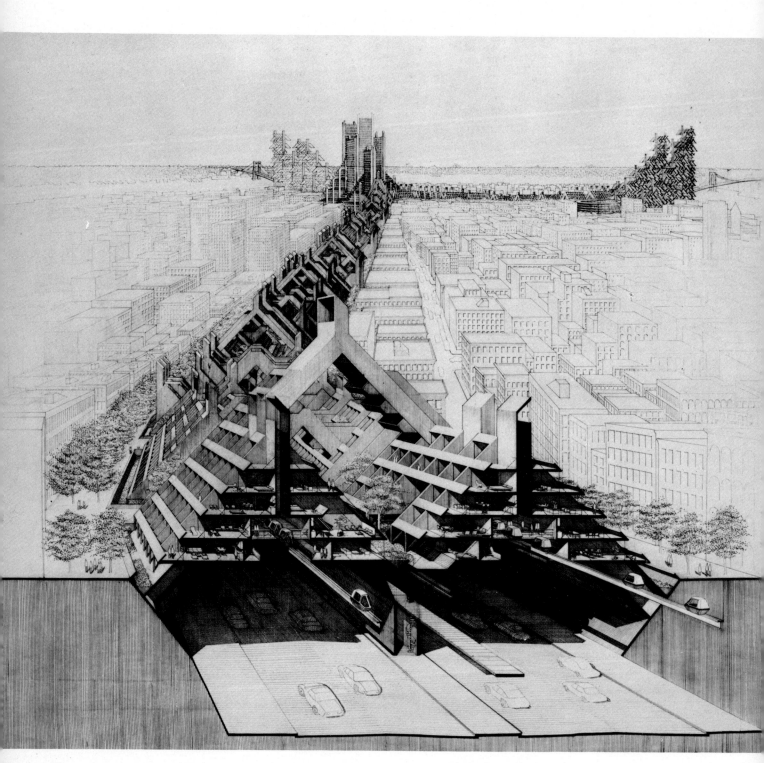

2 Antecedents, Analogies and *Mégastructures trouvées*

Megastructure was born and bred in an epoch of unprecedented historical awareness among modern architects; hardly a single novelty in plan, section or structure was offered in the sixties without being justified (or denigrated) by the citation of some historical antecedent. Megastructure, of course, was no more exempt than any other architectural concept, as appears clearly enough in the following exchange from the diverting book of tape-recorded *Conversations with Architects* in which the authors, John Cook and Heinrich Klotz, question Paul Rudolph:

Cook: What is the dominant tendency in architecture since Mies?
Rudolph: After Mies, the megastructure.
Cook: Are there any models for understanding the megastructure visually? Or does it remain in the realm of ideas. . . . Did you have any examples to work from for this idea?
Rudolph: Oh gosh, a lot of people have worked on megastructure. The best model I have found is the bridge in Florence.
Cook: Ponte Vecchio.
Rudolph: The Ponte Vecchio — the shops along the pedestrian way, and over it marvellous housing. The scale of supports is in keeping with the vehicular way, and then there is a working down of scale. There is nothing new. That is a megastructure, and probably the purest example in traditional architecture. . . .[5]

Thus Rudolph's own megastructures, such as the Lower Manhattan Expressway development (**3**), are put in a double historical context of change (since Mies) and no change (since the Ponte Vecchio, **4**), and anchored there by the reference, justified by detailed analysis, to a well-known but not architect-designed historical precedent.

Whatever one may think of the quality of this little exercise in historical erudition, we must be grateful that the megastructure generation were so prone to cast about for ancient and modern precedents, since this has created an unusually large store of collateral imagery which not only enriches our view of the cultural background to megastructure but also helps to focus the concept by bringing into view allusions that may not have been expressible in words. A megastructure was not only a building which, say, satisfied the four headings of Wilcoxon's definition; a megastructure was also a building which *looked like* a megastructure.

Since no deliberately designed megastructures existed in concrete fact before 1966, resemblances had to be struck with buildings admitted, appointed or discovered to the megastructure canon from past periods if there was to be any conversation at all. The Ponte Vecchio was one of the most distinguished of them, and Rudolph's analysis by no means exhausts its possibilities as a precedent; he might easily have made an issue also of the transience of the

3 *Lower Manhattan Expressway project (Paul Rudolph, 1970). A 'mainstream' megastructure if ever there was one, with its conventional 'A-frame' or Terrassenhäuser section of two sloping stacks of apartments back to back over each carriageway of a giant transportation-artery.*

4

shop structures strutted off its flanks, or the presence of a sealed pedestrian 'circulation duct' leading through its upper works from the Uffizi to the Pitti Palace.

Patriotic Britons, however, needed not look so far afield for convincing medieval precedent. Old London Bridge (**5**) had, from AD 1209 to 1831, presented most of the lineaments of a true megastructure, the basic megaform of the bridge itself supporting changing generations of houses, shops, even a chapel; the coming and going of the subsidiary accommodation recorded in Gordon Home's reconstructions in the London Museum constitutes a kind of capsule history of the life of London. Germany's prime historical exemplar, on the other hand, emphasizes different aspects of megastructure: the Königsbau in Stuttgart (**6**) is a conscious architectural creation — by Knapp and Leins, 1856 — conceived as a multi-functional urban improvement providing, like Cumbernauld Town Centre 110 years later, a vast covered shopping concourse and pedestrian way. Its elevations, however, cast in a contained neo-classical mould, suggest neither extensibility nor adaptability, and thus put it outside the canon visually.

5

6

4, 5, 6 *Urban ancestors of megastructure: (4) the Ponte Vecchio, Florence, with 'temporary' housing and shops bracketed off the sides of a multi-level bridge structure; (5) Old London Bridge (from a painting by Samuel Scott, c. 1750), a Gothic 'megaform' supporting many generations of buildings devoted to functions as diverse as housing, religion and commerce in the six centuries it spanned the Thames; (6) the Königsbau, Stuttgart (Knapp and Leins, 1856), a purpose-designed multi-functional urban structure anticipating by almost exactly a century megastructures of similar function such as Cumbernauld Town Centre (see chapter 8).*

7 *The Cliff Palace, Mesa Verde, Colorado. A pre-Columbian* pueblo *ruin which is often claimed to be even closer to true megastructure than the conventional exemplar of 'group form', the Italian hill-town — chiefly because the carrying structure of the latter (the hill) is usually hidden under the town itself, whereas at Mesa Verde the massive slot in the cliff is clearly seen to carry the smaller accommodations within it, much as the structure of Le Corbusier's Projet 'A' (see 2) carries its private houses.*

American precedents tend to be either pre-Columbian or literally exotic. James Marston Fitch, to cite a conspicuous example, applies the term 'mud masonry megastructure' to Bedouin villages in the Moroccan Sahara,[6] but almost identical phrases can be heard applied conversationally around US architecture schools to such domestic constructs as the *pueblos* of Taos, Pueblo Bonito or Mesa Verde (**7**). What brings these Indian megastructures within the canon is their visible extensibility and adaptability, their lack of obvious regular geometry in spite of the fact that their overall form is usually easy to grasp and their small parts extremely regular. For these reasons, no doubt, *pueblos* ancient and modern were seen as a corrective lesson against the incomprehensible disorder of present American cities — Vincent Scully, for instance, has spoken of the ancient *pueblos* as 'our only native school of urbanism'.[7]

The idea of vernacular architecture as a model of town-building was, as noted, commonplace in the fifties and sixties. Even such sophisticated commentators as Ernesto Rogers could praise the contrivedly stacked housing at Marina Grande on Capri, with its conspicuous external stairways, as 'a valid architecture . . . situated in a valid town plan . . . these two realms of experience have to be blended into a single phenomenon'.[8] Local architects in conversation termed it *megastrutture folcloriche*, pointing out the powerful diagonals of the external staircases, yet another visual consonance with megastructures as consciously designed. We have already noted that Maki had consciously brought Italian hill-towns into the megastructure argument, and similar architecture, disciplined into Teutonic regularity and repackaged as stepped *Terrassenhäuser* (as in the work of K. W. Schmidt and others at Stuttgart), often provided the pretext for the first publication of conscious megastructure designs in German magazines. Maki, however, in pursuit of other examples of group form, also introduced certain types of Japanese agricultural village. These do not present dramatic silhouettes so much as planwise groupings of dwelling units along roadways, comprehensible forms recording growth and change but without overall geometric regularity. Something equally close to megastructure can be seen in the forms of many roadside towns: English coaching towns, for instance, like Marlborough, where the trunk road is widened into a broad market-place with a variety of tributary buildings such as inns and shops 'clipped on' along both sides. These could come and go without affecting the perceived form of the whole; even when viewed from the air, a clearly perceivable structure would persist though there was no regular geometrical town plan in the normal sense.

These vernacular instances, of course, were offered in most cases simply as examples, or praiseworthy examples, of ways of designing towns, only rarely as direct comparisons with megastructures. An example of the latter type of citation occurred when Peter Blake, of *Architectural Forum*, observed that 'Plug-In City's fundamental idea – the city considered as a single organic entity – is as old as Urbino. For here, too, the city was a skeleton of urban spaces (passages, steps, streets, piazzas) which held things together.'[9] But Blake was a conscious promoter of the idea of the city as a unified entity, persistently promoting the images of Lower Manhattan, San Gimignano etc. as examples of 'the city as a single building' or 'the city as a unified work of art', and both Urbino and 'Plug-In City' were grist to that mill. Few others, however, saw 'plug-in' concepts in that light; for most observers they were the very opposite of Urbino, the high-technological as against the handicraft-traditional.

On this there would be general and explicit agreement: the inventors of the plug-in/clip-on concepts themselves filled their eponymous magazine *Archigram* with both obvious and esoteric machine-imagery. This preoccupation of *Archigram*, and of other magazines and megastructural groups of young architects, was widely noted and historically scrutinized. Thus Denise Scott-Brown in 1968:

. . . the claim is made frequently here that the schemes illustrated are based on technological means available or in use even today, though not usually in connection with city-building.
Many of the cities *do* look familiar. They look like the industrial outskirts of American cities, like Jersey tank-farms and cracking towers, or the oil derricks, pumps and cranes of San Pedro harbour, and the Huntington Beach sections of California's Route 1. One may question whether theirs is not, in fact, a nineteenth-century rather than a late-twentieth-century industrial vision?[10]

A good question, rather easily answered by the one word 'Futurism'. The whole revival of a romantic (as opposed to the established neo-classical) vision of modern technology goes in direct parallel with a revival of architectural-historical interest in the Expressionism and above all the Futurism of the early twentieth century. As against the International Style's classicizing view of technology and machinery as neat smooth regular solids of anonymous aspect, the younger megastructuralists clearly saw technology as a visually wild rich mess (**8**) of piping and wiring and struts and cat-walks and bristling radar antennae and supplementary fuel tanks and landing-pads all carried in exposed lattice frames, NASA-style. Much of the intellectual underpinning for this picturesque view of advanced technology came, directly or otherwise, from the

8 *Industrial landscape at Redondo Beach, California. One of the inspirations — or justifications — for the 'clip-on, plug-in' view of megastructure, much observed and commented in the sixties.*

writings and projects of the Futurist architect Antonio Sant'Elia, in spite of the fact that he had been dead since 1916. His projects (**9**) were published in magazines high and low, official and underground, and the forms in them were copied and even built; not only were his *case a gradinate* among the quoted historical precedents for the stepped *Terrassenhäuser* section for apartment-blocks, but his kind of towers also appear in one of the best-known built schemes, the Brunswick Centre in London (discussed in chapter 8).

As for Sant'Elia's writings, they were like direct incitements to action:

We must invent and rebuild *ex novo* our modern city like an immense and tumultuous building site, active, mobile and everywhere dynamic, and the modern building like a gigantic machine . . . lifts must swarm up the façades like serpents of glass and iron . . . [the street must] plunge storeys deep into the earth, collecting the traffic of the metropolis and connected for necessary transfers to metal cat-walks and high-speed conveyor belts.[11]

Projects by the Archigram group (**10**) realize these verbal imperatives more literally than Sant'Elia himself had done, but, more importantly, this rhetoric seemed to send a generation in search of machine/city analogies, both functional and purely visual. Some of these analogies were powerfully direct: the Austrian Hans Hollein's visions of giant machines in Lower Manhattan range from the joky (the Rolls-Royce radiator taller than any skyscraper) to the ambiguously serious, like the half-turbine-shell lying a mile long across the Wall

9 *Milan Central Station project (Antonio Sant'Elia, 1914). Of all the pioneers of the Modern movement, Sant'Elia was the most directly influential on megastructure as an urban concept, the virtual inventor of both the A-frame* Terrassenhäuser *section and the vision of giant buildings spanning over traffic arteries – see 3, but see also 191 for a direct visual comparison with the Milan station project.*

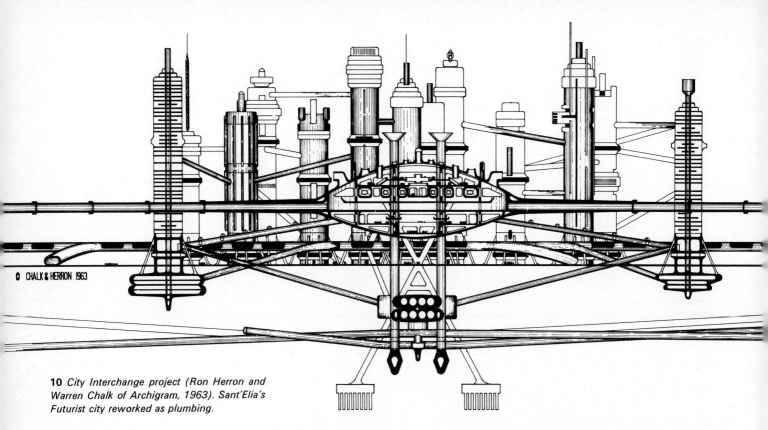

@ CHALK & HERRON 1963

10 *City Interchange project (Ron Herron and Warren Chalk of Archigram, 1963). Sant'Elia's Futurist city reworked as plumbing.*

11 *United Nations complex project, Vienna (Masato Shimazu, 1970). Megastructure as urban machinery, visualized in machine forms.*

Street area and looking remarkably like the large abstract urban projects being devised in those days (1963–4) by Hollein and his partner Walter Pichler. Even these, however, were outbid in their home city by Masato Shimazu's pure 'machine' (**11**) entered for the UN Vienna congress centre competition at the beginning of the seventies. There was, indeed, a steady trickle of such projects throughout the intervening years, their mechanistic inspirations and determined formalism revealed by often crude collaging of unaltered technical illustrations on urban perspectives or aerial views, or by simply redrawing assemblies of machine components in such a way as to make their scale ambiguous and then giving them the well-known 'see-all-them-dots-they're-people' treatment.

Hollein was more subtle and persuasive; his device of showing common transportation equipment like railroad cars magnified to almost unreadable scale and set down in some inoffensive middle-European rural landscape achieved unique architectural resonance. There was apparent urban relevance, too, in the most celebrated of these collages — those that featured aircraft-carriers (**12, 13**). Such dry-land stranding of large vessels to make architectural polemic has respectable ancestry, of course, in the work of Le Corbusier, but Hollein is clearly out to make different points. The overhanging silhouette of the flight deck suggests shelter to what is below, but the top-heavy effect was clearly the mode of the day. Furthermore, the asymmetrical arrangement of the main elements, with the bridge structure at the side of the flight deck instead of axially astride the hull as in Le Corbusier's 'ocean greyhounds', seems to have had consonances with the relationship of public buildings to public spaces. This is more clear in Hollein's second version, where the carrier is sunk hull-deep in the landscape so that the flight deck is flush with the ground surface like the paving

20

of a piazza. In either case the residual silhouette above ground is clearly what rang a bell for the megastructuralists: although the dates make it impossible for these collages to have influenced the design of Cumbernauld Town Centre (they were not exhibited until 1964, when Cumbernauld was under construction), the Centre's designer, Geoffrey Copcutt, frequently used the aircraft-carrier analogy to characterize the intentions of his design.

The hull-deep version, however, has other echoes; the concealed presence of the sunk hull is revealed by cutting a section through the earth that also sections the ship, exhibiting its inner complexities, and this touches another important analogy – the great ship as the container of a complete and self-contained

12, 13 *Aircraft-carrier projects (Hans Hollein, 1964). Nautical imagery brought ashore to give a powerful megasilhouette (12), and buried hull-down in the landscape (13) so that the bridge and flight deck become a public building alongside a piazza, and the entire private life of a community is encapsulated below ground.*

12

13

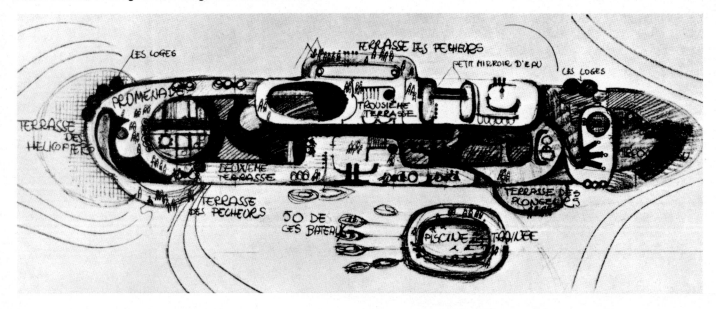

14 *La Tartaruga cruise-ship project (students of Pierluigi Spadolini, Florence, 1969). In a complex reworking of traditional Modern movement imagery in which ocean liners had served as standards of comparison for buildings or whole cities, a liner is here expanded into a megastructure, a floating Fun Palace (see chapter 5) rather than a means of transportation.*

human community (**14**). Again, the idea of a floating town was not new, but it seems to have been time for a revaluation of this established view of great ships. Paolo Soleri, for instance, deliberately claims it as an ancestor for 'Arcology', his own independent version of megastructure, pointing out that both ocean liners and Arcologies share the common characteristics of

compactness and definite boundary; the functional fullness of an organism designed for many, if not most, of man's needs; a definite and unmistakable three-dimensionality. Three main characteristics are not common: the liner is structurally and functionally designed for motion within a fluid; the liner is a shell for a temporary society of unrelated people; the liner is a sealed package connected to the outside only by synthetic information. Relieved of these three tyrannies, the liner, the concept of it, can open up and, retaining its organisational suppleness, become truly a 'machine for living in'. . . .[12]

Other megastructuralists might not have seen these three 'tyrannies' as anything unwelcome; indeed, Soleri himself designed at least one Arcology, 'Asteromo' (**15**), which was to orbit in the 'black void of space' and would therefore have to accept the inevitable constraints of an impermeable exterior skin.

However, as has already been hinted, this was not how space science normally struck the megastructuralists. It was not the sealed envelope that interested them so much as all the clip-ons, the sense of an unconstrained aggregation of functional elements *without* a controlling envelope. But if space travel gave the sanction that rendered picturesque disorder acceptable, that sanction did not have to wait on the facts; a minor revolution in visual sensibility took place on whichever was the exact day when Wernher von Braun replaced the ageing Willy Ley as the West's leading space guru and as the man who wrote the technical briefs for Chesley Bonestell's realistically rendered visions of the immediate space future. Well before the first manned flights, von Braun and Bonestell had driven the sleek, projectile-shaped spaceship image out of currency and replaced it by images of open frameworks (**16**) filled with spherical pressure-vessels, command modules and power-packs. When Armstrong set foot on the moon, the module from which he descended must have looked as familiar as home to the megastructure generation.

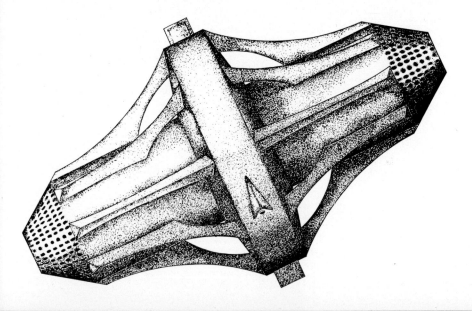

15 *Asteromo orbital Arcology project (Paolo Soleri, 1967). In spite of his hostility to sealed structures for his Arcologies (giant architectural ecologies for whole communities) and the earthbound location of all his other projects, Soleri's continuing fascination with this 'city-as-space-satellite' theme is attested by the fact that he has recently revived Asteromo.*

16 *OGO satellite (NASA, 1965). Typical space-hardware design of the sixties; the clearly articulated component-by-separate-component conception, the expansive composition, were consciously reflected in many megastructure projects.*

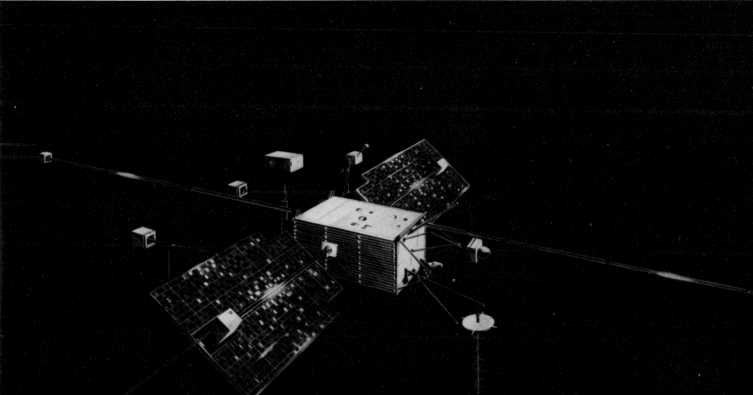

They seem to have been equally at home with undersea technology; Sealab (**17**) rates Skylab in prestige as well as frequency of illustration. The prestige seems to have been different, however; space travel was remote, abstract, élitist, its prestige something that people like architects had to share with men in the street at a respectful distance. Sub-aqua activity, however, was the sort of adventure that more ordinary mortals could get into if moderately affluent. It must have been the sense of possible participation by normal, passionate, desk-bound members of the professional bourgeoisie, rather than the select and perfect passionless puppet-figures of the space race, that gave such glamour to the submarine scene — though the utterance of the word 'submarine' should warn us that this was also the period of the Beatles, and remind us that there were distinct graphic and pictorial analogies between their 'Yellow Submarine' (**18**) and the Archigram wing of the megastructuralists.

Paradoxical as it may seem, this interest in extreme technologies and fashionable Pop art must lead this review of the visual culture of megastructure back to vernaculars of a sort and ultimately to historical studies. One of the main centres of academic megastructuralism in the middle and late sixties was the newly formed graduate urban-design course at the University of California at Los Angeles (UCLA). Its seemingly insatiable demand for teaching talent brought to Los Angeles Denise Scott-Brown (hence the observations on San Pedro already quoted), most of the Archigram team, and a host of others. Many of the visiting teachers, frustrated by the students' failure to exploit the imaginative possibilities of concepts like 'undersea sin cities', would demand to know how they could produce such boring projects when one of the world's great maritime pleasure megastructures was just down at the end of Wilshire Boulevard — Santa Monica Pier (**19**). This venerable (by California standards) amalgam of engineering structure and normal commercial buildings had undergone many megastructural changes over the years, its basic megaform persisting while subsidiary accommodations came and went, without ever ceasing to be both urban and multi-functional; it included even residential accommodation as well as bars, restaurants, entertainments, fishing and harbour facilities and even car-

17 *Sealab (US Navy, 1968). Though less expansive than space hardware, underwater tackle, designed equally additively for an equally hostile environment, was another source of technological form-rhetoric for the mega-structure generation — for an underwater city see chapter 5.*

18 *Yellow Submarine (from the film of the same name, design Heinz Edelman, 1968). Mega-structure belongs historically to the period of 'the Beatles' greatest hits', and the animation of* Yellow Submarine *reflects the graphic style of the period as accurately as do the drawings of Archigram.*

19 *Santa Monica Pier, Los Angeles (1922 onwards). An exemplary classic among accidental megastructures, and still available (unlike Old London Bridge) for inspection by megastructure-oriented students.* Ludique – *'recreational' in English – and supporting buildings that have come and gone over the years while the main structure remains, it embodies two of the main intellectual concepts underlying megastructure. More importantly, in some ways, it visually exemplifies the loosely-assembled Megastructure Look.*

20 *Palace Pier, Brighton (M.R. St George Moore, 1898–9). Though perhaps too formal in its design and too permanent in its smaller structures to satisfy fully the megastructure concept, a great pleasure pier like this possesses the multiplicity of function commonly expected of a megastructure and, better still, its total function is* ludique, *devoted to the games and pleasures of the people – on* Homo ludens *as the proper inhabitant of megastructure, see chapter 4.*

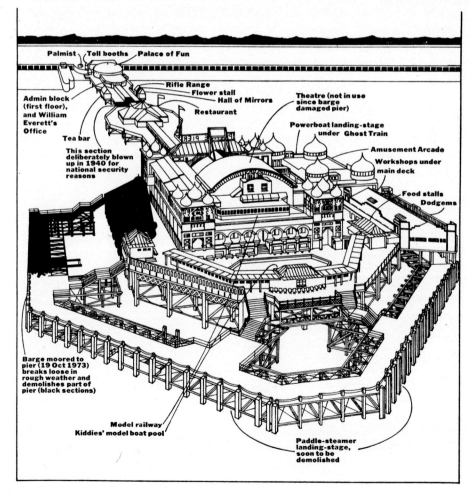

parking — indeed the whole length of the pier could be traversed by car, thus giving it the transportation component that was increasingly taken to be an essential of megastructure. And given the ramp that brought cars down from the cliffs on shore, and the odd external staircase or two, the pier even looked like a megastructure. Thus, viewed in the appointed season and the right frame of mind, Santa Monica Pier was perceived to be a natural grown megastructure produced by the inherent forces of technology and society. Japanese Metabolists might be projecting unrealizable visions of artificial land in Tokyo Bay; the pier already had a vacant lot used for car parking over the Pacific Ocean.

The sense of megastructures being produced thus by natural forces of some sort was obviously an added justification for consciously designing such works, and was constantly reinforced by the discovery of new *mégastructures trouvées.* Other piers entered the canon: Palace Pier at Brighton (**20**) because it was multi-functional and *intégralement ludique*[13] (a criterion to be discussed in chapter 4), Southend Pier because it was multi-functional and had over a mile of internal mechanical transportation; but curiously the new pier at Scheveningen, Holland (**21**), by Maaskant, Dijk and Apen (1964), passed without comment.

Ocean fortifications also received a welcoming press, not only because they contained the whole (if constrained) life of complete communities, but also

21 *Scheveningen New Pier, Holland (Maaskant, Dijk and Apen, 1964). A rare example of a major pier completed in the megastructure period and exhibiting most of the true characteristics of megastructure, from loosely aformal composition to resolutely* ludique *functions, but created outside the 'great international megastructure conversation' and ignored by most of the megaliterature.*

22 *Shivering Sands Fort, off Whitstable, Kent (1943). Non-pleasurable over-water architecture in the Thames estuary, apparently known to some of the Archigram group while they were still children, these additive, articulated structures on diagonal legs supporting the day-to-day life of isolated military communities were rediscovered and much illustrated in periodicals of the later sixties.*

23 *North Sea oil-rig. The growth and development of offshore oil technology, culminating in the American and Russian offshore oil-drilling 'towns', provided a constant stream of 'real-life' exemplars for megastructure design. This relatively modest example, however, has the added point of interest that the living accommodation under the helicopter pad is made up of 'Porta-kabins', proprietary prefabricated industrial buildings which were transported and installed complete — living proof that the 'living capsule' was a workable proposition.*

because of their powerful imagery of loosely connected functional units in purely functional array. One at least of these – Shivering Sands Fort (**22**) in the Thames estuary – has been cited as a possible source for Archigram's famous 'Walking Cities' drawing that caused so much alarm among the elder Establishment of Modernists like Sigfried Giedion. Offshore oil-rigs and drilling platforms were also laid under tribute (**23**), especially the complete over-water drilling towns built by the Russians in the Black Sea and the Caspian. Not only were they complex in their industrial and community functions, but their loosely articulated overall forms seemed to realize the planwise aspects, at least, of Archigram's 'Plug-In City' projects. Since these 'artificial islands', Aryamneft and Neftamye, were not published until some four years after Plug-In City, real life again seemed to confirm the visionaries' dreams.

Finally, one must note two genuinely urban *mégastructures trouvées*, both most appropriately in New York, that city that has contributed so much to the world's stock of images of the city of the future, and both, equally appropriately, under the eye of *Architectural Forum*, the magazine that did more than most to support the idea that megastructures were essential to the future of cities (even if it was slow to acquire the word 'megastructure' to express its intentions). One was Grand Central Station; it emphatically does not look like a megastructure, but its vast and multi-functional ramifications can be experienced as one (**24**), and it is organized like one:

At urban scale, a railroad tycoon, the younger Vanderbilt, achieved the first, and thus far the only, demonstration at precinct scale, of the Futurist City. Behind the Grand Central terminal in New York . . . the architects Reed and Stem, with the engineer Colonel William J. Wilgus, used the 'yard' and its tracks under Park Avenue as the basis of a fantastic interweave. This embraced half a mile of over-and-under trackage, of platforms, bridge streets, ramps, elevateds and subways, pedestrian and vehicular.[14]

Thus wrote old Douglas Haskell in the 'farewell' issue (September 1964) of the original *Forum* of which he had so long been editor. Even without the word,

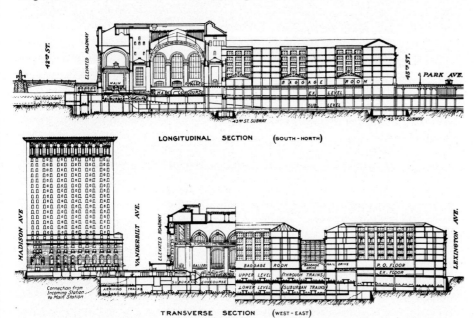

24 *Grand Central Station, New York: transverse and longitudinal sections (Reed and Stem, with William Wilgus, 1903–13). A memorable complex of interconnected concourses, hotels, office accommodation, shopping and railway facilities straddling two levels of tracks and interlaced with roads, Grand Central Station 'can be experienced as a megastructure' (Michael Hollander) even if it hardly looks like one, and is often cited by New Yorkers as proof that megastructure was invented in that city.*

megastructure thinking pervades the whole issue, and Grand Central has since become one of the most commonly cited prototypes for megastructure, especially among patriotic Gothamites eager to claim the concept as a New York invention — a claim that is reinforced by both Penn Central Station and the Rockefeller Center.

Visually, however, they could make an even stronger claim for a structure that really does look like a megastructure in a densely built-up metropolitan setting. Recognition of the status of this unique artefact came slowly and obliquely in the pages of the revived *Architectural Forum* after 1966. Its first claim to attention lay in the use of air-rights over transportation ways as building sites, given the proposition (disputable) that Manhattan is acutely short of building land. So the proposal to erect residential towers over the approachways to the George Washington Bridge was guaranteed some journalistic interest, whatever the quality of the architecture (and it wasn't much!). At about the same time (1965), however, the New York Port Authority, apparently in a bid to improve their image, entrusted the design of the new bus terminal at the bridge to Pierluigi Nervi instead of to their own staff architects, who had by then rather run out of reputation — though they almost contrived to destroy Nervi's powerful design by their detailed finishing off of the structure's minor accommodations.

However, those who tried to stand back far enough from the bridge to assess or photograph the results of these works could not fail to observe that what they saw looked like (and might even function like) a megastructure. The view across the Hudson from the Jersey shore shows the bridge arriving on the Manhattan bluffs in a complicated swirl of superimposed approach spirals and ramps (**25**), with the bus station squatting above them, and backed up by a file of four apartment towers that are clearly part of the same complex but are slightly off line because there is a bend in the double-deck motorway below. This note of geometrical uncertainty, of adaptation to the terrain, couples with the giant scale of the whole (see diagrams on pp. 128–9: each of the apartment towers is as tall as some built megastructures are long!) to produce an overwhelming impression that here is a real megastructure — an impression that is reinforced by some striking resemblances to Sant'Elia's sketches at the point where the motorway plunges under the tower blocks at the eastern entry to the complex.

Yet, in spite of the proliferation of architects' and engineers' names that attaches to the final megavision, it can hardly be said that anybody conceived its design; the GWB complex is more a combination of infrastructure and opportunism, and the result looks like the anonymous forces of urban society combining to prduce a unique and immensely powerful image. In the words of Donald Canty,

the complex is in fact, one of the boldest amalgams of buildings and transport yet built in the USA. . . . The Terminal's presence in the city, amidst the low brick monotony of Washington Heights, is that of a bristling warship moored among tug-boats. . . . Nervi has fulfilled his mandate to bring the drama of the bridge into the city, thus giving New York its only symbolic gateway at a major point of entry.[15]

25 *George Washington Bridge approaches, New York (1927 onwards; bus terminal roof by Pierluigi Nervi, 1965–6). An unco-ordinated accumulation of buildings in the air-rights space above the double-decked approach road to the Manhattan end of Othmar Ahmann's famous bridge resulted in by far the largest (for comparative size see 130, 131) and most visually convincing of all accidental megastructures.*

From 'complex' to 'symbolic', this is the proper language in which megastructures were appreciated, shipping analogies and all! GWB had everything — sheer scale, powerful imagery, housing that could be plugged and unplugged without destroying the megaform, public spaces and services, a 'transportation interchange node' with all its attendant ramps and levels, a transportation spine

underlying and organizing the total form – and it was packed into a dense urban context to which it gave drama, form and a sense of place. It concentrates most of the operational, constructional and visual themes that are otherwise found only thinly distributed through the diffuse body of megafancying of the time.

Diffuse it certainly was; nothing should be allowed to give the impression that architects were out in droves from dawn till dusk, beating the urban bushes for megastructure precedents. On the other hand, when megaprecedents were serendipitously stumbled on, they were keenly taken up and treasured. Again, it should not be assumed that they were immediately and consciously adopted as prototypes for megastructures; the word to focus the concept did not exist until 1964, and was hardly current by the end of 1966.

Nevertheless, this unfocused 'cloud of witness' felt impressive and convincing at the time. The accumulating body of projects and imagery supported a sense that this was the way things should develop, were already developing. Above all it supported the feeling that if architectural design could get into the act somehow, it could help resolve 'the insoluble problem of the modern city'. At a time when social and statistical planning procedures were felt to be dissolving the sense of the city as a physical artefact, when planning seemed to be drifting away from architecture, its supposed parent, these antecedents and precedents were felt to suggest that architecture and its skills were still relevant to the future of the city. In the guise of 'urban design', the exercise of architecture on a very large scale might bridge the gap between the single building and its disintegrating urban context. It was this belief that brought together such unlikely partners as Italian hill-towns, Jersey tank farms, Victorian seaside piers and stranded aircraft-carriers in a single argument. Each in some way asserted that a physically comprehensible form, however rich and indeterminate, exists for urban building problems, as against the 'incomprehensible sprawl' of the simplistic, unfocused, statistical city of single-family dwellings on a million suburban lots. At that point of resolution and despair, the 'city as a single building' became a thinkable concept and megastructure was its appointed form.

3 Beginners and Begetters

What, then, was the first megastructure consciously conceived by the mind of an architect, whether or not that mind contained the word for the concept? Without the word to render ambition precise, it is difficult to know how to draw the line between the more or less accidental and the rather more intentional. To judge from two decades of conversation, however, many of the mega-structuralists themselves would accept a scenario in which the concept begins to emerge from the work of Le Corbusier, well after Fort l'Empereur, but around the time of his projects for La Sainte-Baume and 'Roq et Rob' (26).

26 *Roq et Rob project (Le Corbusier, 1948). Though little more than a regularized version of the Italian hill-town image, this exercise in composition by the accumulation of standard units is taken as one of the true beginnings of megastructure ideas after World War II.*

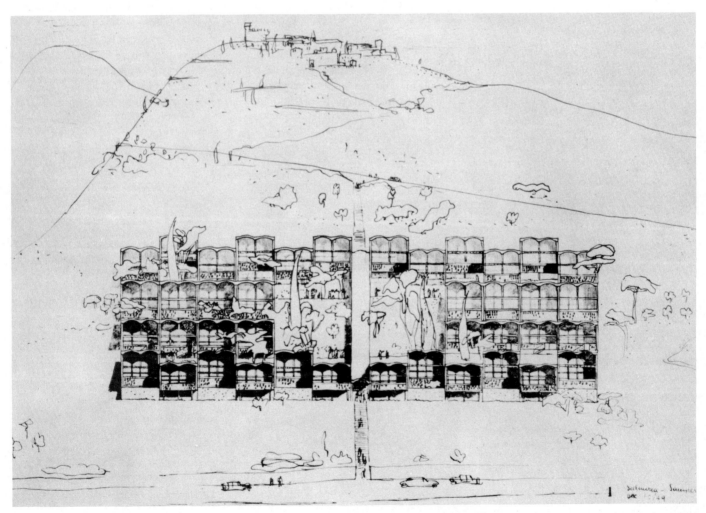

These projects of 1948–9 are not yet megastructures, since there is no substantial permanent structure on which the modular and repetitive dwelling units are built up. This is more like Maki's classification of a 'collective form', a hillside town, aformal and extensible in plan. But if the *œuvre complète* of Le Corbusier is the most likely place for scholiasts to find the true spiritual beginnings of megastructure, observation on the ground would suggest that the nearest thing to a built megastructure in those early days was situated in a place and an architectural context that most of the megastructuralists would regard as dubious, and was the work of an architect they would strenuously repudiate. Yet a long, slightly curved (like the GWB complex), framed structure containing miscellaneous minor accommodations looking as if they might well be interchangeable, and all notoriously based on a romantic view of mechanical transportation, was built in 1951 to the designs of a Scottish architect whom no one in his right mind could ever have mistaken for a young radical. However much later radicals may squirm at the thought, Basil Spence's 'Sea and Ships' pavilion (**27**) at the Festival of Britain exhibition on the South Bank in London has a visible prima facie claim to be considered an early megastructure.

There would be little historical point in making an issue of this one possibly freakish instance were it not for the fact that, somewhere behind its outmoded period decorations, it must connect to at least part of the intellectual tradition that supports later megastructures. In fact, the period detailing is the clue: its detailed aesthetic can be found anticipated in the writings of a modern pundit – Sigfried Giedion – who certainly does belong to the megastructure tradition somewhere. In an essay of 1943, written in *troika* with J. L. Sert and Fernand Léger and entitled 'Nine Points on Monumentality', Giedion's ninth point had been this:

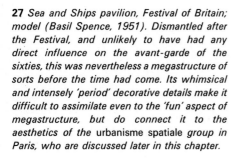

27 *Sea and Ships pavilion, Festival of Britain; model (Basil Spence, 1951). Dismantled after the Festival, and unlikely to have had any direct influence on the avant-garde of the sixties, this was nevertheless a megastructure of sorts before the time had come. Its whimsical and intensely 'period' decorative details make it difficult to assimilate even to the 'fun' aspect of megastructure, but do connect it to the aesthetics of the* urbanisme spatiale *group in Paris, who are discussed later in this chapter.*

Modern materials and new techniques are already to hand, light metal structures, curved laminated wooden arches, panels of different textures, light elements like ceilings which can be suspended from massive trusses . . . mobile elements changing positions and casting different shadows. . . .[16]

All these devices were to be seen at the Festival, and nowhere in greater concentration than in Spence's pavilion, though most were to turn up again, little modified, among the works of the French *urbanisme spatial* movement in the late fifties and early sixties. If it be objected that this essay on monumentality was not published in England until 1958, so that Spence could not have seen it in time, even if the French had, the response must simply be that much of the attitude advanced by Giedion *et al.* was conversationally common property throughout the Modern movement, spread about by Giedion and Sert themselves, and by other CIAM mouthpieces like Ernesto Rogers who were in and out of England during the late forties.

What Spence's pavilion does not reflect, however, is Giedion's concern with monuments as such, especially monuments in relation to their urban settings. Thus point five asserts:

Today modern architects know that buildings cannot be conceived as isolated units, that they have to be incorporated into vaster urban schemes. There are no frontiers between architecture and planning . . . correlation between them is necessary. Monuments should constitute the most powerful elements in these vast schemes.

That is much more like the true voice of the committed megastructuralists a couple of decades later.

Within the context of the book *Architektur und Gemeinschaft* (English version *Architecture, You and Me*) in which Giedion finally and formally published these views, the most explicit example of a modern urban scheme fulfilling all his desiderata (urban scale, functional complexity, social concern etc.) is the 1953 Boston Center complex projected by Gropius and The Architects' Collaborative. Architecturally it cannot be read as a megastructure because it is too obviously a composition of separate buildings on a common podium. Paradoxically, the despised podium *can* be read as a megastructure of sorts: spanning over streets and subways, it incorporates shops, pedestrian spaces, parking and transportation. In many ways, the rise of megastructure was to be the symbolic revenge of this underworld of lowly service-infrastructures on the 'fine-art' architecture which had previously monopolized the sunshine and the public view.

During this period, however, the only part of the world that seemed to have a mind seriously to build anything like megastructure was Latin America. Whatever the arguable megastatus of the celebrated but unfinishable *Helicoide* in Caracas, the project for the new university in Tucumán by Horacio Caminos has multiple claims. One strong claim is that its giant scale and ambitions set the intellectual tone for a whole generation of Tucumán graduates, including Cesar Pelli who figured largely in the Los Angeles school of megastructuralists – the project that made Pelli famous, the Sunset Mountain scheme of 1964 for the Daniel, Mann, Johnson & Meldenhall office, took a whole mountain as its site. But if that was bold for the mid-sixties, Caminos's project was, for 1952, absolutely sensational. It involved levelling the top of the mountain, covering part of it with a modular system of triangular umbrella units two storeys high (**28**), and framing it with multi-storey slabs of enormous length – the student hostel (**29**) was to be two thousand feet long – with their own internal

28, 29 *Tucumán University project (Horacio Caminos, 1951–2). Latin America's first major bid at a megastructure, this gigantic hill-top complex in Argentina got as far as retaining walls and site works, but little further. If completed as designed, it would have covered the levelled mountain-top with a system of concrete umbrellas large enough to shelter most of the campus, framed by buildings of enormous length — the student hostel (29) was to be 2,000 feet long.*

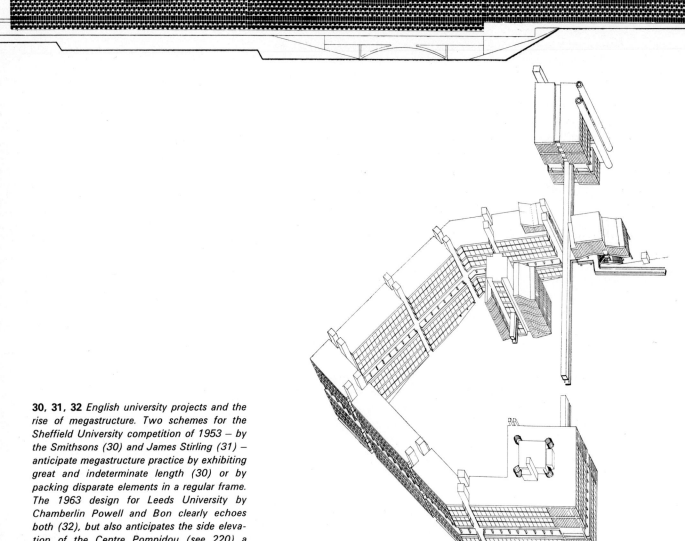

30, 31, 32 *English university projects and the rise of megastructure. Two schemes for the Sheffield University competition of 1953 — by the Smithsons (30) and James Stirling (31) — anticipate megastructure practice by exhibiting great and indeterminate length (30) or by packing disparate elements in a regular frame. The 1963 design for Leeds University by Chamberlin Powell and Bon clearly echoes both (32), but also anticipates the side elevation of the Centre Pompidou (see 220) a decade later.*

30

circulation patterns. Though sternly rectilinear, these cliff-edge blocks probably owe something to the snake-plan ridge-top apartments of Affonso Reidy's Pedregulho scheme of 1947. But whereas Pedregulho was completed, little was done beyond preliminaries and some neat faculty houses on the lower slopes at Tucumán. Nevertheless, its scale and ruthlessness guarantee it a place somewhere in the megastructure canon.

A place 'somewhere in the canon' would also have to be found for some British competition schemes of the early fifties – the Smithson (**30**) and Stirling (**31**) schemes for Sheffield University, for instance, both of which seem to have left traces on the somewhat megastructural design for Leeds University produced by Chamberlin Powell and Bon around a decade later in 1963 (**32**). By the mid-fifties, however, more specifically megastructural projects were beginning to surface here and there. In 1955, for instance, a remarkable project for an art museum in Antwerp (**33**) by François Jamagne[17] demonstrated quite explicitly the concept of a diagonally braced framework supporting high-technology 'capsules' in pursuit of maximum flexibility and interchangeability. Though it anticipated the later frame-and-capsule projects of, say, Wolfgang Döring, there seems to be no connection, in spite of the publication of Jamagne's design in the influential magazine *Bauen + Wohnen.*

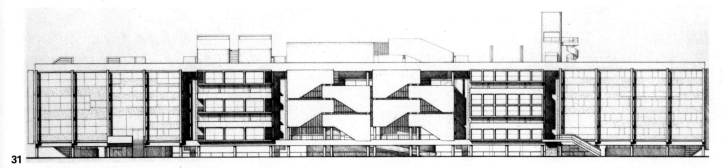

31

32

33 *Art Museum project, Antwerp (François Jamagne, 1955). Again the Centre Pompidou is anticipated, this time in the diagonally braced vertical frame of Jamagne's remarkably forward-looking project, which also anticipates most versions of the 'high technology capsule' type of megastructure in which enclosed cells (here sections of display galleries) of great technical sophistication are hung at will in a simple carrying frame.*

34 *Tomorrow's City Hall project (Louis Kahn, 1952 onwards; model 1958). One of two prime sources (see also 37) for the diagonal frame so frequently proposed for megastructures, and the first of Kahn's studies of the replanning of Philadelphia which collectively were to exercise great influence on the megastructure movement.*

The upright rectilinear frame with diagonal bracings is only one of a number of almost standardized solutions for basic carrying structures which can serve as visual signals that there are megastructural intentions afoot. Another and equally influential one was the frame composed entirely of diagonal structural members. Though this had at least one respectable ancestor in bridge design, the direct inspiration among megastructures almost certainly came from Louis Kahn and his schemes for 'Tomorrow's City Hall'. The best-known version of this is the model of 1958 (**34**), but published versions go back as far as 1952.

All versions of this project must be seen, in hindsight, as contributory to Kahn's great plans for Philadelphia, which gave far more convincing visual form to Giedion's demands for a more monumental urbanism than did the projects of any of Giedion's more direct followers. As against the lightweight, coloured, mobile vision promoted by Giedion, Kahn offers a city dominated by a ring of dark, coarse, massive towers like classical ruins — hollow incomplete cylinders, truncated pyramids, perforated cubes, the diagonalized city hall — and each the size of a city block (**35**). None could quite be called a megastructure in itself (most were only parking-garages), but the total effect was megastructural, and when Kahn returned to the theme in the famous 'viaduct' plan for Philadelphia (**36**) the result was something that Vincent Scully had no compunction in referring back to Le Corbusier's Fort l'Empereur and acclaiming as a megastructure.

35 *Center City Philadelphia project (Louis Kahn, 1952). A ring of vast, solidly monumental structures clustering around the city's heart, none strictly a megastructure, but together conjuring an urban imagery that inspired many megastructure projects.*

36 *Viaduct plan, Philadelphia (Louis Kahn, 1964). Traffic works barely considered ten years earlier here expand into mighty viaducts of ancient Roman or high Victorian scale, with results that are more nearly megastructure than anything else of Kahn's to which the term has been applied.*

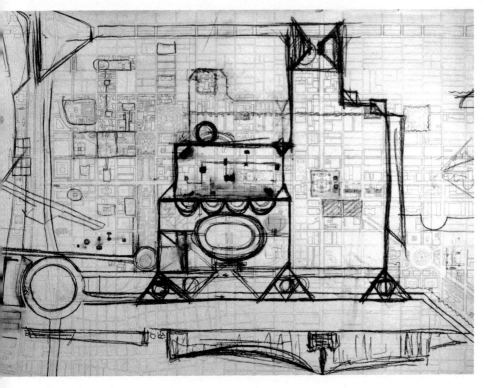

37 *Atomium, Brussels Expo (A. and J. Pollak and A. Waterkeyn, 1958). The restaurants and viewing platforms in the upper spheres of this 'theme building' (based on an enlarged atomic model) were reached through the diagonal tubes — a rare built version of the concept of circulation through diagonal structure that was to sustain many a megastructure proposal.*

The other obvious and contemporary source for the concept of a massive diagonal structural system was the 'Atomium' (**37**) at the Brussels Expo '58. Its intentions were far from megastructural, though seen over the roofs of the surrounding suburbia it does have something of the overscale and landmark qualities that many megastructures were later intended to present. More to the point, however, is that the designers of this 165×10^6 enlargement of a ball-and-stick molecular model — A. and J. Pollak with the engineer Waterkeyn — put most of the vertical circulation inside the steel tubes that made the 'sticks' of their tetrahedral composition — the admitted prototype for putting stairs and escalators inside the diagonal elements of many later structures, such as Archigram's Plug-In City.

There is another aspect of Kahn's Philadelphia projects that needs to be noted here. The towers were largely for car-parking, and grew both functionally and formally out of the traffic-circulation proposals that underpin nearly all these schemes. One such drawing, showing downtown traffic as canalizations of

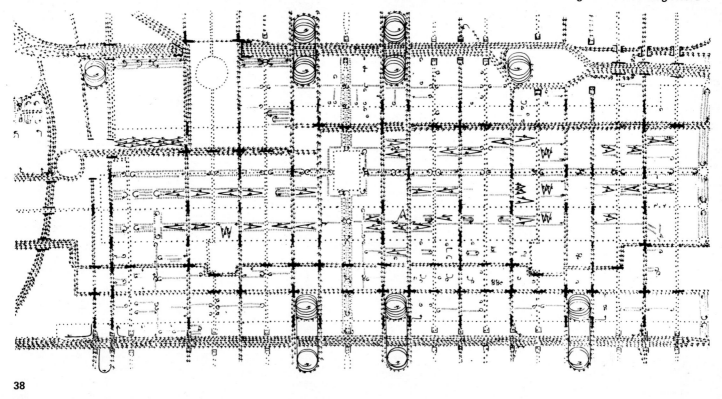

38

39

draughtsman's arrows pursuing one another along the streets as close as cars in the rush-hour and spiralling up into the parking structures (**38**), became a kind of icon in the eyes of architects two generations younger than Kahn, both as a beloved image in its own right and as a symbol of the aspiration of architects to 'do something about the traffic problem'.

This ambition can be traced back through Le Corbusier to Sant'Elia and beyond, but with new urgency it now became the excuse or justification for many a projected megastructure, especially in the United States. There, however, they could claim a rather surprising pre-war ancestor in Frank Lloyd Wright's Broadacre City projects. In spite of the city's ultra-low and seemingly more rural than urban densities, the plan is traversed by a monumental, multi-level traffic facility – the 'great arterial way', in Wright's period prose – which concentrates all express through traffic by rail and road (**39**), together with warehousing and other subsidiaries, and rejoices in some extremely complex overpasses and connectors.

38 *Reformed traffic circulation project, Philadelphia (Louis Kahn, 1952). An ideal diagram which became a 'key image', giving visual form to a widespread feeling that the energies of traffic movement, suitably directed, could give large-scale form to the modern city.*

39 *Great Arterial Way; model (Frank Lloyd Wright, 1936–7). A surprising anticipation of much later traffic-generated megaforms, the more unexpected because its location, in Wright's mind, was not a highly concentrated metropolis but his extremely low density Broadacre City project.*

40 *Downtown Fort Worth project; model/collage (Victor Gruen Associates, 1956). The first of the 'business-district-on-a-podium' projects that inspired megastructuralists, the scheme offered pedestrian circulation on the main podium level and vehicular parking below. Widely published, it set a standard of detailed elaboration and sheer vastness of ambition that all later projects had to match if they were to be taken seriously.*

A more widely noticed US traffic-based project was Victor Gruen's scheme for downtown Forth Worth (**40**), also as early as 1956. The full impact of Gruen, his works and writings will be discussed in the next chapter, but Forth Worth needs more than a passing mention here. Like many later proposals, it frames downtown in a necklace of freeways and parking-garages, the latter mostly under the edges of an extensive pedestrian level which provides a new 'artificial ground level' on which most of the 'Central Business District' is to be redeveloped. Basically it is of the same family as Gropius's Boston Center, with an equally conventional grouping of office-slabs and other customary modern building types, but its scale and absoluteness were stunning: it covered the entire Central District, and proposed to exclude all automobile circulation from that area completely. If not a megastructure, it was of the same school of thought in its determination to dispose of the automobile. So, paradoxically, was its effective opposite, Reginald Malcolmson's 'metro-linear' city project (**41**), which took the need for giant traffic arteries as the generating principle of its whole architectural concept.

Besides traffic, there was one other constraint that could be exploited to justify proto-megastructures: the need for extreme environmental insulation. Thus the published photographs of Egon Eiermann's 1953 project for the Stuttgart *Funkhaus* (broadcasting house) show something that certainly looks like a megastructure of sorts — two long parallel slabs of offices enclosing between them a sandwich of irregularly shaped studios and other sensitive installations that need to be protected against noise and external disturbances. The variability of these forms, and the literal 'open-endedness' of the sandwich, give an air of provisionality and extensibility that may have been intentional.

Thermally extreme environments could be even more megastimulating. In the late fifties the French magazine *Cahiers du centre scientifique et technique du*

41 *Metro-linear City project (Reginald Malcolmson, 1957). The link between the linear cities of the pioneers of the twenties and the 'unlimited', extensible megastructures of the sixties was provided by this widely known proposal for a continuous transportation-strip building flanked by regularly spaced tower blocks. It was a true descendant of early versions of Le Corbusier's* Ville Radieuse, *modified by the ideas of the old German urbanist Ludwig Hilbersheimer, with whom Malcolmson worked in Chicago.*

42 Cité-paquebot *project (Wladimir Gordeef, 1956). Intended to make life comfortable for white colonials in the Sahara Desert — it is not necessary to go into outer space or the ocean deeps to find an environment that is hostile to somebody! — sealed and self-contained like an ocean liner or* paquebot, *Gordeef's luxury living machine had its apartments opening off a vast air-conditioned communal space. When external climatic conditions were favourable (at night, for instance) the exposed outer ends of the apartments could be opened up instead of the inner, air-conditioned faces.*

bâtiment published a series of studies for buildings for European inhabitants of the Sahara. Most were conventionally sensible reworkings of the *Terrassenhäuser* section for shade and cross-ventilation, but one more visionary scheme proposed to make the apartments serve as one wall of a large, high volume of conditioned air containing gardens and public facilities, the apartments being opened up to the external or internal atmosphere, whichever was the more desirable or habitable (**42**). The entire living area would thus be, for most of the time, a sealed system, 'compact' within its 'definite boundary' — and these words used by Soleri about ships are very appropriate, since the project was titled, either by the magazine or by its designer Wladimir Gordeef, the *Cité-paquebot* ('liner city') ![18]

By this time, however, the sixties were in sight, and so were true megastructures. The Smithsons' entry for the *Hauptstadt Berlin* ('Berlin — capital city') competition of 1957 proposed a vast wandering pedestrian deck with clipped-on office towers, all at variance with the given Berlin street grid at ground level. Two years later, some of the entries for the rebuilding of Marszalkowska Street in Warsaw came close to being megastructures in their overall organization, if still a bit Fort Worth in their forms. More provokingly, and also in 1959, Gino Valle's first design for the Zannussi-Rex office block in Pordenone (**43**) came close to megastructure in its forms, the seemingly extensible ends carried high on columns above the ground, its flanks adorned with the boldly expressed diagonals of staircases.

More importantly, 1959 saw the publication by Kenzo Tange and his students at the Massachusetts Institute of Technology (MIT) of the Boston Harbor project, widely regarded as the first true megastructure, certainly the first Japanese one. With its publication, megastructure emerged from the limbo of

almost-formulated ideas, and with it came the Japanese 'Metabolist' school of megastructuralists. At almost exactly the same time there emerged equally well-defined-looking schools of French and Italian megadesign. These three virtually unconnected bodies of work deserve separate treatment before they merge into the general body of megastructuralism after 1964.

Metabolism

The special relationship of Japan to megastructure has always been admitted. Not only was the word finally invented by a Japanese, but the launching of the Metabolist manifestoes at the World Design Conference in Tokyo in 1960 can now be seen as an attempt to launch megastructure as a unique Japanese contribution to modern architecture, marking the maturity of Japanese architecture and its independence of other cultures' 'neo-colonialist' views of what it ought to be.

Whatever the West's previous suppositions about the nature and future of modern Japanese architecture, the effect of the launching of Metabolism was galvanic, and, as Robin Middleton sarcastically observed:

Architects in the West were rendered almost senseless with emotion . . . it seemed that wondrous new megacities would be created high above the old towns, avoiding all the complexities of usage, land-ownership and bureaucracy. . . .[19]

If this is cynicism justified by hindsight, Metabolism as such is only part of the story; the changed perception of Japanese architecture desired and effected by the Metabolists (and their financial backers) was equally due to the emergence of a massive new monumental manner of using concrete, Corbusian in its origins but unmistakably Japanese – now – in its visual impact.

43 *Zanussi-Rex office block, Pordenone (Studio Valle, 1959–60). The Megastructure Look at the beginning of the megastructure decade: long and extensible, repetitively but aformally composed along a spine of communications, externally hung with projecting elements and the diagonals of staircases – but not reckoned a megastructure because of its single administrative function.*

44 *Ocean City project; model (Kiyonoru Kiku-take, 1962). One of the prime visions of the Japanese Metabolist group: vast cylindrical towers forming the 'trees' on which the individual dwellings come and go like seasonal 'leaves', each according to the natural time-scale of its own proper 'metabolism', and all standing on floating concrete islands in order to relieve the pressure on Japan's scarce supplies of urban land.*

So the West, which had previously expected Japanese modern architecture to be characterized by a spare, Miesian continuation of the austere native tradition of domestic simplicity, had to adjust to a Japanese architecture that was bulky, brutalist, ponderous and irregular. This was no strain; Western modern architecture was moving in the same direction stylistically, so the work of the Metabolist group promised not only exciting by-passes through the impasses of town planning, but a detailed aesthetic that was monumentally appealing. The Metabolists were underwriting the megastructural ambitions of their Western contemporaries, and they knew it.

Thus the first clear exposition of a Metabolist project outside Japan was to an appropriately symptomatic audience at the Otterloo CIAM/Team-X congress of 1959. Kenzo Tange, an invited participant, showed not only one of his own pre-Metabolist projects, but also two by Kiyonoru Kikutake, one of which was the 'Sea City': 'land for man to live; sea for machine to function'. The drawing reproduced in the official report of the congress seems to be a condensation of two different earlier Kikutake schemes: the 'Marine City' of 1958, with its cylindrical residential towers built down into the water beneath concrete islands, and the 'Tower City' of 1959 with similar towers built upwards from island bases. The two concepts were combined again in the 1962 'Ocean City' model (**44**) — and finally realized in miniature caricature on dry land (**45**) by Kurokawa in his 1967 'Yamagata Hawaii Dreamland' swimming-pool complex!

In introducing Kikutake's projects in 1959, Tange made all the standard Metabolist points, though without using the word 'metabolism' itself:

Tokyo is expanding but there is no more land so we shall have to expand into the sea. . . . Every day people come into the centre of the city, and must then return in the evening to their homes outside the city. For the average man the time required for this trip is an hour.

In this project the architect is thinking of the future of the city. He has divided it into two elements, one permanent and one temporary.

The structural element is thought of as a tree – a permanent element, with the dwelling units as leaves – temporary elements which fall down and are renewed according to the needs of the moment. The buildings can grow within this structure and die and grow again – but the structure remains.[20]

From the opening exposition of Tokyo as an urban crisis to the closing analogy of the metabolism of urban structure, Tange here covers the whole Metabolist argument in capsule form. Very little was added in the whole bulk of the movement's later writings to the two basic propositions: that artificial building land must be created in overcrowded cities, and that the different built elements of the city have different natural rates of metabolic change. The mind-numbing simplicity of this 'theoretical programme' probably had as much to do with the international impact of Metabolism as did the seductive monumentalism of its huge visionary forms. Nothing comparable was on offer in either Europe or North America, yet it was in North America that Tange himself produced the project so often acclaimed as the first real megastructure.

45 *Yamagata Hawaii Dreamland (Kisho Kurokawa, 1967). Ocean City was among the Metabolist visions that achieved built form at a drastically reduced scale and in mild travesty as leisure installations – here, a swimming pool.*

47

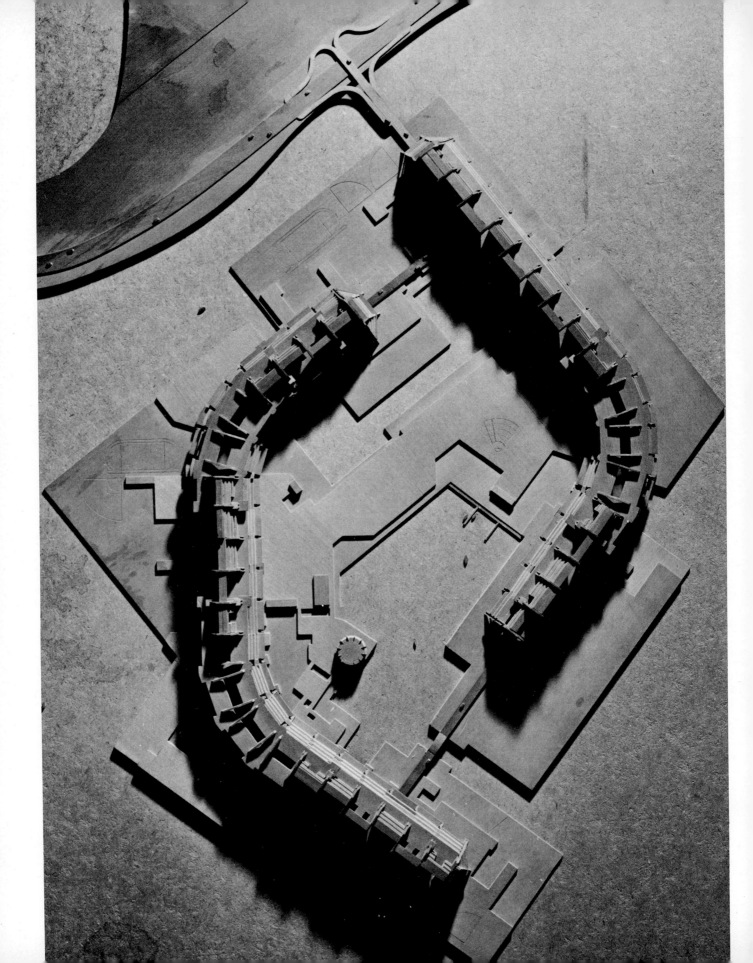

The reasons for the accepted primacy of the MIT Boston Harbor project (**46**) are clearly multiple. Firstly, it could not be brushed off as a pretty flash-in-the-pan improvization, but was a finely detailed model based on extensive and detailed design studies. This, secondly, gave it an air of buildability and probability; as did, thirdly, the fact that Tange himself was a known and respected institution by this date. So, fourthly, was the Massachusetts Institute of Technology, which, fifthly, was conveniently close to such centres of architectural communication and influence as New York, ever a major market-place of megastructural ideas. The sixth consideration is somewhat imponderable but needs to be pondered: that by its early date, this scheme probably did much to shape the concept of megastructure as generally understood, so that all attempts to locate the origins of the concept would tend to lead back to Boston Harbor.

For instance, it cannot but appear as the immediate parent of that magisterial project for Tokyo Bay which is probably Tange's – and certainly Metabolism's – greatest contribution to twentieth-century town-planning ideas, though it seems more likely in fact that both evolved almost simultaneously from a common stock of ideas. Of these ideas, the most important were those of terraced housing stacked back to back over transportation ways, with the important proviso that what both the projects offer is in fact terraced housing *land*, and location over a body of water conveniently adjacent to a major urban centre. The use of the 'A-frame' section was not new, of course; Tange seems to have known the Sant'Elia version, if not the innumerable derivatives like Gropius's enigmatic *Wohnberg* ('housing mountain') of 1928 (see p. 203). In Tange's version, however, this combination of housing facing outwards from the tent-like inner space within the A-frame, and transportation and other services within the space (**47**), has a new-minted freshness that derives partly from his detailed re-examination of the concept and the powerful formal inventiveness he brought to bear on it – especially in the Tokyo Bay version,

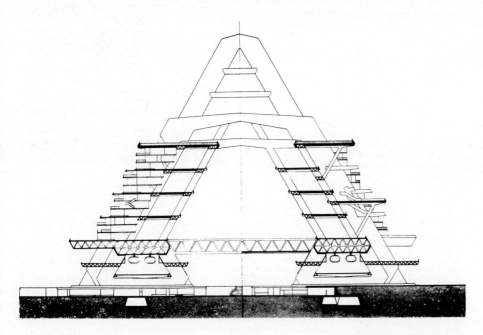

46, 47 *Boston Harbor development project (Kenzo Tange and students at MIT, 1959). One of Tange's two definitive megastructure projects, both distinguished by clarity of overall form and elaboration of design. In the Boston Harbor version, the two almost matching housing blocks are of the conventional A-frame section (47), straddling the loop of roads and rapid transport that comes out from the shore. The A-frame, however, is already seen more as a shelving system on which a variety of residential accommodation can be built than as a coherent* Terrassenhäuser *structure.*

where the curvature of the terraced section gives a genuinely tent-like and sheltering effect. The Boston version, presumed to be earlier, had plain straight-sided A-frames, but each of the two equal but opposite structures had a distinct curve in the middle of its plan, so that a partially closed public space was formed between them. The Tokyo versions were straight in plan, literally open-ended and extensible. Far from being the defining elements of the grand design, as in Boston, they were tributary to a more generalized concept, mere attachments of a vastly greater structure.

That greater structure must surely constitute one of the most heroic visions of town planning to appear in this century. Irrespective of whether it could be built or lived in (and many would regard it as an inhuman monument to Tange's megalomania), it marks a definitive break with all previous urban design concepts, however vast (**48**). The contrast with Lucio Costa's only slightly earlier plan for Brasilia (**49**) is instructive. Both schemes feature a central 'monumental axis' of governmental and other public buildings along a pair of parallel highways, but Costa's are seen as separate blocks in orderly geometrical ranks, whereas Tange's link up into irregular chains. Furthermore, where there would seem to be an irrefutable case for a megastructure at Brasilia, at the point where the monumental and residential axes cross in a complex intersection-cum-bus-terminal, there is none, whereas Tange's scheme is *all* megastructure – an enormous over-water communications structure connecting megastructures, served by megastructures, and made of megastructures.

48 *Tokyo Bay project (Kenzo Tange, 1960). Almost before the megastructure movement was under way, Tange had produced what looked like remaining the movement's major masterpiece – an urban structure extending downtown Tokyo some eighteen kilometres across the bay, and filling much of the remaining area of water with associated housing structures. Like Gruen's Fort Worth, it raised the threshold of credibility for urban planning projects, but put traffic works to entirely new uses in creating form (each sub-district of the scheme is framed in a loop of freeways), and thus made Japan the fount of inspiration for architectural and urban visionaries for most of the sixties.*

49 *Brasilia master-plan (Lucio Costa, 1956). The best that conventional Modern movement planning wisdom had achieved before 1960, but timid and constrained by comparison with Tange's gigantic vision for Tokyo.*

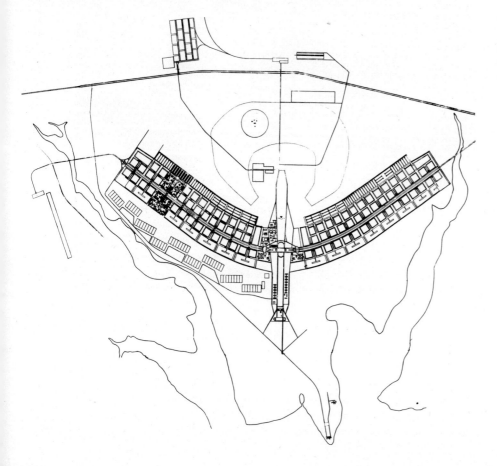

The idea of building over water in Tokyo Bay did not originate with Tange; it had a respectable, if short, history going back explicitly to April 1958, when Kyuro Kano, president of the Japan Housing Corporation, suggested filling in some eighty thousand hectares of the northern part of the bay. But, as the *Japan Architect* noted a year later, 'the extra space would be welcome, but many architects and urban designers believe that simple reclamation would be too crude and in the long run ineffective'.[21] This reaction seems to have been the trigger, not only for Tange's Tokyo scheme, but for those of Kikutake already mentioned, as well as Masato Otaka's proposals for a series of roughly parallel offshore strips of 'artificial land' carried on massive piles.

The Tange version, however, is vastly more sophisticated than any of the others. Described in the simplest possible terms, it consists of a chain of roughly rectangular freeway loops, the first of which would frame the existing Central Business District on shore. The next would overstep the shoreline, and the third and fourth would be entirely over water. Each link would have its parallel straight sides composed of sequences of suspension bridges, for which the

50, 51 *Tokyo Bay project: Central Business District and (51) housing structures. The overall design is so vast a megastructure that many of its individual parts would qualify as megastructures themselves in a different context: the business buildings consist of multi-storey bridges carried between massive service towers, while each of the tent-like structures providing the 'artificial ground' on which housing may be built is in itself larger than the whole Boston Harbor project (see 46).*

obvious prototype is the Oakland/Bay bridge sequence in San Francisco — one of a number of signs that Tange's American experiences were giving him a technical and dimensional boldness to match the Corbusian boldness of his detailed forms. Within these links would be the office buildings etc., generally conceived as megastructures of habitable bridge trusses (**50**) spanning between skyscraping service towers arranged on a regular square planning grid. Beyond the fourth link the project changes its urban character, though the freeway bridge system continues its uninterrupted march across the bay. The empty fifth link contains only a harbour, after which the space within the links is again occupied by offices and public buildings; but now subsidiary bridges depart at right-angles to the main line of the chain of freeway links, connecting to clusters of the tent-like residential units spread across the broader waters of that part of the bay (**51**).

Tange has offered numerous social and financial justifications for this eighteen-kilometre adventure, but none of them does more than provide excuses on a suitably vast numerical scale for what can almost be left to justify

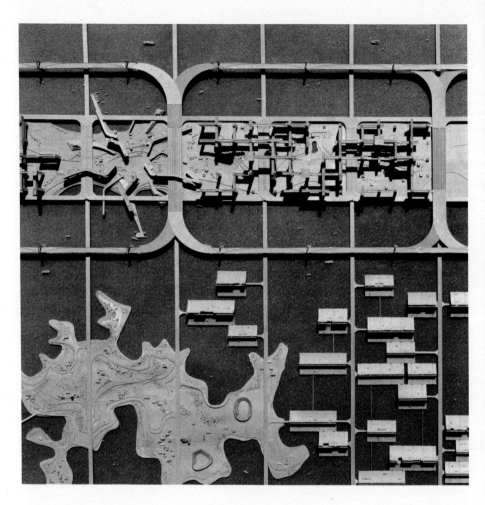

52 *Tokyo Bay project: view of over-water structures. Perhaps the best indication of the scale of the project is the subsidiary role played by suspension bridges the size of the George Washington Bridge. Many critics have feared that, as a consequence, the scheme, while comprehensible as a model, might be incomprehensible to ordinary human beings if built at the scale of real life.*

itself as a *création pur de l'esprit humain* (as Le Corbusier would phrase it), a work of art in its own right that can be left to stand up for itself as a monument to a particular intersection of time and national culture. It is unmistakably Japanese, from the overall conception of an urban metabolism in which all parts have their own rates of growth and change to the detailed design of the dwellings on the shelves of the tent-like residential structures. Yet it demands to be judged at an international level; Europe and America have been laid under tribute, and have responded by almost universal approbation and emulation.

The sense of scale is unnerving; so is the formal control over all the parts of the professedly aformal and uncontrollable megaform (**52**). The project has an air of authority not be be recaptured in any of Tange's later works (except possibly the arguably megastructural Yamanishi headquarters building at Kofu, **53–5**) nor ever to be equalled by his younger contemporaries who formed the Metabolist group proper. Frankly, their visionary sketches look sloppy and half-baked by comparison, even when they too are taken as far as model form, as were Kikutake's 'Sea City', Kurokawa's 'Helicoids' (**56**), or Isozaki's 'Space City' (**57**) of housing bracketed out from cylindrical towers, or when the projects were closely tied to real, about-to-be-developed building sites of realistic scale, as in the much redesigned Ohtemachi or Shinjuku developments.

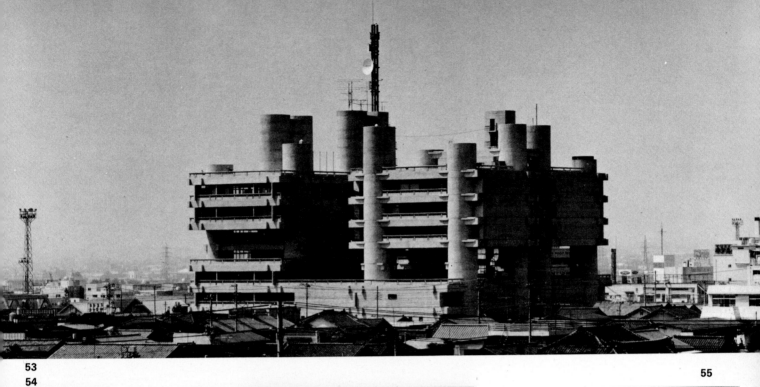

53
54

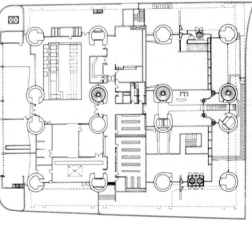

53, 54, 55 *Yamanishi Communications Centre, Kofu (Kenzo Tange, 1967). The nearest thing to a megastructure that Tange was to build, its extensibility is by implication vertical, since the towers (53) terminate at different heights, while 55 shows that they form an effectively closed composition in plan. The usable accommodation (broadcasting studios, offices, etc.) appears to be housed in removable concrete boxes, but the construction is in fact conventional, so that the result (as at Habitat, Montreal, see chapter 6) is really a monolithic statue commemorating an ideal of adaptability that was practically impossible to realize in built fact.*

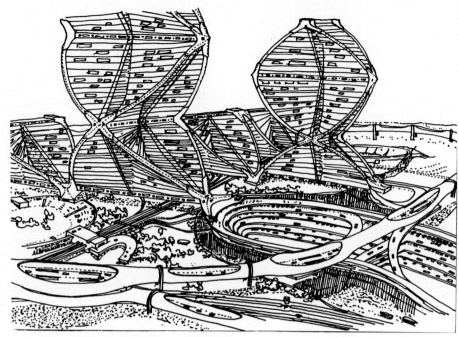

56 *Helicoids project (Kisho Kurokawa, 1961). Perhaps the best-known and most immediately recognizable of Japanese Metabolist projects, it was originally intended as a proposal for the rebuilding of the Ginza district of Tokyo, but subsequently developed an independent life in the magazines as the ultimate symbol of Metabolism.*

57 *Space City project; collage (Arato Isozaki, 1960). Another famous, almost totemic image of Metabolism, with the habitable bridges of the new city disdainfully overstepping the tumbled ruins of older urban cultures and the polluted present — a procedure also proposed by others outside Japan, especially Yona Friedman (see 60, 61).*

Tange's Tokyo Bay simply raised the scale of the megastructure argument to a level of monumental vastness from which it could not get down again. The other architects, schools and movements who were already moving in the same direction could only pay it the sincere flattery of imitation, and in the process proved that, like the minor Metabolists, they had neither the formal vision nor the sustained inventive capacity required. The Japanese megastructure movement had only a very short life of genuine creativity – its 'academicism of Utopias'[22] was already apparent to Manfredo Tafuri as early as 1966 – but its effect on the two contemporary European movements in France and Italy seems to have been entirely destructive; their decline seems to date from the moment when they became aware of the enormity of what the Japanese had already achieved.

Urbanisme spatial

The concept of a French 'school' of megastructuralists may have been only a figment of journalistic imagination. Nevertheless, it looked pretty convincing around 1960–62 in the pages of *Architecture d'aujourd'hui*, and in Michel Ragon's book *Où vivrons-nous demain?* ('where shall we be living tomorrow?') of 1963. Ragon's book, which seems to have had some influence on later megaliterature, covers practically every aspect of experimental and visionary architecture visible at that time from a viewpoint in Paris – that viewpoint being, in practice, the pages of *Architecture d'aujourd'hui*, of which the book is really a concise and vastly better written summary aimed at the general reader. Much of the material covered has nothing much to do with the rise of megastructure, but quite a lot is directly relevant and is couched in journalistic phraseology of admirable punchiness which encapsulates much megathought – *l'augmentation de la concentration urbaine/villes-galaxies/le problème des circulations/la recherche de la dimension/nouveaux matériaux, nouvelles formes* – all under the sign of *l'ère tertiaire*, for which the truest English translation is probably 'the post-industrial age'.

The phrase *urbanisme spatial* gives the title to Ragon's fifth and most widely noted chapter, and also provides the handiest phrase to characterize what French megastructuralism was about. From outside the normal Paris network the chapter covers only Kahn, Kurokawa and Soleri among names of consequence, while from within the network it covers Edouard Albert, Nicholas Schoffer, Janusz Deryng, Walter Jonas, Paul Maymont and Yona Friedman, and opens with a quotation from Alexandre Persitz, editor of *Architecture d'aujourd'hui*:

Imagine, not a single Eiffel Tower, but ten, twenty or even more, like an immense metal forest, connected by bridges, roads and platforms. Within this gigantic 'three-dimensional' spider-web are ranged dwellings, schools, theatres, commercial enterprises. . . . The structure is lighter and more transparent than Eiffel could have dreamed in 1887. All the tension members are cables; those in compression are few, essentially lattice pylons. Scintillating coloured materials, lighter and smaller forms are threaded through this *Cité Spatiale*. . . .[23]

This, almost visibly, is the kind of aesthetic proposed by Giedion *et al.* in 1943 and discussed at the beginning of this chapter, and with minor variations of structural methods it is the aesthetic of *urbanisme spatial*: a very lightweight network carrying multi-level and usually changeable provisions for the whole life of a city. Of all megastructure visions it is the most abstract, least material and

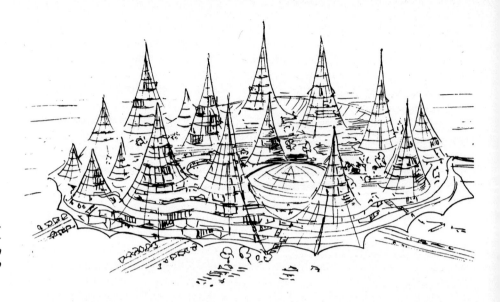

58 *Suspended City project (Frei Otto, 1960). Though German, Otto produced the first pictorial images that fulfilled the French dream of a non-rectangular, three-dimensional spider-web city hung from a forest of Eiffel Towers.*

most conventionally 'elegant', and is called *spatial* only because it adds a third, vertical dimension to the customary two of the planner's flat paper surface to give a three-dimensional planning grid liberating the plan from the ground.

As a concept this was not new; what distinguished *urbanisme spatial* from previous ideas of the sort was the proposal to build a physical grid of this sort in a form light enough for it to look no more than an abstract grid. Persitz's insistence on extreme lightness in his description of this vision (presumably based on a project by Frei Otto (**58**) or Paul Maymont) was a doomed fantasy, but at the time compulsive and engaging. It may be called 'doomed' for two reasons. Firstly, the aesthetic it expresses was already thoroughly out of date (and probably had been ever since its partial realization in 1951), and was about to be crushed throughout the world by the more 'crumbly' Brutalist aesthetic of raw concrete and massive monumentality that was the normal mode of megastructural expression. Secondly, it was not constructible as envisaged; Persitz's supposition that the compression members could be a few light lattice pylons had already been shown to be unfeasible as far back as 1951 (differences between first sketches and final version of the Festival of Britain 'Skylon'), and this was being demonstrated again in many contemporary projects such as the Snowdon/Price/Newby aviary for the London Zoo. In all experience of tension structures the compression members tend to be thicker, more numerous and visually more obtrusive than the first pencil sketches had hopefully proposed, yet the myth persists.

What made the myth look convincing enough to support *urbanisme spatial* was a particularly brilliant and adventurous phase of lattice structures, and one or two tension models, produced around the end of the fifties by French engineers like Robert le Ricolais, René Sarger and Jean-Louis Sarf — and an acquaintance, at least photographic, with the work of Frei Otto, Buckminster Fuller and the likes of Eckhard Schulze-Fielitz. By concentrating on the more extreme and visionary schemes devised by such a remarkable array of talents, the Urban Spatialists were able to maintain an air of verisimilitude in their projects. Although Frei Otto was the only engineer who produced schemes which directly support the vision propounded by Persitz, Sarger and Le Ricolais were more immediately to hand – especially Sarger, who was virtually 'engineer in residence' at *Architecture d'aujourd'hui* at the time.

One of his projects in particular seems to have had almost talismanic standing among architects of this connection: the first version of his projected roof structure for the new parliament building in Teheran, which is illustrated in Ragon as a pure structure, stripped of both its functional accommodations and its name. As a kind of pure structural vision, it has both ancestry and progeny. Given its obvious diagonality and open lattices, its ancestor must be Sarger's own structure for the French pavilion at Brussels Expo '58, which offered tangible proof that this kind of structure was practical and would stand up (**59**). The progeny must include the projects of Paul Maymont, for which Sarger virtually admitted direct paternity in a laudatory note in 1962, but also the *Neo-Babylone* of Constant Niewenhuis, whose social programme may be his own (see next chapter) but whose aggressively diagonal (and in part tensional) structure seems to be descended at least visually from this reading of Sarger's Brussels design.

59 *French pavilion, Brussels Expo (René Sarger, engineer, 1958). A number of brilliant French engineers like Sarger, in innumerable speculative studies and a few built prototypes like the Brussels pavilion, gave 'objective' warrant for the obsessive diagonalism of a whole generation of lightweight megastructure projects.*

However, these tensile propositions do not provide a three-dimensional planning grid that is easy to use, since they tend to generate circular plans, and to produce sagging diagonals in section. *Architecture d'aujourd'hui* therefore kept its eye on rectangular developments as well: the stackable capsules of Pascal Hauesermann, the early versions of Toulouse le Mirail and other projects by Candilis/Josic/Woods, the 'Spatial City' of Schulze-Fielitz and, above all, the *urbanisme mobile* of Yona Friedman.

Of all the Urban Spatialists, Friedman is by far the best-known internationally; indeed he is one of the best-known of all megastructure theorists, whose influence and personal impact can be attested by eye-witness accounts from most parts of the megastructure world. The reasons for this international renown are largely his own energetic self-promotion, together with a body of ideas that are few, relatively unchanging, and easy to grasp in spite of much flourishing of mathematics and 'scientific' method. It would be unfair to call him a 'one-idea man', but a very restricted register of basic propositions and images pervades all his published work and leads always to the same type of architectural/urbanistic conclusion. His basic concepts are mobility and change, which thus put him in a similar position to the Metabolists in some ways, though not in one fundamental way: Friedman sees mobility and change as basic human needs — change within the house, and mobility of the house's location. These ideas, which emerged as early as 1958, were soon linked to the concepts of 'the democratization of the city' (permitting every citizen to choose his habitation by computer) and of 'play' or 'amusement' — Friedman is the first of the megastructuralists to invoke the name of Johan Huizinga, theorist of the importance of play in the history of civilization, though he does not cite the title of Huizinga's book *Homo Ludens*[24] — 'man at play' — which became very current in European megacircles (see next chapter).

The concept of the megacity as the playground of a new leisured class informs theories as diverse as those of Niewenhuis and of Archigram, but in Friedman's reading it leads not to diversity but to concentration on a single, double-headed proposition: *architecture mobile*, which enables the citizen to change the plan and equipment of his dwelling, and *urbanisme mobile*, which enables the citizens collectively to change the grouping and location of their dwellings within the urban frame. The essential supports, almost in the Habraken sense, for this double adaptability are to be:

Urbanisme Spatial . . . techniques for mobile architecture and mobile urbanism. It consists of a three-dimensional infrastructure (multi-deck space-frame grid). The usable volumes for homes, offices etc. occupy the voids of this infrastructure, and their arrangement or rearrangement follows the will of the inhabitants. . . .

Infrastructure Spatiale . . . a three-dimensional grid, raised on pilotis above ground level. Lightweight uses are located in the interstices of this structure, in the elevated part. Heavyweight uses (industry, large meetings, circulation) occupy the ground surface, under the Three-dimensional grid, and between the widely-spaced pilotis — which contain vertical circulation and services (lifts, stairs, mains distribution, ducts).[25]

Friedman's explanatory sketches confirm and re-confirm this unitary, simplistic solution, at once convincing and universal. Whether the ground surface is occupied by Paris, New York (**60**), Algiers (**61**), London dockland or even the English Channel (**62**), above it spreads the same generalized 3-D grid in which *Homo ludens friedmanensis* can play his universal but personalized metagame of 'let's make a city'. The grid, whatever its ultimate source (probably Mies van

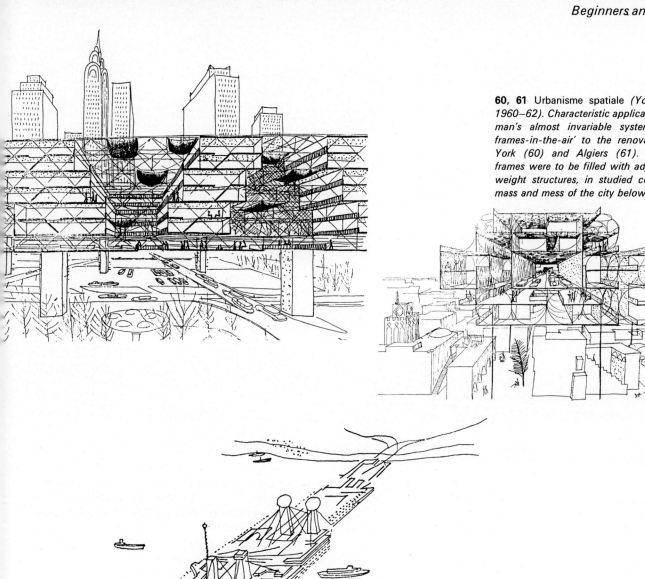

60, 61 Urbanisme spatiale *(Yona Friedman, 1960–62). Characteristic applications of Friedman's almost invariable system of 'space-frames-in-the-air' to the renovation of New York (60) and Algiers (61). The elevated frames were to be filled with adjustable light-weight structures, in studied contrast to the mass and mess of the city below.*

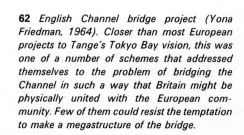

62 *English Channel bridge project (Yona Friedman, 1964). Closer than most European projects to Tange's Tokyo Bay vision, this was one of a number of schemes that addressed themselves to the problem of bridging the Channel in such a way that Britain might be physically united with the European community. Few of them could resist the temptation to make a megastructure of the bridge.*

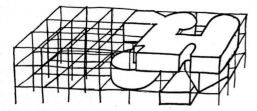

63 *New Central Station, Ottawa (J. B. Parkin and Associates, 1966). Frames like those proposed by Friedman could indeed be built, but most turned out to be handsome ceremonial structures (see also 106) into which it would have been almost impossible to insert habitable structures.*

64 Architecture mobile *(Yona Friedman, 1962). Within the apparent liberties offered by the empty space-frames of his* urbanisme spatiale, *Friedman's architectural offerings tend to look curiously constrained: here he stirs little beyond the elementary geometrical forms and earthbound floor-by-floor planning practised by Le Corbusier in house designs of thirty years earlier.*

der Rohe, though his students at the Illinois Institute of Technology, Chicago, were later to find it unbuildable) bears little relationship to structural probabilities; it more nearly resembles the 3-D chessboards that some architecture schools were toying with at the time. It also resembles architecture (**64**), far more than do, say, the absolute grids of Schulze-Fielitz, which come right down to ground level and leave no clear space between pilotis beneath. Friedman's grids on legs could be related to a number of available archetypes (**63**), and something like them was to be built, for quite unrelated reasons, in cases as different as Ezra Ehrenkrantz's prototype 'system-built' school at Stanford University or Tange's central 'Theme Piazza' at Osaka Expo '70.

This, at least, was a concept negotiable outside France in a world going Metabolist; the fastidious way it overstepped the mess of existing cities was obviously comparable to the way in which Isozaki's 'Space City' elegantly bypassed the planners' usual problems of condemnation and demolition. Friedman's grids, though structurally as skinny as Maymont's, proposed an image that would be acceptable to the maturing megamood of the sixties. The rest of *urbanisme spatial,* linked to an outmoded aesthetic, had nothing comparable to offer, especially in the forms in which it was promoted by *Architecture d'aujourd'hui.*

One or two talents, like Maymont who had been to Tokyo and could now do islands, Kurokawa-style (**65**), and even Hollein-type proposals such as a rather neat project for a linear city under the river Seine (**66**), remained afloat for a year or two, but the whole Parisian grouping was becoming less effective and more defensive as the sixties went on. Thus in 1964 a special issue of their magazine

65 *Floating Island project, Monaco (Paul Maymont, 1963). One of the few Parisian Urban Spatialists who had been in direct contact with the Metabolists, Maymont had something of their formal sophistication — and for that reason his projects began to look better and better as the sixties proceeded.*

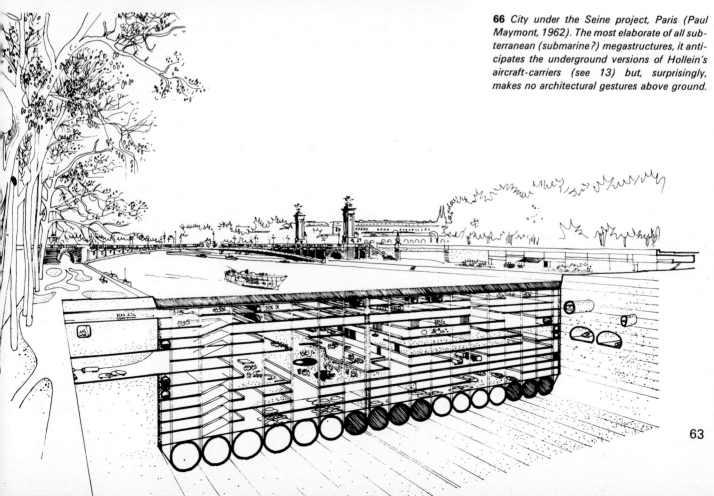

66 *City under the Seine project, Paris (Paul Maymont, 1962). The most elaborate of all subterranean (submarine?) megastructures, it anticipates the underground versions of Hollein's aircraft-carriers (see 13) but, surprisingly, makes no architectural gestures above ground.*

63

devoted to *Recherches* (the usual names plus English newcomers) was followed in November of that year by one in which Persitz paid the same English names – now recognizable as Archigram – the supreme compliment of attack, albeit equivocally:

It would be vain to tax these studies with utopianism, absurdity or impossibility. Effectively they have nothing to·do with concrete responses to problems, but are manifestations of violent defiance. They are also an expression of a vitality that one cannot but find encouraging and sympathetic. But to pedantic spirits and architecture students one must make it clear that these studies are not offered to inspire Diploma projects, nor as models for cities of the future. . . .[26]

This is an instructive response from an editor who had never been tempted to tax Niewenhuis, Soleri or Kurokawa with Utopianism, absurdity or impossibility; but these three could, at an editorial pinch, be assimilated to some of the themes that had preoccupied the magazine in the preceding five years. Archigram and their generation could not; they were after something different, as will emerge two chapters hence. They threatened the comfortable cultural chauvinism that had for so long seen Paris as the centre for all things modern. The Metabolists with an effort could still be assimilated, Archigram could not and was attacked; but what is even more striking is that the Italian megastructuralists were totally ignored until their movement was almost spent.

Città-territorio

In fairness to Persitz, however, it must be admitted that the Italian movement of the early sixties is probably easier to see now, in retrospect, than it was at the time, when any general ideas about Italian megastructuralism were likely to be focused on one single designer who was hardly ever personally present in Italy. This was Paolo Soleri who, while still commuting across the Atlantic occasionally, was increasingly committed to America, and was becoming most widely known for his first large specifically American project, the 'Mesa City' drawings of 1960 which became public property after the 'Visionary Architecture' exhibition sent on tour by the Museum of Modern Art, New York, the next year.

That show contained no work by the grouping of Italians who will be labelled for present purposes with the phrase *città-territorio*. Manfredo Tafuri seems to have been the originator of the phrase, which he used in print to review a collection of discussion papers emanating from a round-table and fifth-year studio project given at the Faculty of Architecture in Rome in the academic session 1961–2. The ostensible subject of this concentration of academic activity and talent was a project for the *centro direzionale* (subsidiary business district) proposed for a site at Centocello astride the then unbuilt and therefore modifiable *Autostrada del Sole* outside Rome. The contributors to the round-table were a very distinguished body indeed, including (besides Tafuri) Alberto Samona, Lodovico Quaroni, Carlo Aymonimo, Vieri Quillici and others. The discussions were open and remarkably free in form by the standards of Italian university procedures at that time, and ranged over the entire *problematica* of urban redevelopment as then perceived by the participants. Even so, the student projects that resulted are remarkable and unexpected in their variety and attack. Some are plainly derivative, from powerful foreign sources like Metabolism or potent and present Italian talents like Quaroni; but the published designs also

67 Centro direzionale *project, Centocello, Rome (Antonioli, Tonelli and other students at Rome Faculty of Architecture, 1961—2). A proposed subsidiary business centre astride the autostrada near Cinecittà, south of Rome, this seems to have been the first European project to come near to rivalling the formal inventiveness of the Metabolists. The diagonal space-frame is of an innovative type, but, in what must seem a typically Italian manner, it serves more as ceremonial scene-setting than as the support of usable accommodations.*

include tension structures, some remarkably opened-up and aformal planning, and at least one diagonal frame (**67**) that anticipates Archigram rather than following Kahn. And all but two can comfortably be categorized as megastructures of some sort, which is truly remarkable for Europe at that early date.

One reason for this apparent precocity may well have been the quality of discussions at the round-table, which encouraged far-out speculation, energetically supported by Tafuri and his working partners in their design office 'Studio-AUA'. For this team in particular, *città-territorio* was a body of concepts about the relationships between what happens inside the city and what happens outside, a situation with which the established planning concepts (zoning, neighbourhood units and so forth) could not cope. Tafuri and his associates proposed to concentrate planning activity at the points where the real action was happening: the transportation channels where the business moved to and fro, and especially the suburban sites where the radial channels met the peripheral ones around the city. At these sites they proposed to harness the economic and social activities that served city and territory alike – the economic tertiaries like marketing and management, the social secondaries like education and entertainment – and Centocello exhibited all these possibilities.

But to seize those possibilities, they maintained, required a *salto culturale*, a cultural leap, in scale with the quantum jump in the sheer size of urban problems. Since, however, they were architects, they still envisaged that *salto culturale* in purely architectural terms:

The city remains for us, beyond its functions as the propulsive force of social life and the economic nucleus of the territory, a point of physical concentration for architectural and spatial values . . . a *centro direzionale*, seen in these terms, will become the expressive and symbolic seat of the multiple functions of the city. . . .[27]

But in a characteristically Italo-Utopistic manner, while acknowledging that such *centri* will not deliver the urban goods, nor be built according to their precepts, without 'a new political dimension, a new administrative structure in which democracy will not be a slogan but a reality' – acknowledging all that, they propose not to wait for the glorious revolution, but to get on with the elaboration of their projects. 'Architecture or revolution?' For them, as for Le Corbusier forty years earlier, architecture was still the city's last best hope, and megastructure was architecture's last best hope.

For, if concentrated and literate debate was one stimulus to these precocious student projects, another was the whole profession's sustained practice in producing just such projects. *Centri direzionali* were common propositions in the legally required master-plans of Italian cities, and the omnipresence of this particular problem may already have done something both to shape Italian perceptions of town planning in a particular way and to concentrate attention on problems of this order. The time-span in which this process could have happened must have been short but decisive, since the first really relevant competition was as late as 1958–9. The strict subject-matter was housing, the site – La Barene at Mestre on the edge of the Venetian lagoon – was a classic case: it was peripheral (Mestre affords no other type), in an unmanaged conurbation (Mestre was a by-word), and right on a transportation channel between city and territory (the causeway to Venice itself). The winning design, by a team headed by Quaroni, presents a cluster of very large residential slabs laid out as part-cylinders of very large radius – the largest is over four hundred metres across. These are grouped by the head of the causeway and are big enough to be impressive even when seen from Venice, and a splendid, simplifying perspective sketch shows them thus, reflected in the waters of the lagoon (**68**).

This was indeed a concentration of 'architectural and spatial values', and it would probably have influenced the Centocello projects even if Quaroni himself had not been present. After it followed a steady succession of competitions and propositions, understandably of varying interest, but adding up to a flow of projects by talents as important, intellectually as well as architecturally, as Benevolo, de Carlo, Tafuri or Tentori, in which the overall tendency is always the same: towards a single comprehensive construction covering most of the site and embracing all of its required functions. Given these developments of 1959–63, the students who produced the Centocello projects must be seen as

68 *La Barene housing project, Mestre (Lodovico Quaroni and design team, 1958). One brilliant sketch of the proposed housing mirrored in the waters of the Venetian lagoon sums up the formal discipline – and formalistic ambitions – of this monumental concept, in which the residences are laid out in solid circular sweeps up to a quarter of a mile in diameter.*

only a little ahead of the Italian game. Neither were they the only players, even in their own age-group. . . .

Thus in 1961-2 a team of Milanese students headed by Giorgio Bay tackled another classic site, at Chiesa Rossa on the southern outskirts of the city, with a noble intention: 'The southward extension of the subway is a symbol of the city moving toward the countryside without degrading it';[28] and though the result may lack the formal adventure of the Romans, the complexity and ambition are both there (**69**). Again, though the overall project looks at first sight like separate housing blocks in parallel formation, the connections between them at various levels, and with the subway station and other subsidiaries, result in what is effectively a single building extensible along its major axis. By 1963 the magazine *Casabella* was publishing projects of this order at an average rate of one a month until, in the summer of that year, the whole situation changed suddenly. With the publication of the competition projects for the *quartiere direzionale* in Turin, *città-territorio* ceased to be a purely local and Italian affair. The editors of *Casabella* sensed that this was 'one of the outstanding cultural events in the architecture of our time',[29] and the rest of the world took notice, at least of the winning scheme, by Quaroni and team once more (**70**). To the rest of the world it was an extraordinarily rich and complex, masterly and inventive urban renewal scheme, and no more than that. Few non-Italian commentators were stirred to remark much beyond its skilful multi-level traffic arrangements, and it

69 *Chiesa Rossa housing project, Milan (Giorgio Bay and other students at Milan Polytechnic, 1961—2). Another classic Italian peripheral site, opened up by the extension of the Metropolitan railway towards the countryside. Although the scheme was apparently conceived conventionally as separate housing blocks in parallel array, the connection of the blocks to the underground station, with its concourses and facilities, effectively unites the whole into a megastructure of sorts.*

70, 71 Quartiere direzionale *project, Turin; winning competition entry (Lodovico Quaroni and design team, 1963). The culmination – and tombstone – of the pioneering phase of Italian megastructure, much published and admired, but too much like the 'everywhere-the-same' type of downtown that was to bore the later sixties.*

seems more than possible that its widespread acclaim may be closely connected with an elusively Sant'Elian quality about the perspectives (**71**) that chimed in well with the revival of interest in Futurism and other newly established *idées reçues.*

For those who had been following the progress of the concept of *città-territorio*, however, some of the other schemes might have seemed more significant. Those in particular by the Samona team, by Aymonimo and Achilli, by Tafuri and Studio-AUA (**72**) (all of the original Roman round-table, like the winner) would have looked more striking formally and more penetrating intellectually, more determined to concentrate architectural and spatial values. And all three of them were among that majority of submissions that could be classified without embarrassment as megastructures.

As so often happens, recognition and exhaustion seemed to arrive together; this was the end of the road, as well as the supreme moment, for the Italian City-Territorialists. Quaroni's winning Turin scheme joined a select band of officially esteemed exemplars of the New Town Planning (Toulouse le Mirail and some of the entries for the Venice-Tronchetto (**73**) and Tel Aviv-Yafo competitions were others) in a limbo of approval where they no longer had the power to stir men's minds. The torch of progress passed, by general consensus, to the 'radicals' of Florence, but its flashes of illumination seemed to reveal Italian megastructuralism stuck in the same attitudes for almost a decade. This too was an 'academicism of Utopias'.

72 Quartiere direzionale *project, Turin; competition entry (Manfredo Tafuri and Studio-AUA, 1963). This project by the prime theorists of the peripheral business centre is not only more obviously Italian and megastructural than Quaroni's winning design (70, 71), but also seems to look forward to 'radical megastructures' (see 154–6).*

73 *Tronchetto Island development project, Venice; competition entry (Manfredi Nicoletti and design team, 1963). Another piece of appropriately megastructural design for a typically megastructural cluster of functions — parking and harbour facilities on an artificial island.*

4 Megayear 1964

The rising tide of proto-megastructural activity in the early sixties was clearly headed for a peak of creativity before the middle of the decade, but in retrospect it seems that the *annus mirabilis* for ideas and projects was 1964.

This was the year, for a start, when Fumihiko Maki first used the word 'megastructure' itself in print; when key issues of *Bauen + Wohnen* and *Architectural Forum* helped to crystallize the body of ideas involved; when a number of new forces like Archigram made their first real impact; and in which most of the megastructures actually built had been designed. Some of them were about to go to the working detail stage, one or two were already being built; one is tempted to add to Wilcoxon's four-part definition cited in chapter 1 some such final clause as

5   and designed before Christmas 1964.

However, the availability of the word marks a new and conscious beginning. Maki himself supposes that it had been in colloquial use for some time in the eastern US, where he had done a fair amount of teaching, before he committed it to print in *Investigations in Collective Form.* This seems likely; at least one story alleges that the word was used as early as 1962 by Charles W. Moore when, as visiting critic at Yale, he is reported to have exclaimed to a student: 'Oh, *up* your megastructure!' — or some such form of exasperated words. However, it is not traceable in print before Maki's use, and it is noticeable that even magazines close to the heart of the action did not dispose of the word that year; *Architectural Forum* got as close as 'megacity' and 'macrostructure', but no nearer.

As to the derivation of the word, there seems to be general agreement on the etymology guessed at by Wilcoxon in his *Bibliography*: *mega* as in 'megaton' from atomic weaponry, 'megalopolis' from Jean Gottman's book of that name, or 'megabucks' from any number of rueful jokes about government expenditure; and *structure* as in 'infrastructure' most clearly, possibly as in Habraken's 'support structure', and generally and almost subliminally as in all the ancient structural mystiques of the architectural profession — though megastructuralists were somewhat divided on what explicit importance should be accorded to structure, as will be seen in later chapters.

It is not too important, in fact, even in Maki's book, even if some of his Metabolist contemporaries appear practically obsessed by sheer monumental structure. If one regards the book simply as a source for megastructure, Maki too might seem to view matters thus, but the complete book, pictures and text (of which some parts were written with Masato Otaka and others with Jerry Goldberg) covers many different aspects of 'collective form' including some totally non-megastructural variants. The opening essay, 'Collective Form: Three Paradigms', offers two other paradigms beside megastructure, thus:

1 Compositional Form: groups of buildings composed according to traditional Modern Movement precepts (e.g. Brasilia).
2 Mega-Structure: a large frame containing all the functions of a city, mostly housed in transient short-term containers.
3 Group Form: accumulation of identical spatial or structural elements into larger complexes (Italian hill-towns).

Maki neither approves nor condemns 'compositional form'; he simply notes that it is a familiar and understood procedure that can be left to 'stand on its merits', while he expounds the other two approaches in some detail, and describes how

Urban designers are attracted to the megastructure concept because it offers a legitimate way to order massive grouped functions. One need only look at the work in the recent Museum of Modern Art show of 'Visionary Architecture' to sense the excitement generated among designers by mega-form. While some of the ideas displayed in the show demonstrate structural virtuosity at the expense of human scale and functional needs, others have a quality which suggests no divergence between compacted economic function and human use.[30]

He does not itemize the designs which fall into these two contrasted categories, but the kind he seems to regard as beneficial can be deduced from the schemes (none from the Museum of Modern Art show, one notes) that he illustrates in the book. These include Tange's Boston Harbor and Tokyo Bay schemes and – under the specific denomination of 'megastructure' – Kurokawa's low, rectangular-gridded 'Agricultural City' project (**74**), a remarkably undramatic image in this company.

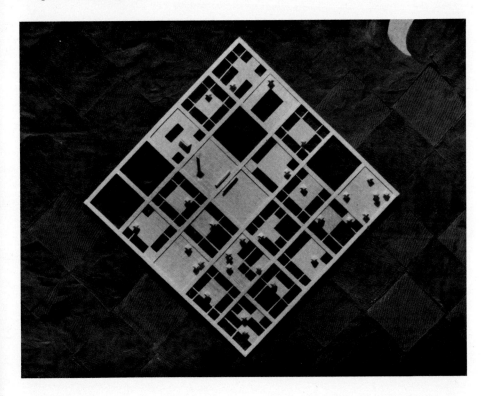

74 *Agricultural City project (Kisho Kurokawa, 1961). An extensible, low-profile 'mat-building' intended to be at one with the agricultural community it serves – but, because land is the very basis of an agricultural economy, raised on legs to leave the ground surface unencumbered.*

Maki also adds to the central concept of megastructure some subsidiary categorizations such as 'hierarchical' and 'open-ended' megaform (though most later megastructuralists would have repudiated the hierarchical version by arguments similar to those set out in Christopher Alexander's *A City is not a Tree*[31]). Like some of the French Urban Spatialists, he also proposes large-scale environmental and climatic control within megastructures, and that the large basic works for megastructures — earth-moving, artificial ground, circulation systems — should be charged to public accounts, seeming to imply that smaller and more transient structures could be left to private investment.

Much of the book is taken up with illustrations, visual and verbal, of historical examples of collective form, though he also shows his own and Otaka's joint projects for the Shinjuku (**75**), Dohima and Tokyo 'K' sites, the last looking the most like a megastructure as normally understood. At first sight, however, the most surprising illustration is a diagrammatic version of the central area of the proposed New Town at Hook in Surrey, designed by the architects of the London County Council (**76**).

Britain is not normally seen as a significant contributor to visionary architecture at this period, more as a nation of earnest grey functionaries designing socially responsible architecture for the people; but this very illusion gave curious power to anything that the British did contribute. Maki's inclusion of Hook is perfectly congruent with the rest of his argument, and coming from

75 *Shinjuku redevelopment project, Tokyo (Maki and Otaka, 1962). Exemplary version of what became almost a standard solution to urban design problems when the Metabolists applied their principles to real sites and plausible financing: the creation of an 'artificial ground platform' to raise buildings clear of the ground and of traffic.*

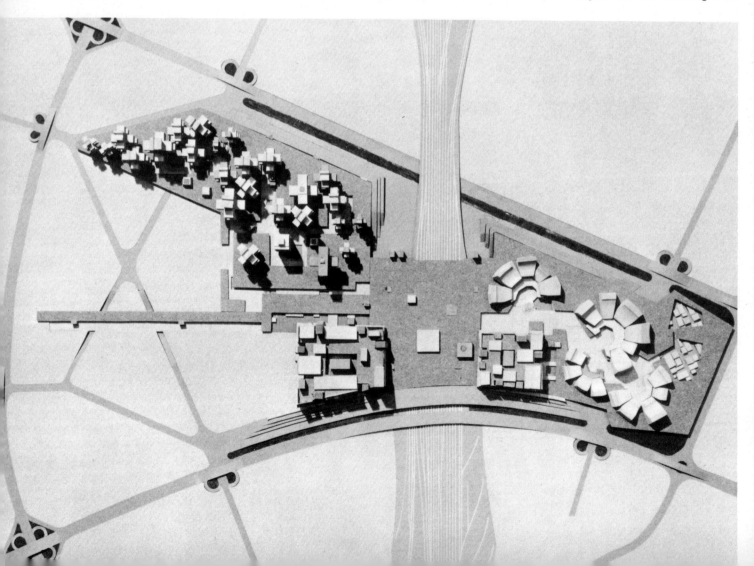

Britain the project lent a certain sober authority to his arguments. At a time when most men of 'good common sense' would have dismissed megastructures as overwrought and impractical visions, three documents had appeared in Britain which seemed to give practical and responsible support to such ideas.

All three can be seen as belonging to 1964 in terms of their impact, though in terms of publication dates they spread from 1962 – *The Planning of a New Town* (Hook Report), through 1963 – *Traffic in Towns* (the Buchanan Report) to late 1964 – Victor Gruen's *The Heart of Our Cities*. The first two appeared to suggest that megastructures could be socially responsible products of social democratic régimes, the third – given Gruen's reputation as a successful designer of shopping centres – that they could be profitable propositions in a hard-nosed market economy. These apparent suggestions were in some sense justified. Later critics who complained that Royston Landau, in *New Directions in British Architecture*, had made 'the Archigram Computer City rub shoulders with such

76 *Central area proposals, Hook New Town (London County Council Architects' Department, 1961–2). Never built, the Hook project nevertheless exercised considerable influence; its spine of concentrated social and shopping facilities on a raised pedestrian podium above the traffic circulation summed up the best town-planning ideas in good currency at the time, and showed that megastructural solutions were thinkable even to British bureaucrats.*

practically-based research projects as the outline plan for Hook . . . or the Buchanan Report'[32] showed considerably less awareness of recent history than Landau did. It is not just temporal distancing that makes these various projects and proposals of 1964 look so much alike; there is a real megastructural boldness and, indeed, bloody-mindedness about the Hook scheme, and even more so about the last area-study in the Buchanan Report, which proposed to turn a large area of London's West End into a single multi-level complex almost half a mile from north to south, framed in a garnish of giant freeway intersections that neither Detroit nor Los Angeles could hope to emulate.

It is important and salutary to remember that in the early sixties British official reports, not normally noted for visionary fervours, could propose such vast designs as models for municipal emulation and stir hardly a murmur of disapproval (whatever outcries may have arisen later). The mood of established architects was sanguine, and in the small world of London architecture ideas circulated rapidly between them and the visionaries. Today's student 'raver' could become tomorrow's civil servant: in the case of the Buchanan report, for example, the team who made the proposals for London's West End had gone to Buchanan's staff from the fifth year at the Architectural Association School, where they had been working on an even more megastructural version of the Hook plan.

The situation with Gruen was different, obviously, and his impact more diffuse. His Fort Worth scheme has already been mentioned as a possible megastructure prototype; his East Island project (**77**) was the first of a long line of schemes from various hands which would have turned New York's Welfare Island (now Roosevelt Island) into a residential megastructure, more or less as is happening in a garbled version (**78**) at the time of this writing; and his office was to become avowedly megastructural at the end of the sixties, when Cesar Pelli joined it to design their submission to the UN Vienna competition discussed in

77, 78 *East Island, New York (otherwise Welfare Island, now Roosevelt Island) has been a constant incitement to American architects to make a megastructure in the East River. 77 is Victor Gruen's early-sixties proposal for a unifying enclosed shopping street and transportation channel running the full length of the island. 78 shows the state of development in late 1975, with buildings by various hands agglomerating into a megastructure of sorts along the line of a central street surviving from an earlier plan by Philip Johnson.*

77

Chapter 8. The real reason for his impact, however, may lie simply in the fact that within this aggressively successful commercial designer there lurked – as *The Heart of Our Cities* reveals on page after page – a Viennese aesthete who shared most of the urban design aspirations and architectural prejudices (such as hatred of cars) of his more visionary colleagues. This apparent combination of commercial success and sound cultural preferences was fairly irresistible, and worked at the time to support megastructuralism more than any of the other received ideas that Gruen was promoting.

However, one must admit that what was being proposed by Gruen or the British public agencies was tame stuff by comparison with the projects of Maki or the Metabolists. There is a very wide gulf of intentions between Gruen's mechanically advanced but architecturally bland East Island scheme and, say, Plug-In City by the London Archigram group, which hit the magazines in 1964 and radically altered the style and tone of megastructuralism for the rest of the decade. Plug-In City was to appear in many publications beside *Archigram* itself, but nowhere more influentially than in the farewell issue of *Architectural Forum* (August/September 1964), to which reference has already been made.

That issue was an occasion, almost a testamentary statement. Douglas Haskell's encomium on Grand Central Station was quoted in chapter 2, but in the rest of that article Haskell develops the theme that the whole of Manhattan should be managed in the same way:

New York, for lack of steady reminders, forgot about carrying any further its sudden invention in smooth, high-density urban movement, and to this day goes in for daily tie-ups, frustration, lost tempers, and violence, running everything pre-Columbian style on a base mostly at one level, which has to serve buildings which may soon reach 200 floors...[33]

– a statement which sums up most of the established concerns which gave megastructural thinking its 'constituency' among older generations. The basis of its constituency among younger established opinion appears continuously, if sometimes obliquely, in the rest of the issue. This was the responsibility of Peter Blake, who succeeded Haskell as the magazine was about to collapse and edited it through two, if not three, subsequent incarnations. Blake's contribution begins with a scrapbook (which later historians may well peruse with amazement and enlightenment) of favourite architectural images – a sequence that begins with Archigram and all but ends with Archigram; the last image is, in fact, of Urbino seen from the air, but the penultimate one is of Plug-In City (hence the comparison discussed earlier).

The linking caption on this concluding page begins by quoting Barbara Ward Jackson on the need for a 'shaping imagination, the liberating idea' in the future of cities, and then identifies Plug-In City as 'a symbol-sketch for what is being built right now in such places as Cumbernauld, Scotland; le Mirail, France, and West Berlin'. It goes on to propose the comparison with Urbino on the grounds that in both cases the city is 'a skeleton of open spaces ... which hold things together'. The comparison will not wash; Plug-In City's powerful diagonal grid is intentional, and precedes the creation of the individual accommodations within it, whereas at Urbino the piazza, say, is simply the ground left over after the Montefeltro dukes had finished building the palace, cathedral etc. True or false, however, the comparison is advanced in support of Blake's theme of the city considered as a single organic entity, a theme pursued in relentless detail in the last thirty-eight editorial pages of the issue.

79 *Downtown Frankfurt am Main project; competition entry (Candilis/Josic/Woods, 1962). A mat-building (compare 74) whose basic conception was to reappear a year later as the same architects' successful entry for the design of the Free University of Berlin.*

80 *Megacity project (students at Cooper Union, 1963). Megastructure returns home to New York, in a historically aware blend of Sant'Elia's Futurism, Russian Constructivism and the traditional imagery of Manhattan itself.*

Here, under the rubric *Cities – the New Scale* ('. . . new scale of architectural concern, taking in nothing less than the entire urban environment'), the argument begins with articles setting out the approved concerns about 'The Urban Emergency' (replete with quotations from President Johnson and the mandatory pictures of dereliction and disorders), continues by examining the textbook case of Philadelphia (where the problems of Market Street were to inspire a variety of megastructural proposals before the decade was out), and by a few more short steps arrives at 'The City as a Single Structure':

To make the city work, urban designers are exploring big new multilevel frameworks which combine concentration, separation and flexibility. Some of the concepts behind such macrostructures are evident in this winning redevelopment scheme for the center of Turin.

Having thus introduced Quaroni's *quartiere direzionale*, Blake groups with it the Frankfurt scheme of Candilis/Josic/Woods (**79**), Cumbernauld Town Centre, a 'South Cove Infrastructure' by two Harvard students, and a student 'Megacity' from Cooper Union (**80**). Taken as a whole, this was the largest collection of megastructures and related concepts to be published together up until that time in their own right and as moderately sensible and buildable propositions. What is conspicuously missing from the whole issue, however, is the work of the Metabolists, their concept of the long-term frame and short-term subsidiaries, and the word 'megastructure' itself. It may be that this was deliberate exclusion, since Blake appeared conversationally at that time to be preoccupied with the concept of 'the city as a single work of art', citing San Gimignano and the Lower Manhattan skyline as examples – finished and perfected examples, rather than the provisional and approximate silhouettes that Metabolism would seem to imply. Even so, the absence of the word 'megastructure' itself is puzzling. Blake reads German, so that even if he had failed to pick up the word directly from Maki, he might well have taken it from *Bauwelt* of April 1964, where it was first used in print by a non-Metabolist in a celebrated article on the group by Günther Nitschke. The same article appeared in English

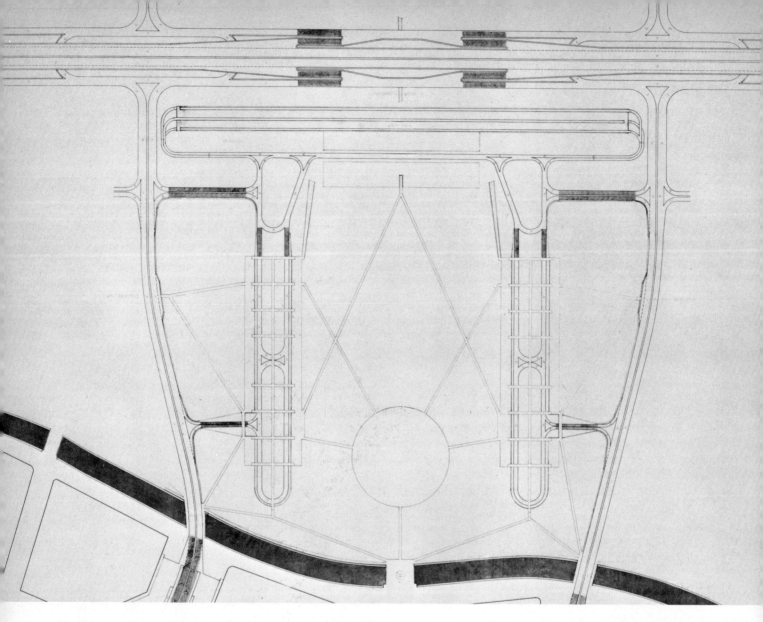

81 *Mehringplatz project, Berlin; competition entry (Alison and Peter Smithson, with Günther Nitschke, 1963). Large-scale traffic works to support a pair of long office blocks: a continuing fascination with mechanical movement patterns as the generators, or justifiers, of dramatic urban form, as might be expected from a team that included the 'discoverer' of Metabolism.*

translation, though too late for Blake, in *Architectural Design* for October of the same year, a steady flow of interest in the pages of the professional magazines being another sign that this was the megayear.

Yet another sign was the emergence of a kind of canon of large-scale projects that were persistently published, and usually together, in almost any kind of study of town planning from the most flat-footed to the most wildly visionary. These included the winning and other entries for Turin as already mentioned, for the Tel Aviv-Yafo housing, the Bochum and Berlin free universities, the Berlin-Mehringplatz (**81**) and the Venice-Tronchetto schemes. Many were megastructures only in comparative scale, and some by visual analogy, while some came closer to Maki's definitions; but they combined to give a sense of something new emerging — though it should be noted that whatever was emerging as the word and the diffuse cloud of projects began to gel could hardly affect the megastructures that were to be built, since most of these were already in the last stages of design. For this reason, there was always to be a gap between any completed works at which one could point — even at Montreal Expo '67, where one was often stuck for any word but 'megastructure' to describe what was pointed at — and what was sensed to be a vast and potent vision of the city as a single work of imagination.

That vast and potent vision could hardly avoid being called 'Utopian' sooner or later, but the manner of its calling was strange and indirect, and raises some critical side-issues. Although it occurred mostly later than 1964, it is best dealt with here because the pursuit of this topic will lead back ultimately to 1964 and to one of the most revealing but unsettling proposals about the function of megastructure to be made in any year at all.

The word 'Utopia' could hardly fail to be applied to megastructures, since their earliest publication was often in a context such as *Fantastic Architecture* (1960), by Conrads and Sperlich, which has the word 'Utopian' in its subtitle and somewhat nonchalantly packages Soleri, the Brussels Atomium, Sant'Elia, Frei Otto and others with the *utopistisch* Berlin visionaries of the early twenties. Furthermore, under the heading 'Utopia today' it avers that

Thirty years later . . . ideas are taken up again which were frequently hinted at in the 'Utopian letters' of 1919–20, even if motivated by different considerations . . . 'mobile architecture' and 'adaptable building' are studied.[34]

This, clearly, is a conventionally sloppy usage of the word 'Utopia' as meaning little more than visionary or improbable; few of the projects under discussion here were seriously engaged in the task of proposing a radical new and perfected social order.

Nevertheless, even in German literature the 'Utopian' tag clings to megastructure, first appearing consciously so attached in a special issue of *Bauen + Wohnen* of January 1964 entitled 'Reality and Utopia in Town Planning'. In the concluding paragraph of his introductory essay the editor, Jürgen Joedicke, claims:

Where [the sociologist Josef] Lehmbrock takes his stand on the deficiencies of present city-building, so Tange indicates the other pole of thought, the Utopian . . . not the familiar form of Utopia, consciously trying to outdo the real facts, but the other sort, the unconscious Utopia. Tange begins with the problems of today, proceeds to the problems of tomorrow, and seeks to solve them on the basis of an ever-evolving technology. This progressive development of ideas from today to tomorrow differs sharply from the mere sensationalism that often disguises itself as Utopia. . . .

Throughout the introduction, however, Joedicke seems to be trying to disentangle two, three or even more versions of Utopia. One is the traditional one descended from Sir Thomas More, which frequently does try to overturn the real facts simply by reversing the present polarities of men and society; another is the so-called New Utopianism of French and American professional futurologists, which often merely amplifies present trends in society; a third would be what Joedicke calls 'blind visions' unrelated to any known or anticipated condition of man or his society. How these last ever became assimilated to any socially relevant Utopianism is a peculiar historical problem of Modern architecture in Germany, as suggested above, but it left its marks on German attitudes to megastructure.

This confusion of aims and end-products was ultimately productive, however, because it drove German writers to try and disentangle the purposes and social destinations of megastructures. In 1972, for instance, Tomás Maldonado, following what was by then established German tradition, discussed mega-structuralists as 'Old Utopians of the present day', intending thus to distinguish them from the 'New Utopian' futurologists. By this phrase, Maldonado explains,

we mean those planners, especially architects and urban planners, who are formulating ideal models of future cities which they call megastructures. We choose to call them 'Old Utopians' because they have accepted the attitude of traditional Utopianism. On the one hand they refuse to undertake any action that implies a planning compromise with the environmental needs and pressures of the present, and on the other hand they refuse to hypothesize any sort of decision-taking trajectory that might make these megastructures realizable in the future. . . .[35]

Clearly, even Tange is neither a Utopian nor even a megastructuralist by this definition. If one turns to the footnote where Maldonado offers examples of what he takes to be megastructures, the list is so short and so emphatically visionary (e.g. Kurokawa's 'Helicoids', Archigram's 'Walking City') that it excludes more than ninety per cent of the schemes that might relevantly be discussed in this book. Yet, in passing, Maldonado offers what must be the true adjective on megastructures: the word 'ideal'.

An ideal city, as proposed by the Renaissance progenitors of the concept like Alberti and Filarete, was a buildable geometrical layout related to one of the perfect forms of the Platonic tradition. It was often conspicuously indifferent to the social system to which it gave shelter, whereas Utopia, by contrast (in the view offered by Colin Rowe, Françoise Choay and other recent scholars), is often obsessional about the proposed social system, but not too concerned about architectural form. Only in the nineteenth century, according to Rowe, did the two kinds of ideal become conflated (as in the vision of a Bellamy or a Howard), and only in the twenties was social Utopia confused with 'architec-tural adventurism'.

In terms of the Rowe/Choay type of distinction between ideal cities and Utopias, megastructures can probably be defined as ideal cities intended to house somebody else's Utopias — the New Utopias of the futurologists. The point emerges clearly, if almost unwittingly, in Mechthild Schumpp's *Stadtbau-Utopien und Gesellschaft* ('town-planning Utopias and society') of 1972, in which the megastructuralists appear as a kind of coda to a learned study of Utopianism from Thomas More to the Bauhaus. On the basis of a better acquaintance with the literature than Maldonado exhibits, she identifies three characteristic propositions 'dominating three distinguishable types of modern planning Utopias'.

The first is the Metabolist distinction between the permanent and the transient; the third is a technological vision of the city (as in Hollein, Katavolos, Schoffer); but the middle one is 'the concept of a "mobile leisure population" as the point of departure for the modelling of the town-planning future'.[36] The point is well made; not only was leisure hopefully identified as a prime feature of life in a post-industrial culture by the futurologists, but the concept labels a very large category of megastructure attitudes from Friedman to Archigram — even if the reasons why Archigram appears so preoccupied with leisure prove, in the last analysis, to be so trivial as to drive a serious historian to despair. Friedman, however, asserts the existence of a *nécessité biologique de l'amusement* which claims a *liberté de choix sans aucune opposition* that in its turn can be delivered only by his *architecture/urbanisme mobile.* The concept is important because it implies another reason for the changeability of the subsidiary accommodations in his, or anybody's, megastructures: they were to change not only because of the termination of their original functions or structural integrity, like the leaves of Tange's metabolist tree, but also so that they should not obstruct the *vie ludique*, the 'play life', of the citizenry. The answer to Denise Scott-Brown's 1968 question, both rhetorical and satirical, 'What is everybody doing up there with everybody else in those megastructures?'[37] might prove, only half satirically, to be: rearranging the equipment for the next game!

Megastructures as the architecture of 'fun' belong to the next chapter, but one must note here a very serious proposition about the functions of megastructure that brings us back to megayear 1964: the identification of the proper inhabitant of megastructure as *Homo ludens,* the archetypal 'man at play'. The identification was made in a lecture given in that year on his *Neo-Babylone* by Constant Niewenhuis; the lecture may have earlier versions, but the text read in London early in 1964 is the one which achieved the permanence of print and an English translation, and was the most widely noticed at the time.

Constant's interest in 'ludic' activities derived not only from his fellow-Dutchman Johan Huizinga, but also from his membership of the *Internationale situationniste*, that lively crew of entirely serious political and aesthetic pranksters whose best-known members were the painter Asger Jorn and the poet Guy Debord. As a group they were interested in town planning, not only in their abstract demands for an impossibly Utopistic *urbanisme unitaire* 'determined by the uninterrupted and complex activity through which man's environment is consciously re-created', but also in a remarkable sensitivity to the nature and behaviour of cities as they exist on the ground epitomized by Debord's accounts of being driven through the streets of Paris by forces of 'psycho-geographical drift'.

Somewhere between the absolute future they desired and the compromised present they inhabited the Situationists proposed their concept of the *situation construite ,* 'the creation of a transitory micro-world and – for a single moment in the life of a few – a play of events' of which the prime example, in the end, was to be the *événements* of May 1968 in Paris. Pending the unforeseeable outcome of that entirely unforeseen super-situation, their smaller 'happenings' would have to serve as steps toward *urbanisme unitaire*, the indispensable basis for a liberated society where life would be a work of art.

Neo-Babylone represents Constant's attempt to project structures in which such transitory micro-worlds could best be produced, intended to provide

the environment the homo ludens is supposed to live in. For it should be clear that the functional cities that have been created during the long period of history in which human lives were consecrated to utility, would by no means suit the totally different needs of the creative race of homo ludens. The environment of homo ludens has first of all to be flexible, changeable, assuring any movement, any change of place or change of mood, any mode of behaviour. . . .

In a surprisingly conventional way, he then goes through a litany of standard concerns over population growth, the building over of the countryside and the congestion of traffic circulation. He finally reveals that *Neo-Babylone* will consist of a series of structures called 'sectors', which his illustrations (**82, 83**) show to be an inventive and exaggerated form of the giant space-frames of Sarger or Le Ricolais, explaining that

the sector itself – whose dimensions are much bigger than those of any present building – is a system of levels that leave the ground-level free for an intensive fast traffic . . . the

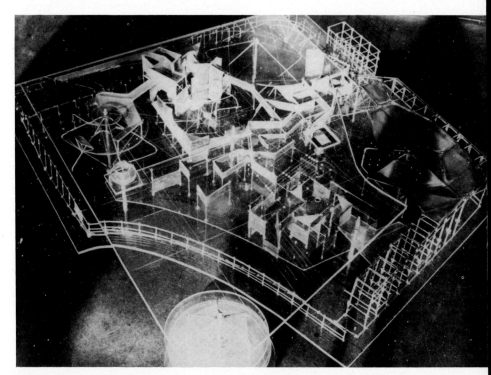

82, 83 *'Sectors' of the* Neo-Babylone *project (Constant Niewenhuis, 1962–3). These vast structures, very much in the mode of* urbanisme spatiale *as far as their frame-works were concerned (83), were intended, paradoxically, to support the lightest of human activities – urban life viewed as the playing out of an open game, giant playgrounds for* Homo ludens.

sector floors are primarily empty. They represent a sort of extension of the Earth's surface, a new skin that covers the earth and multiplies its living space ... the unfunctional character of this playground-like construction makes any logical subdivision of its inner spaces senseless. We should rather think of a quite chaotic arrangement of small and bigger spaces that are constantly mounted and dismounted by means of standardised mobile construction elements, like walls, floors and staircases.[38]

Or is it Habraken who is echoed here? These are his same 'mobile construction elements'. For all the nobility of this *ludique* vision, it comes down in the end to bricks and mortar, and it may well have been this concluding note of bourgeois practicality that enraged his fellow Situationists, who derided Constant until he quit the movement. According to their absolute and Simon-Pure philosophical standards, his building of actual models only served to excuse the *techniciens de la forme architecturale*, while the attempt to propose actual mechanisms for *la vie ludique* merely played into the hands of a consumer economy.

In one sense they were right; once you begin to clothe the naked concept of *Homo Iudens* in usable equipment, and to connect the constructed situations to the power mains, the result is liable to look remarkably like a swinging affluent society and its mobile, leisure-seeking citizens. At the time of the lecture's publication it would have been almost possible to test the propositions of *Neo-Babylone* against the buildable facts: by 1964, a working model of sorts of the 'Fun Palace' had been built in London for Joan Littlewood, and on the other side of the Atlantic Guy Desbarats, Guntis Plesums and others had more or less finalized the detail design of the 'Theme Pavilions' for Montreal Expo '67. Both will be dealt with later, but it is instructive to note here that the Fun Palace was intended to deliver, almost detail for detail, the kind of ludic flexibility demanded of *Neo-Babylone*, and that the Theme Pavilions were to demonstrate, albeit accidentally and in only general terms, the environment of large empty platforms carried above the earth's surface on complex diagonal structures. Constant's vision of *Homo Iudens* at home in the megastructure was as timely as the hour in megayear 1964.

5 Fun and Flexibility

Tradition has it that the word 'fun' entered the British megastructure argument as early as September 1962, though not on British soil. As far as can be ascertained, the phrase 'Fun Palace' was coined, and applied to the project Cedric Price was designing for Joan Littlewood, on the sidewalk in 42nd Street during a visit they paid to New York in that year. Once applied, however, the word stuck, and the fun content of British megastructure ideas was one of the factors that guaranteed their worldwide penetration and distribution in the middle sixties, with or without the assistance of the Beatles, Mary Quant, the legend of Swinging London and all the rest of it. But there is another and probably more important reason for this impact: detailing.

Looking back over the first half of the sixties and the characteristic megastructures of the period, it is noticeable – alarming even – how few of them actually offer any nut-and-bolt proposals as to how the transient elements should be secured to the megaform, or what precise devices and services are required for the playful activities of *Homo ludens*. The general level of technical information and precision in the first half of the decade can be typified by Kikutake's proposal about what should happen in 'Marine City' after the main cylinders had been built:

When the cylinder was completed, the factory would then convert itself to the production of prefabricated housing units, which would be lifted by a crane and literally plugged in to the surface of the cylinder.[39]

Even allowing for the accidents of translation, 'literally plugged in to the surface', in the absence of anything even faintly resembling working drawings, is very low indeed on practical information. All too frequently the Metabolists, Urban Spatialists and Italian megastructuralists seemed deliberately to avoid taking responsibility for any of those minutiae which, in the eyes of the 'Old Masters' of Modern architecture like Mies van der Rohe and Auguste Perret, were the very probity of architecture: 'God is in the Details'!

The reasons why the British alone seemed prone to finnick over detailing are diverse and often personal, but do seem somewhat connected to a national tendency to take refuge from ideology in pragmatics. Even so, it must be recognized that the Fun Palace, for instance, had to be taken to the point of detailed structural calculations and the satisfaction of fire regulations, while Archigram, by contrast, seemed to be motivated by sheer manic pleasure in proliferating drawings (**84**). In either case, the absence of any explicit ideology was found disturbing, or at least baffling, outside Britain; on the other hand, the presence of detailing was almost universally welcomed, especially in the stunning graphic forms in which Archigram could present it.

Of course, neither Price nor the diverse talents of the Archigram group had sprung rootless from an architectural vacuum. The earliest project for anything

84 *Walking City project (Ron Herron and Brian Harvey of Archigram, 1963). Most celebrated of early Archigram projects, largely because of the alarm caused among the older planning Establishment by the thought of 'elements of the capital city' being put on legs and set to roam the world. Their location here in the East River, with the towers of Manhattan in the background, suggests a deliberate challenge to older visions of the future — but it was always dangerous to take Archigram too seriously, or at apparent face value.*

resembling a megastructure that I remember seeing was a student group project produced at the Architectural Association as early as 1952; for some fifteen years after that, comparable schemes were among every summer's final thesis projects, getting more and more like megastructures and more and more elaborately well drawn with each successive year. At the same time, there was a developing body of speculation about the philosophy of endlessness in architecture which was to arrive, nowhere quite independently of the mega-structure tendency, at the hospital projects of John Weeks, London-based architect and theorist of an 'indeterminate architecture' of extensibility and adaptability. Throughout the period, too, there were rumours and possibilities of commissions for large and conspicuous projects; some were to result in material landmarks like Cumbernauld Town Centre or the Tricorn shopping centre in Portsmouth, while others were to hang fire seemingly for ever as large and beautifully detailed models, as in the case of Colin St John Wilson's Liverpool civic complex.

Even without this rich and sustaining background, however, it is possible that the Fun Palace might still have turned out much as it did, from the very nature of the original concept. What Joan Littlewood sought from her architect Cedric Price, engineer Frank Newby and systems consultant Gordon Pask was less a building than a 'facility', a 'service', a 'space-mobile', a 'giant toy'. None of this was surprising, since much of Littlewood's theatrical experience was concerned with improvisatory performance, public participation and the like, in a manner which, though it had nineteenth-century roots in traditional popular theatre, also had affinities, easier to see now than they were then, with the ludic situations of Constant and the Situationists as set out in the last chapter. Such affinities could be obscured by Joan Littlewood's tendency to cosily British and traditional phraseology:

... a place intended to be open twenty-four hours a day for every kind of recreation and enjoyment, a permissive place which could be used by some as 'a university of the street', by others as 'a latterday Vauxhall Gardens where one might meet one's Nell Gwynne'.[40]

But Price could write the prose of the day, and in his version it sounds nearer to the twentieth century as inhabited by the megastructure generation:

This complex, which enables self-participatory education and entertainment can only work – and then only for a finite time – if it is not only accessible to those living and working in the immediate neighbourhood but also, through its varied communication links, accessible as a regional and national amenity.

The siting exploits existing communication networks and gives a clue to the potential enrichment of life through increasing mobility at present un-realised in large urban communities. The sense of confinement on the site is reduced by the deliberate extension of the visible limits. The activities designed for the site should be experimental, the place itself expendable and changeable. The organisation of space and the objects occupying it should, on the one hand, challenge the participants' mental and physical dexterity and, on the other, allow for a flow of space and time, in which passive and active pleasure is provoked.[41]

The physical realization of this 'educreative' environment offered by Price for the particular site under consideration, in the Lea valley north-east of London, involved an open frame of very large dimensions (**85**), on the scale of a shipyard and not unlike a shipyard to look at: five rows of fifteen latticed steel towers each, connected at their heads by trackways to carry travelling gantry cranes capable of transporting gear and equipment to and from all parts of the site. The whole was to cover a rectangle of some 855 × 375 feet – about twice the size of Place Bonaventure in Montreal. Permanent piped and conduited services were to be supplied vertically through the supporting towers, but all horizontal elements – services, roofs, floors – all walling elements, environmental equipment, escalators etc. were to be impermanent, movable and interchangeable (**86–8**).

85 *Fun Palace project; model (Cedric Price, Frank Newby, Gordon Pask, 1962). One end of a two-bay feasibility model is seen here, with the travelling gantry crane spanning over the system of service towers and horizontal trusses that were to form the carrying frame within which the adaptable accommodations could be hung. Note the absence of fixed floor levels, a 'freedom' which no other megastructuralists permitted themselves.*

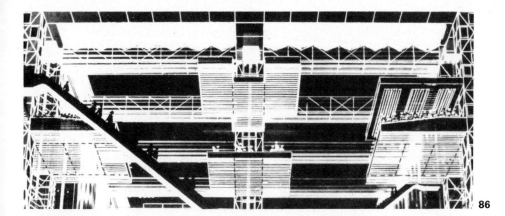

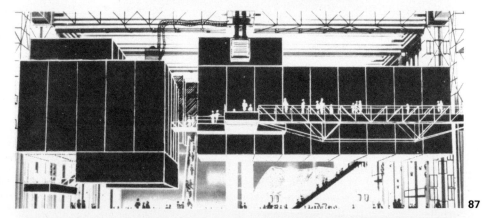

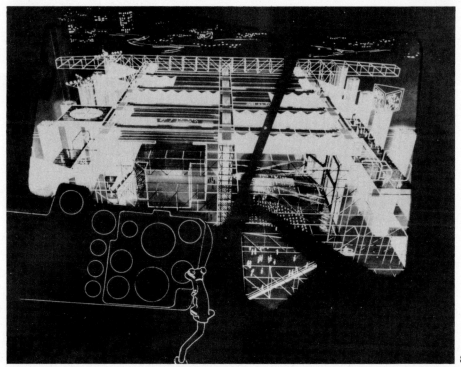

86, 87, 88 *Fun Palace in various arrangements: (86) open platforms and ramped seating as for a major spectacle; (87) enclosed volumes for activities requiring controlled environments; (88) mandatory 'period' view from approaching helicopter — like most* ludique *projects of the time, the Fun Palace predicated a far higher degree of mechanical 'mobility-on-demand' than any conventional planner dared contemplate.*

The range of variability envisaged by the Fun Palace team went spectacularly beyond what had been proposed by Constant for *Neo-Babylone*, where there were at least fixed floors, even if everything else was provisional. The Fun Palace was seen as an adaptable volume, to be floored, roofed, walled and serviced at will with the minimum of restraints in any of its three dimensions. Whether any strolling *Homo ludens* could have rearranged any but the smallest of Price's proposed units at individual, unaided whim seems extremely doubtful. The rapid creation of a six-hundred-seat auditorium, say, with entrances at the 37'6" datum, reached by escalators from street level, clearly implies the collaboration of a sizeable force of technical assistants. For this reason, the whole proposition would probably have been unacceptable to Constant, and anathema to the hard-line Situationists – but not unacceptable to someone raised in the tradition of theatre, nor to English progressive professionals of the Left; neither group would see anything wrong with a little professional backstage assistance to the people's participatory pleasures out front.

As in Buckminster Fuller's almost contemporary and also unbuilt 'World Game', public participation would have consisted largely of manipulating the controls of sophisticated technical installations managed by expert staff, massively computerized and connected to national electronic linkages. Hostile critics might dismiss it as 'no more than a glorified slot-machine arcade', but the Fun Palace team, pragmatists to a man, were not minded to wait for the Revolution to make a perfect *palais ludique* possible; they would have a practicable Fun Palace here and now, as a way of raising public consciousness to the level where a Revolution might be found to have happened.

Such reservations accepted, however, there remains one aspect of the Fun Palace which is more radical than is the case in any other proposed megastructure of that vintage: the time-scale of its 'metabolism'. Whereas the Japanese, for example, do not seem to have imagined the transient accommodations lasting for much less than the duration of a fashion in entertainment or the span of a human generation, those in the Fun Palace were envisaged as being assembled and broken up more than once in a day, if necessary. And whereas the supporting megaforms of the Metabolists appear to be intended to endure perhaps for centuries, the life of the basic frame of the Fun Palace was estimated as ten years by Price, only nine by Littlewood!

Such a high rate of changeability was seen as implying a high rate of recoverability. The transient accommodations were to be built from a limited repertoire of recoverable elements, which would be stored when not in use in areas of the structure which were equally and coincidentally not in use (a neat, self-trimming equation: the fewer functional volumes assembled, the more space left over for storing the elements). All this, as has been said, was worked out in great and quantified detail, though only rather generalized drawings were ever published. The complexities of the kit of parts and their supporting systems were formidable, but the design had been pushed to the point of satisfying, for instance, the remarkably tough and outmoded London fire regulations before the project was allowed to drop for lack of ready finance.

Throughout the period 1962–7, however, it represented a challenge and a design-education, a radical exemplar and an unfailing focus of interest for the immediately succeeding generation, including the Archigram group, their friends and connections, and the students only slightly younger than themselves whom they taught in various architecture schools in the London area. For this generation Price served locally as an 'instant guru', and was often given a page to himself in *Archigram* itself — the architectural broadsheet/magazine/information-package which was, for the second half of the sixties, the essential organ of the worldwide 'junior' megastructure movement.

Though international in scope, *Archigram* was started by Peter Cook in London in 1961 as an information-sheet whose intention was, largely, to salvage from oblivion certain admired student projects and failed competition entries which would otherwise have passed unrecorded. The reasons for doing so were only partly concerned with taking revenge on the Establishment, though *Archigram* I was ornamented with phrases like: 'We have chosen to by-pass the decaying Bauhaus image, which is an insult to Functionalism.' Much more important to the group was the dissemination of information, a way of telling students and young architects about all the extraordinary goings-on which their teachers and the official professional press were 'concealing' from them. For this reason, the early issues in particular give an invaluable survey of the interests of radical young megastructuralists of the time. Thus, while issues I and II were largely concerned with projects by *Archigram's* editors and their friends and contemporaries, issue III onwards featured Buckminster Fuller, Cedric Price, mobile homes, Arthur Quarmby's plastic structures, Ionel Schein, George Nelson, Yona Friedman, under-sea and outer-space equipment and a number of historically disreputable characters: Berlin Expressionists, Russian Fantasists of the twenties, the Futurists. By the time of *Archigram* V, late in 1964, the register included a whole range of megastructuralists — Frei Otto, Paul Maymont, Paolo Soleri, Isozaki, Leopold Gerstel, Schulze-Fielitz, Constant Niewenhuis — and even some of the student projects from the Rome round-table of 1961–2.

The intention, as has been said, was to circulate information, but the effect — given the temper of the times and the manner of presentation — was to create the illusion of the existence of some kind of 'Megastructure International'. The illusion was greatly reinforced by the clamorous success of the conference organized at Folkestone by Archigram in 1966 under the title of IDEA — International Dialogues on Experimental Architecture. As the title shows, it was not intended to be specifically megastructural, nor did many of the known megastructuralists actually turn up to speak, but Archigram and their projects were very much in the international eye from then on.

Even the group itself was something of a 'historical illusion' produced by the magazine, at least in its early years. The full membership which produced the classic projects of 1963 onwards did not come together until 1963, when they were gathered together by Theo Crosby (not a member of the group, older than them and already well known) to produce projects for a major British building and developing company. It was under this aegis that the first megastructural designs were evolved: the Fulham Study and the Montreal 'Entertainments Tower'.

The Fulham Study (named after its location in London) is of lesser interest here, though its informal grouping of *Terrassenhäuser* blocks along a wandering pedestrian way (**89**) probably provided the unfortunate prototype for much sloppily planned pseudo-megastructure housing built in Britain after 1970. The Entertainments Tower (actually the work of Peter Cook alone) was a different matter, the first clear manifestation of Archigram's persuasive strain of megafantasy (**90**).

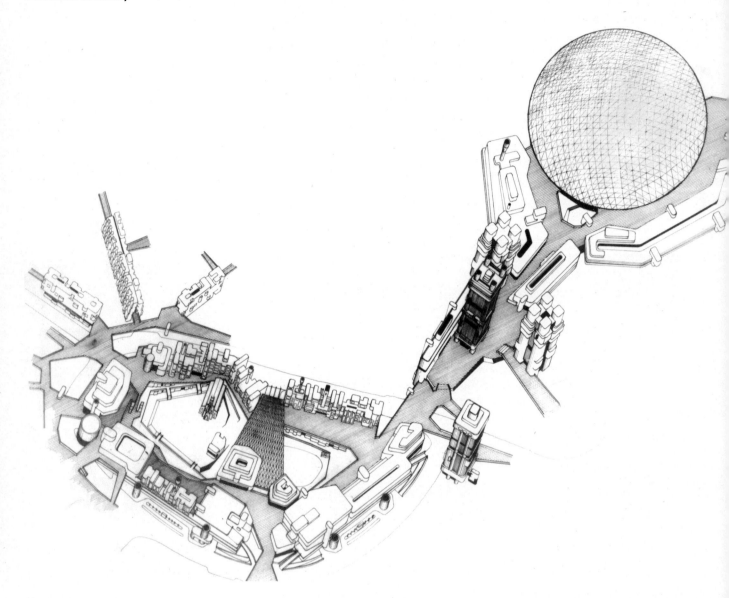

89 *Central area, Fulham Study project (Archigram for Taylor Woodrow, 1963). Undertaken for a major builder–developer, this first extended design by Archigram as a group is still close conceptually to admired London student work of the period. The general response of British periodicals was to ignore the central area ('merely fantastication') and concentrate on the spurs of housing which can be seen top left, the least adventurous part of the project and the unwitting ancestor, it seems, of much dull and unlovable pseudo-megastructure housing since.*

Its basis was to be a standardized pre-cast tubular concrete television tower that the developer hoped to mass-produce and market all over the world – a notable fantasy this, since, at just over six hundred feet high, it would be the largest factory-made component in the history of architecture. Further to this strain of manufacturer's fantasy, the giant cylinder was to be sealed at both ends to make it watertight, and then towed across the Atlantic to be erected as a central feature at Montreal Expo '67. These proposals are worth spelling out in detail, because they give some idea of the kind of 'hard-headed' business propositions on which the megastructuralists' fantasies were supported. In this case, of course, 'support' is to be taken literally; the tower was to carry a considerable weight of entirely buildable etceteras (**91**) wrapped round it by Peter Cook – 'diagrid' sub-structures, oblique elevator tubes, geodesic domes forming a complex of auditoria, aquaria, shops, offices and other facilities.

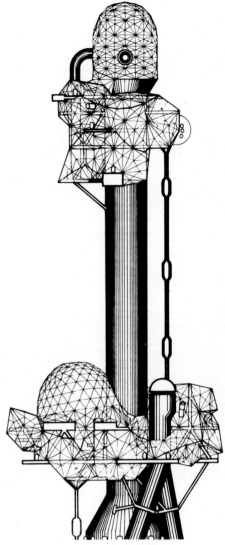

90, 91 *Montreal Entertainments Tower project (Peter Cook for Taylor Woodrow, 1963). Elaborately modelled and obsessively drawn out in detail (91), this 600-foot fantasy was firmly grounded in a serious proposal to pre-fabricate the central core for use as a TV transmitter tower all over the world. To make the ludique version proposed for the Montreal Expo of 1967, Peter Cook has hung it with the most admired architectural goodies of the time, from lattice domes to diagonal elevator ducts.*

92 *Sin Centre project (Mike Webb, 1958–62).
The pioneer English proposal for a* palais
ludique, *anticipating both* Neo-Babylone *and
the Fun Palace, enshrining Archigram's view of
the 'living city' as a zone of pleasurable disorder
– but concealing in its interstices some hard and
original thinking about both structure and
mechanical services.*

Most of the formal and structural elements were obviously derived from
elsewhere, but this would not worry Archigram, who always handled other
people's coinages as if they were common currency. More relevant here are the
larger concepts employed and their origins. Thus 'entertainment' is a natural
enough concept in an exhibition building, but it was particularly apt in the
Archigram context, having been preceded by Mike Webb's 'Sin Centre' (**92**), a
much reworked student project of 1958–62 which may have formed part of the
inspiration for the Fun Palace as well. But in 1963 Webb, Cook and the rest of
the group were also working on the exhibition 'The Living City' which
advanced, in the teeth of conventional planning wisdom, a view of cities which
celebrated disorder, fun, chance, consumerism and entertainment. This particular understanding of the functions of cities was to inform all the significant
projects by the group, was to drive them into megastructure and then to drive
them out again.

Beside *entertainment*, another leading concept, though differently expressed,
is *jointing*: the Montreal tower, the somewhat related 'Transportation Interchange' by Ron Herron and Warren Chalk (**10**), the 'Walking City' by Herron
and Bryan Harvey (**84**), the 'Underwater City' by Chalk (**94**), all exhibit more or
less extensively a related set of idioms of jointing and connecting obviously

required by an architecture of tubes and capsules. Though this can hardly be called detailing as early as this (1964), it was already far more precisely worked out than anything that had appeared up to that date in the work of the Metabolists or the Urban Spatialists. The reason for this seems to be that Archigram were always at least as interested in the parts (and their sub-parts) as in the whole, and also passionately interested in draughtsmanship, which, for various reasons, they had plenty of time to drive to a high level of elaboration. Both sets of interests were to become even more evident in the project that made Archigram famous: Plug-In City.

The scheme in all its versions and ramifications was, again, entirely Peter Cook's. Its impact derived partly from the spectacular qualities of the project itself, partly from the package in which it was first delivered to the world: *Archigram* IV or, to give the full title on the cover, *Amazing Archigram 4 Zoom issue.* The theme of the whole issue was the relevance of fantasy, specifically science-fiction fantasy, to 'real architecture'; and the message was hammered home by page after collaged page of space-comic imagery (**93**), Fantasists of the twenties, underwater and deep-space technology (much of that, too, fictional), a sprinkling of contemporary projects including their own, and a central pop-up scene of fantastic towers related to the Montreal scheme.

The message was also punched home by the running text, which was sometimes set out as normal editorial material, sometimes contained in the think-balloons emerging from the heads of space-comic figures as they went, otherwise undisturbed, about their customary extra-galactic ways. Says one character who has just been given the gift of tongues by a 'menticizer':

The search for radical valid images goes on — leads in many directions. The SPACE COMIC universe great in its complexity is just one such direction, can inspire and encourage the emergence of more courageous concepts. . . .

This technique is somewhat related to that used a little earlier by the Situationists in their magazines, but they had preferred to leave the original

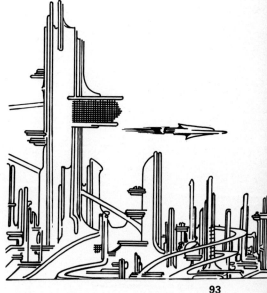

93

94

93, 94 *Archigram as pure fantasy. Blasting off from the 'Futuristic' or even 'Modernistic' cities of science fiction — here (93) redrawn by Warren Chalk for* Archigram IV — *the group's draughtsmanly obsessions drove them wherever the foot of man had not yet properly trod, whether outer space or under sea: 94 is a Warren Chalk drawing of 1964 for a submarine city, the first of many such to be dreamed up on the fanatic fringes of megastructure-land.*

dialogue in its pristine weirdness (always more striking in French translation) and to destroy bourgeois capitalism by way of the captions or the texts alongside. Archigram preferred to mix the two, and were fully aware of what was going into the mixture. An intercalated Marilyn Monroe figure announces:

A respectfull salute in the general direction of Roy Lichtenstein and we're off – ZOOM ARCHIGRAM goes into orbit with the SPACE-COMIC/SCIENCE-FICTION BIT. Interesting is the fact that these goodies produced outside the conventional closed architect/aesthete situation show a marked intuative grasp of principles underlying current in-thinking. Which is great. . . .

If this passage falls below the levels of ponderous literacy and pedantically accurate spelling frequently found in other megaprose, the use of imagery has a knowing exactitude which overleaps conventional architecture-magazine rhetoric of the period, by-passes the reader's normal verbal defence mechanisms, and thus produced a distinct shift in sensibility:

I can't think of any one identifiable event that broadened my own perceptions as drastically as the advent of Archigram. At least in the area of architecture and related matters. Until the day when the first Archigram manifesto appeared on my desk, I had been working and thinking pretty much in the standard establishment manner. . . . Then Archigram struck and the world hasn't been the same since. I took off for Cape Kennedy. . . .[42]

That, admittedly, was the editor of *Architectural Forum* paying formal compliments to Archigram, but having witnessed the expression on Peter Blake's face as he perused that first (*sic*: it was *Archigram* IV) manifesto which I had just placed on his desk, I can vouch for its impact. What is interesting, however, is that in spite of what Blake says about its perception-broadening effect, he began by trying to assimilate it to his 'standard establishment manner', making the comparisons between Urbino and Plug-In City which have already been discussed.

Other reprintings of the Plug-In City drawings were much less compromised; the impact comes through pretty nakedly, without any *post facto* apologia, and this, together with the Walking City drawings which so terrorized the ageing masters of CIAM, became the best-known of all the group's images. The grand axonometric (**95**) from *Archigram* IV and the systematic section showing all the kit of parts for Plug-In City together presented an unprecedentedly comprehensive view of a megacity taken down to a fairly fine level of detailing. Cook's own commentaries are worth quoting in part:

The axonometric is usually assumed to be the definitive image, for obviously classical reasons. It is 'Heroic', apparently an alternative to known city form, containing 'futurist' but recognisable hierarchies and elements. Craggy but directional. Mechanistic but scaleable. It was based on a drawn plan, which placed a structural grid on a square plan at 45° to a monorail route that was to connect existing cities. Alongside ran a giant routeway for hovercraft (the ultimate mobile buildings), the notion being that some major functions of the several linked parts could travel between them. The essential physical operations are stressed; the crane-ways and the bad-weather balloons; and the lift overruns are deliberately exaggerated. But overriding all this was the deliberate *varietousness* of each major building outcrop; whatever else it was to be, it was not going to be a deadly piece of built mathematics. . . .

Of the systematic section he observed that, whereas some other drawings may appear to belie the implication that Plug-In City is open-ended in conception, this particular drawing's achievement is that it makes the implication clear:

95 *Plug-In City project (Peter Cook of Archigram, 1963–4). The vision that made Archigram famous, and changed the direction of megastructure thinking, this enormous and much wrought axonometric drawing assembles the whole 'kit of parts' (a favourite Archigram phrase), from diagonal frames (bottom left) to the mobile office towers on the super-highway (right), and the obsessive 'capsule' housing unit which is plugged in to practically every structure in the drawing, and the cranes employed to move the capsules about.*

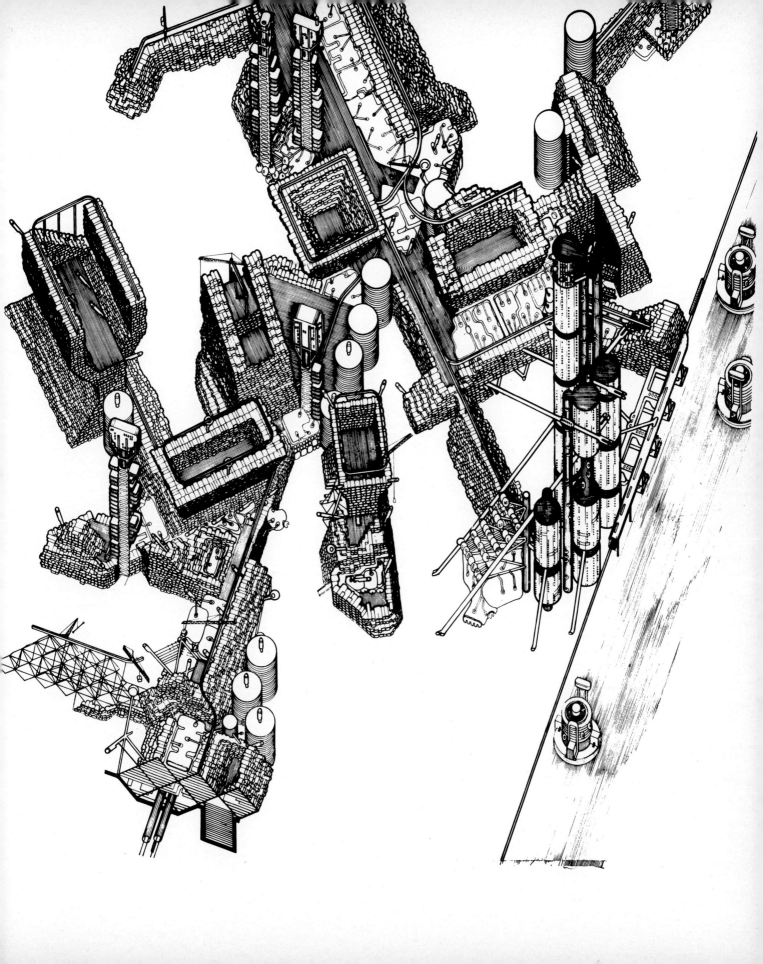

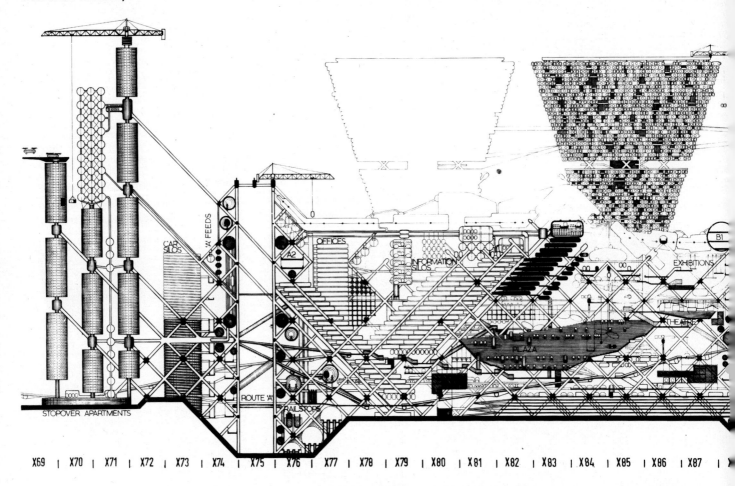

STOPOVER APARTMENTS · OFFICES · CAR SILOS · 'A' FEEDS · INFORMATION SILOS · A2 · ROUTE 'A' · RAILSTOPS · PLAZA · THEATRE · EXHIBITIONS · B1

X69 | X70 | X71 | X72 | X73 | X74 | X75 | X76 | X77 | X78 | X79 | X80 | X81 | X82 | X83 | X84 | X85 | X86 | X87 |

If any occurrence can overlay any other, and the boundaries of taste and use are to be eliminated by individual wishes, then any section must not only be capable of extreme limits of absorbtion, but should try to illustrate them.[43]

Resisting the temptation to make a major linguistic detour through these passages (though phrases like 'craggy but directional' are worth pondering), it is important to fix on those two concepts of 'eliminated by individual wishes' and 'try to illustrate them', because they are the essentials of Archigram's vision from Plug-In City onwards, striving for a city structure that would yield to individual desires more pliantly than previous forms of cities, and would derive its aesthetic from a demonstration of that compliance. Everything about the two drawings suggested permissive change and variability, but the systematic section showed in detail how this was to be achieved. Here were giant diagrid frames (**96**) of inclined service/communication tubes, among which were hung removable roads and railways and public spaces covered, in bad weather, by inflatable roofs. Here were capsules identifiable as shops and homes and offices, and here along the skyline were the mobile cranes to lift and shift, stack and rack all the plug-in units (**97**). Here, for the first time, were megastructure drawings from which one could construct a *working* model.

The mental landscape of the megastructure movement could never be the same again. From 1964 onwards, any project which hoped to be taken seriously

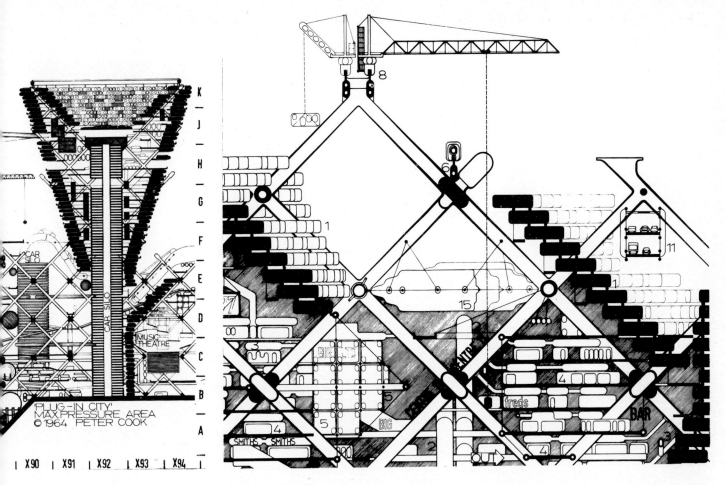

had to be detailed down to the window corners and the jointing gaskets. Since this was the period when the first 'real' megastructures to be built (e.g. those at Montreal Expo '67) were also in the detailing stage, one could claim that Archigram at this point were only 'marching in step with the mind of the age', and Cook, looking back from 1972, did emphasize the 'conventional' aspects of some versions of Plug-In City, which he said was 'very much of its period; the classic A-frame with community space in the centre'. But if these echoes of the conventional *Terrassenhäuser* formula did make the design easier to accept, practically everything else about it represented what the period was pleased to call a 'quantum jump' in architectural sensibility.

The rest of the megastructure connection could also make that jump, but Archigram promptly made another, right out of megastructure, leaving a baffled sense of paradox behind. Having produced one of those masterly images which 'immortalize a moment, typify their age' and so on, they spent the rest of the decade doing something else, heading in a different direction from that taken by the very movement to which that master-image was most meaningful. They themselves may not have recognized this situation until later — though they now tend to claim that for them the *structure* part of megastructure was less important than the illustrated promise of permissiveness, it is difficult to see why, in that case, the structure should have been so persistently detailed with the

96, 97 *Plug-In City in closer detail. The wide-screen sectional drawing (in brilliant primary colours in the original) of the 'max. pressure area' exemplifies the degree of ingenuity with which the consequences of this kind of planning were worked out. The exact functions of the various parts were often only summarily indicated, but the architectural format was extremely precise, and the fitting together of the various parts of the kit (97) shows a variability and control of three-dimensional complexity rare among 'Utopian' projects of the period.*

98 *Megastructure model kit (from* Archigram *VII, 1967). The stabilized megastructure image after Archigram had finished with it – capsules, diagonal frames, cranes, towers, communication ducts, icosohedra, living-pods, platforms – the complete kit of parts for a do-it-yourself megastructure.*

same loving attention as the individual capsules or inflatables – but the change of emphasis was certainly becoming visible only a couple of years later.

Thus, when they were laying out the graphics for *Archigram* VII in 1966, they included two sheets of a cut-out model megastructure kit (**98**) as a joke, a self-satire, on the grounds that 'everyone can do megastructures now, make your own'. The design was but little advanced from Plug-In City, and was arabesqued with in-group jokes about Cedric Price and Buckminster Fuller. The joke was to backfire on them, however; any issue of *Archigram* was by now too sacred a text to be cut up or otherwise mutilated. Copies were carefully preserved, were already being kept by architecture school libraries 'in mint condition in original plastic pack', and as far as is known none of the models was made up at the time except where fringe members of the group or other hangers-on had access to spare copies of the sheets. At all events, the message, though missed by the overwhelming bulk of the readership, was that megastructure was now a bore.

The topic they were pursuing instead – and it manifested itself relentlessly, project by project – was some kind of autonomous living unit, of maximum flexibility, adaptability, mobility and non-monumentality, that could exist independently without assistance from megastructure or any other permanent support systems. Development in this direction began, most specifically, with David Greene's totally autonomous 'Living Pod' of 1965–6, and rushed to its logical conclusion as early as 1968 with Greene's 'Suitaloon', shown in approximate prototype at the Triennale di Milano of that year — an all-enveloping garment which could be inflated to form a small pneumatic dome in which the wearer could recline or just about stand up. This very basic unit of instant shelter was to be worn while moving from place to place on a 'Cushicle', a ground effect vehicle the size of a dentist's chair (and looking not unlike one) which would provide all necessary entertainment, information and life-support systems. In the extreme case, the suitalooned cushicleer could recline at ease in his mobile bubble (**99**), while the associated systems provided him with heat, light, music etc., and papered the inside of the bubble with projected imagery, in total and autonomous insulation from the outside world and the rest of the human race.

This preoccupation of Greene's was clearly nothing to do with megastructure, which by implication at least is social as well as monumental. The other members of the group produced any number of intermediate projects in which the high-technology capsules were patently important, but not at the total expense of support structures and urbanity: Warren Chalk's 'Capsule Homes' tower, Ron Herron's 'Capsule Pier', Chalk and Herron's 'Gasket' housing (**101**) and Peter Cook's 'Hornsey' capsules, all of 1966; Mike Webb's 'Drive-In' housing of the next year; the 'Control and Choice' project (**100**) done by the group as a whole for the Paris Biennale de la jeunesse of 1967; and Ron Herron's 1968 'Oasis (free time node)' (**102**).

Elaborately presented projects like these helped to sustain the impression that Archigram was still part of the 'Megastructure International'; in the process they were putting a remarkably unserious face on the movement, because these elaborate perspectives increasingly presented the most compelling imagery of fun and leisure that architecture had ever produced. From Folkestone onwards, it seemed to be nothing but dolly-girls of every race and hue twisting or frugging

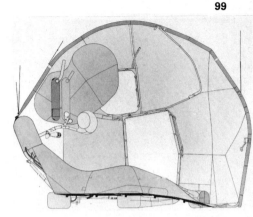

99, 100, 101 *The liberation of the capsule. By 1967 the structural aspects of megastructure had begun to seem merely obstructive to Archigram; the free capsule, exemplified by devices such as David Greene's Cushicle (99) of 1968 — a mobile reclining couch in a private inflatable dome — had been emerging for some time as their preferred environment. Already in 1967, in the Control and Choice model (100), the capsules could move about the structure, and as early as Chalk and Herron's 1965 Capsule Housing (101) the individual units had been so sophisticated and self-contained that their independence was always possible.*

100

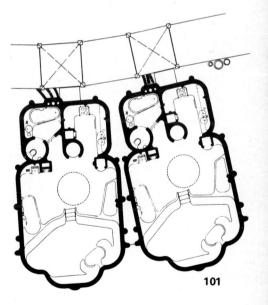

101

102 *Oasis project (Ron Herron, 1968). With its slogans of emancipation and choice, the 'fun' structure invades, liberates, displaces the architecture of the conventional city — but in the process its own substance is dissolving away and the 'leisure people' move into the foreground.*

in their modish microskirts or striped mini-dresses, exclaiming their delight at visiphone messages, relaxing in capsules, while smiling families promenaded the deck spaces, children danced ring-a-roses, crowds surged before giant images of pop stars on vast eidophore screens; everywhere were sunglasses, freaky hair, wild clothes. Not for nothing was Roger Vadim's *Barbarella* a cult-movie of this generation, for it presented their imagery of an *urbanisme ludique* in moving colour; indeed, Vadim's sinful city of Sogo (**103**) reappeared, lightly punned over, as 'Saghor, ville ludique' in a post-Archigram project by Benoit and Valdares published in France in 1970.

However, as an eye-witness of all this, I must lay down a firm *caveat* against making too much of this fun-imagery. Influential it may have been, but it may also have been rather oblique to the basic intentions of the group's members. These images were only borrowed; they were not of Archigram's own devising. Voracious consumers of collageable material with which to populate and animate their drawings, they raided the illustrations and advertisements in

103 *The city of Sogo (from* Barbarella, *directed by Roger Vadim, production design Mario Garbuglia, 1968). Based on Jean-Claude Forest's intellectual comic-strip, Vadim's sexploitation space-opera knowingly caught the mood of the year. The sinful city of Sogo was convincingly megastructural, both inside and out, rising above the sea of encroaching horrors much as Isozaki's Space City (57) had picked its way over the relics of earlier urbanisms.*

colour magazines and came up, inevitably, with 'leisure people', because colour magazines in those affluent years contained little else. Nothing could more aptly illustrate the proposition that megastructures were ideal cities containing other people's Utopias, the leisured post-industrial world of the New Utopians. Equally, nothing could more neatly illustrate the dangers of mistaking a piece of British graphic opportunism for an ideological programme. The presence of all these leisure people in Archigram's permissive cities is as much an empirical solution to the problem of finding someone – anyone! – to populate them as it is a theoretical proposal for who *should* populate them.

In practice, however, the latter reading was the customary one outside the Archigram circle. From Mechthild Schumpp (see previous chapter) through worried students in Argentina who asked me 'How are the theoric propositions of Archigram realized in the daily life?' to the *Utopie* group and other left-wing critics, everyone saw the Archigram vision of the Plug-In City of permissive pleasure as a complete and homogeneous proposal for an ideal future.

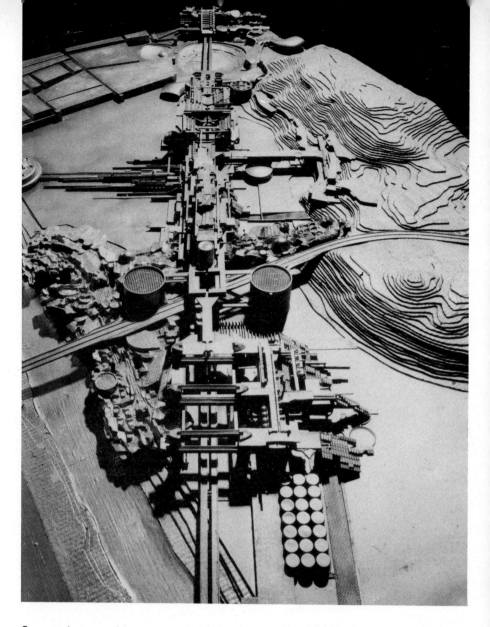

104 *The Archigram influence: Italy. Urban Structure project (students of Leonardo Savioli, Florence, 1966–7). Although it was for interiors that Savioli's students were specifically directed to look at Archigram designs, it is not difficult to see the influence also in the overall forms and detailed model-making quality of this megastructure.*

Successive graphic approximations to an evolving view of man and his environment, many of them tentative or composed *ad hoc* out of bits and pieces already to hand, were frozen, academicized as permanent prototypes of the New City. As Archigram phased themselves out of megastructure, their projects began to acquire the status of the 'ancient monuments' to be emulated in the new 'Academy of Utopias'.

The academic phase of megastructure will be discussed later, but the directness of the dependence deserves to be noted here. Not only did Archigram's first Italian successor-group take the name 'Archizoom' in direct emulation, but architecture students in Florence working under Leonardo Savioli in the academic session 1966–7 were specifically directed to study Archigram drawings during the famous design exercises (**104**) based on the 'psychedelic' Piper-clubs. It was in Japan, however, that the impact of Archigram was most spectacular and most widely noted. In 1966 the Shinkenjiku Residential Competition, organized by *Shinkenjiku* magazine (*Japan*

Architect) and judged by no less than Kenzo Tange himself, was won by a conspicuously Archigram-influenced project complete with cranes and capsules (**105**), and similar tendencies were distributed right through the four-hundred-odd entries.[44] The winner of the next year's competition was closer to the Metabolist tradition, but once again Archigram graphics and many Archigram architectural usages could be found all through the published entries. As a result, the world at large gained the impression that the great and original Japanese megastructure tradition was already exhausted, replaced by academic elaborations of ideas that Archigram had already left behind.

From the publication of these competition results onwards, the world's attitude to Japan was conspicuously changed. No longer were architects 'almost senseless with emotion'. With narrowed eyes, they (or at least their magazines) now chronicled the failure of Metabolism to deliver the goods it had appeared to promise, year by year, down to and including Osaka Expo '70; Osaka ought, at face value, to have been a triumphant tenth anniversary of the Metabolists' bid for world status in 1960, but somehow it was not. The mood had changed about megastructures, and too much seemed to have been plagiarized – notably Isozaki's two entertainment-robots (**106**) in the Festival Plaza, enlarged in form and function from two domestic robots exhibited by Archigram four years earlier.

More than this, everything about Osaka Expo '70 that smacked of megastructure, such as Tange's vast lattice space-grid over the whole Festival Plaza, was now seen as simply repeating an Expo formula that had peaked out, unrepeatably, at Montreal three years before. If Archigram had permanently changed the imagery of megastructure, Montreal Expo '67 had come close to exhausting all the megastructure imagery that could effectively be built at the time, and thus, like Archigram, had left the whole concept permanently altered.

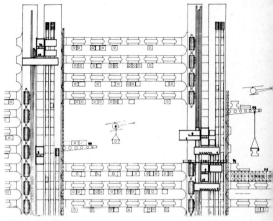

105, 106 *The Archigram influence: Japan. The waning of Japanese hegemony in megastructure seems to date from the publication of the winning design (105) in the 1966 housing competition sponsored by the magazine* Shinkenjiku (Japan Architect), *in which Archigram usages were immediately identifiable – particularly the cranes and capsules. The influence was still evident in the Osaka Expo of 1970 (to which Archigram were invited to contribute): practically everything under Kenzo Tange's Festival Plaza space-frame (106), including Isozaki's entertainment-robots, could be seen as Archigram 'rationalised and strained through the systematic design process of the Japanese'* (Charles Jencks).

6 Megacity Montreal

The megastructure vintage of 1967 was classic, rich and bountiful. That year produced the nearest-ever realization of the promise of Metabolism: the Yamanishi communications centre in Kofu (**53**), by Kenzo Tange. Massive and rhetorical, its concrete-box capsules apparently hung from brackets on the sides of sixteen cylindrical towers arranged in four parallel ranks but rising to different 'indeterminate' heights, it implied vertical rather than lengthwise extension — though remaining 'craggy but directional', in Peter Cook's phrase.

The same year also saw the effective completion of the savagely reduced but still craggily impressive final version of Geoffrey Copcutt's originally vast design for Cumbernauld New Town Centre (**181**), 'the most complete megastructure to be built' and the nearest thing yet to a canonical megastructure that one can actually visit or inhabit. Further, 1967 also gave us Scarborough College (**134**), by John Andrews with Page and Steel, the most immediately striking of all academic megastructures. Scarborough is located outside Toronto, and being Canadian is one of the marks of the true vintage of 1967. Even so, Scarborough is an exception; though Canadian, it is not in Montreal, where the Expo of that year crowned with a flourish of exhibition megastructures a city which was showing powerful megatendencies throughout. At least one of the Expo structures, Moshe Safdie's 'Habitat' housing, is extensively documented, both through massive magazine coverage and through Safdie's own book which, though called *Beyond Habitat*, is largely about the saga of adventures and misadventures that led to the building's construction.

The other megas on and off the Expo site were much less well recorded. This is to be regretted, since it is helpful to be able to see Mega-Montreal of the mid-sixties as a complete historical phenomenon, inclusive enough in its ramifications to cover, among other things, architectural education at McGill University; the topography of downtown; the atmosphere of optimism induced by the onset of Expo preparations; the mysterious power of the local money establishment to promote major property adventures; a bilingual culture with unexpected world linkages; the land use policy of Canadian National Railways; and yet stranger affairs, including the personality of Mayor Drapeau. In the end, however, this historical phenomenon must be defined by its products; however diverse in detail, *les mégas de Montréal* were perceived as a comprehensible grouping of architecture united by ambition, ingenuity and the ground on which they stood.

The reference to the ground on which they stood must be interpreted as having several layers of meaning, mostly literal, quite apart from the obvious geographical one. For instance, the actual site of Expo was on two islands (**107**), one of them entirely artificial, and a spit of land extending outwards from the bank of the St Lawrence which was partly man-made, as was the second island. All were joined by bridges above water and Metro tunnels below ground,

107 *Megacity Montreal: a comprehensive air-view of almost everything that made Montreal the capital city of megastructure in Expo year 1967. In the foreground, the tetrahedral structures of the Theme Pavilion 'Man the Producer', with its attached station from which the rails snake away across the other artificial island to join the landspit on which stands Habitat (off picture to left). Behind the harbour beyond rises one of the giant grain elevators that were seen as proof that 'megastructures grow wild in Montreal', and beyond that again are the towers of downtown, their foundations tangled in a web of underground circulations that made it possible to regard the whole central city as one accidental megastructure.*

so that the whole site could be seen as a megaform in the Metabolist sense. Again, the major claimant to the title of megastructure in downtown was downtown itself, unified by a subterranean network of shopping malls, pedestrian tunnels, Metro stations and parking silos, like eight kilometres of an underground root system of which the office towers and hotels above ground were mere outgrowths. And since the Metro was an active ingredient in both downtown and Expo, it could be seen, if you had so intellectualizing a turn of mind, as the meta-form behind the megaforms.

In all this, the well-publicized Habitat was the real odd man out, semi-detached from both mainland and Expo islands on the peninsular Place d'Accueil, the parking-lot entry to the Expo site, to most of which it was connected not by the Metro but by the subsidiary Expo Express, an independent line which started life as a construction spur. Yet the magazine coverage seems to suggest that most of the world's architectural correspondents got no further than Habitat before rushing back to write their reports on Expo. They cannot really be blamed; it was almost exactly the kind of thing they most wanted to see at such an occasion, a building that most neatly expressed the overt architectural ambitions of its time. If megastructure ever was 'the child of informed opinion', then it was at Habitat, conceived in the academic groves of McGill, idolized by the magazines, and taken up by academics (including dissident student bodies, be it noted) as the model of the good urban architecture of the future.

The very title of the McGill sixth-year thesis from which Safdie developed the project is a summation of some well-established ideas of the epoch: 'A Three-Dimensional Modular Building System'. The reported response of no less a pundit than the distinguished London architect Jane Drew — 'That's fantastic. There's nothing I can tell you; you know what you're doing' — shows how immediately acceptable this conception was at the level of established progressive thought in architecture. However, the '3-D Mod B-system' as it stood in 1961 was not yet Habitat. The model had a visible system of close-spaced structural uprights with habitable capsules slotted between them in a manner that visually recalls Le Corbusier's 'bottle-rack' model of the *Unité d'habitation* at Marseilles; a conspicuous difference, however, was the large amount of empty space interspersed among the capsules, a sure sign of megastructural thinking, however primitive and romantic at this stage.

Safdie's chance to build a version of this conception came while he was away in Philadelphia in 1963, studying under Louis Kahn and in contact with Anne Tyng, whose interests in tetrahedral and pyramidal geometries had already, it seems, affected Kahn's 'City Hall' project (see p. 38). On Safdie's own admission, her ideas had a crucial effect on the first project for Habitat, in which the house-capsules are stacked directly on one another in a staggered formation that gives a version of the *Terrassenhäuser* section, but on a plan which butts them together in a similar kind of stagger, giving a ziggurat or 'stepped die' profile (**108**) that was to rattle around for some years as a possible megastructure format. It occurs again in the projects of Kahn's fellow-Israelis Leopold Gerstel and Zwi Hecker (the latter came to Montreal in due course, cementing a kind of Montreal/Tel Aviv axis), in the project studies for the *Ciudad en el Espacio* of the Taller Bofill group in Spain, and indeed wherever there was any interest in the mathematics of closest-packing figures.

What was eventually built (**109**) was a drastically reduced version of the stepped-die model, only eleven storeys high as against the proposed twenty-

108 *Habitat, Montreal; model (Safdie, David, Barrott, Boulva, 1967). A savagely reduced version of Safdie's original vision of a vast housing scheme at the entrance to Expo, the built version still retained enough of the original admixture of complexities and simplicities to make it about the most compelling building of the year. The basic simplicity is in the proposition to build the whole by piling up standard concrete-box capsules; the complexity begins with the impossibility of having all capsules identical if they are to add up to 158 apartments of different plans, and to survive the consequent asymmetrical loadings, and is rendered more complex by the need to add a substructure of supports, circulations and services because a mere stacking of capsules cannot be habitably self-sufficient or structurally stable. Yet simplicity returns when it is perceived that the whole composition depends on two simple repeats of symmetrical clusterings, balanced about a central axis that is rarely discerned from ground level.*

two, and with a much modified form of the supporting A-frame system, which had originally been supposed to contain oblique elevators and services, Archigram-style. Very little of this, however, could be understood from a first sight of the finished building: an irregular skyline and a complex and involved stacking pattern combined to produce a seemingly disorderly elevation. Furthermore, the residual support system was so tucked under the back of the stacked capsules that its presence could hardly be suspected from the usual frontal viewpoints along the road at the foot of the structure. The overall effect of

109 *Habitat: the western end under construction, showing the immediate first impression of an apparently picturesque, open-ended and aformal agglomeration of units that was also the most lasting memory of Habitat that most visitors took away.*

these piled concrete boxes with their diminutive roof-terraces was one of picturesque disorder, the ever-popular Mediterranean village imagery. In fact, this apparent disorder contained some almost painfully obvious ordering principles in the form of old-fashioned *Beaux-Arts* symmetries balanced around the lift-stacks (**110**), but you had to know where to stand to see them, and most visitors to Expo never stood in those places. For them, the correct term of comparison was Le Corbusier's phrase about the *villes dites d'art*, the 'famous cities of art' of the eastern Mediterranean — 'chaos overall, order and discipline in the parts' — or Maki's group form, which 'evolves from a system of generative elements in space'. At Habitat there was but one generative form, the standard-sized pre-cast concrete box (**111**) which was the basic unit of accommodation for everything in the scheme. If one is to judge from lay comments, and especially the numerous cartoons and jokes made for or against this absolute identity of elements, this basic unit came through clearly as a 'unique selling-point', a 'packaging gimmick' or an 'ingredient X'.

110, 111 *Habitat: interior-scapes. As soon as the supporting structures are seen (110), Habitat reveals itself as being much nearer to the frame-and-capsule norms of its time (which had in fact been anticipated by some of Safdie's earliest projects); but on the exposed and habitable side of the complex (111) the would-be vernacular, Italian hill-town image reasserts itself — high density, regular domestic cells, sociable terraces.*

112 *Habitat: pre-cast room unit being hoisted into place. Not only was the basic housing proposition of Habitat in good currency in 1967, but its structural concept of room-by-room prefabrication and 'building with boxes' was hailed in the press as an 'idea whose time has come'. One of the main reasons why its time had* not *come can be seen here: the boxes had to vary so much in quite major details, such as the placing of openings and the consequent distribution of reinforcing steel inside the concrete, that most of the promised economies of standardization were mislaid.*

For most of the architectural commentators, however, the identity (more apparent than real) of the elements was less important than the fact of their being cast in one piece on the ground and hoisted complete into place (**112**). At a time when North American constructional theorists were about to go for broke on 'system-building', 'factory-built', 'industrialized' or 'prefabricated' housing, Habitat was, as *Architectural Forum* declared, 'an idea whose time has come'. *Forum*'s faith in 'building with boxes' was sustained and passionate; Habitat's justification was seen, in the last resort and in defiance of its elevated costs, as a necessary prototyping and research exercise for a new phase of North American constructional technology, as development work which the industry could or would not finance for itself.

What ultimately came out of this aspect of Habitat was an illusion, a myth, that heavy prefabrication would 'solve the crisis of the American city'. Once this myth was established as an 'idea in good currency' (and therefore dead, as American economist Donald Schon once put it), it became politically viable in the guise of 'Operation Breakthrough' housing programmes; it became academically viable as a fund-gathering mechanism for ambitious Deans and

Chairmen of Architecture; it provided the supposed economic justification for a number of belated megastructure projects – and ultimately it delivered almost nothing commensurate with the size of the myth that had been built up.

None of this was Habitat's fault, of course, except insofar as Safdie had built such hopes on it. He certainly believed that it had some reforming powers:

I came to the conclusion that one couldn't rehouse all the families living in slums in Chicago ... in single-family housing – it wouldn't work because of the numbers of people and areas of land you would need for it.

Yet high rise wouldn't work either. We saw it in the most dramatic form, kids clinging to wire-mesh balcony railings on the thirtieth floor ... people complaining about the horrible life. For the first time I experienced the life of a newly-built slum. It made you feel compassion for the people; it made you hate those buildings.

In retrospect, I had set out on this trip with preconceived ideas, feeling suburbia was bad – after all, the Mediterranean cities were my background. But my conclusion was new; I felt we had to find new forms of housing that would recreate, in a high density environment, the relationships and the amenities of the house and the village. . . .[45]

It is clear from the later pages of *Beyond Habitat* that Safdie believed that this particular brand of cellular geometry could deliver a radically new kind of urban environment; but, looking at what he actually built, one cannot help feeling that he had merely backed up into his autobiography and built an image of his pro-Mediterranean prejudices, and that this was the real reason for its success, since that was about the most widely entertained prejudice then current in architecture. Even the admitted and clearly observed problems of exposed access and lack of privacy seemed to be excusable because these, after all, were the urban conditions that were supposed to lead to that desirable vitality displayed by the communities that inhabited real Mediterranean villages. Habitat was the most immediately accepted of all the Montreal megas because it was the least radical.

It would be unfair, of course, to advance these criticisms of Habitat as criticisms of Safdie's whole work; beyond the horizons of this present study, he was to elaborate his ideas and his geometries further, especially systems of flattened hexagons that produce sections not unlike those advocated by Claude Parent in France in *Vivre à l'oblique* ('oblique living', Paris, 1970). Flattened hexagons are also a favoured closest-packing figure, of course, but Safdie has – bafflingly – said more than once that he is not particularly interested in systematic geometries.

Not so Guntis Plesums, whose geometrical preoccupations date from well before Expo and still continue in his present academic career in Oregon. One of the 'unknown names' of Expo, and an Estonian by origin, Plesums worked with Guy Desbarats of ARCOP (Affleck, Desbarats, Lebensold and Size) on the development and design of the two 'Theme Pavilions' – structures that were themselves the residue of a scheme (one of many; practically every architect in Montreal seems to have nurtured one) to put the whole of Expo in a single megastructural frame of some sort. Both pavilions – 'Man the Explorer' and 'Man the Producer' (**113**) – depended, in gross form and in detailed construction, on that best-loved of close-packing solids, the tetrahedron, though in these cases with a smaller tetrahedron lopped off each of its apices. As a geometrical device (**114**) it worked magnificently in both cases, giving a coherence of totality and parts that must be unique in the recent history of open trusses or space-structures (though neither of these terms is quite apposite to this *sui generis* structural concept). This coherence (**117**) shines through the mutilations

113, 114, 115 (overleaf) *Theme Pavilion, 'Man the Producer', Montreal Expo (Guy Desbarats of Affleck, Desbarats, Lebensold and Size, 1967). The entire structural system was evolved from a single geometrical element (114) devised by Guntis Plesums – a regular tetrahedron with its corners cropped off. Trussed floors and diagonal beams of these elements came to earth in a regular pattern of triangles and hexagons in plan (113). However, local concentrations of load, at points of support and elsewhere, made it impossible to use identical structural members throughout, and the thickness of these elements was therefore varied according to load – a usage that makes the behaviour of the structure readable (115), in spite of its great complexity.*

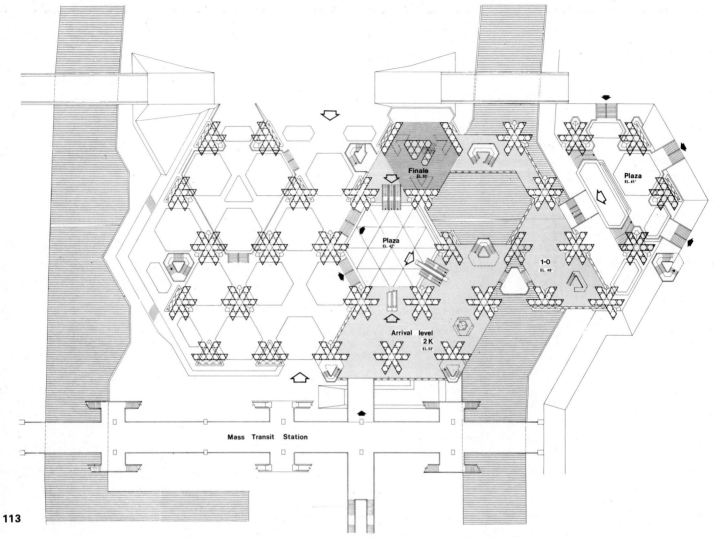

113

114

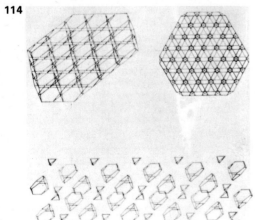

caused to the original conceptions by the usual fire-safety requirements and by the further, less expected, problems caused by distinguished exhibition designers who claimed they could not work in tetrahedral spaces, demanding both total enclosure and vertical walls in some cases.

However, the truncated tetrahedral geometry itself proved difficult to handle as a structural 'brick'. In both pavilions the system had to be compromised to make it structurally usable and constructionally manageable.[46] Extensive give-and-take was required between the architects and the engineers (Eskenazi, Baracs, de Stein and Associates), between the engineers and the fabricators (Dominion Bridge Company), and finally between them and the two construction companies involved. The design process is remembered as taking place in three distinct phases — the architectural conception, followed by the structural design, and then the elaboration of a constructional system — all conducted against a background of only partial knowledge of the exhibits to be contained in 'Man the Explorer' and a complete absence of any knowledge at all of the proposed contents of 'Man the Producer'.

116 *'Man the Producer' under construction. Before the external cladding was put in place, the whole pavilion could still be seen as an open structure carrying floor planes at various levels – a zone of possibilities almost equal to those demanded by Constant Niewenhuis for his Neo-Babylone (see chapter 4).*

Nevertheless, the tetrahedral conception came through powerfully (**115**), if not always clearly, as a strong, convincing architectural rhetoric. At the points of maximum loading, where the structures were secured to their foundations, the tetrahedra were more solid steel plate than they were open space, appearing as closed boxes with circular holes relieved in each of their faces. Higher up, where loads were lighter, they were more like what is commonly expected of such a structure, open trusses with fairly massive members and corners gussetted to varying depths according to local stresses, while at the very highest levels that the visitor could normally perceive the visual effect was more nearly like Plesums's original linear conceptual diagrams, the basic geometry made manifest in its pure form.

In an Expo where, as usual, most pavilions were made of 'architecture' faked up over a hidden and unacknowledged structural frame, such honesty and clarity were impressive, and were made doubly so by the fact that the steel was left exposed and unpainted so that it could weather and oxidize as it liked without looking cheap or un-cared-for. Rather, it gained the kind of authority which accrues to major engineering works, which are also normally expected to exhibit this kind of 'take it or leave it' air; and to describe 'Man the Producer', where the clearly visible concrete block foundations enhanced the effect, as looking like 'a collapsed and rusting Eiffel Tower' was to pay it a compliment.

The foundation blocks were visible because they stood in or at the side of one of the navigable canals which passed beneath the pavilion, which also had under its wing one of the rather complex Expo Express stations, with its concourse above ground level but below the railroad tracks and platforms. These involvements with transportation, and the sense of overstepping other planning considerations, combined with the powerful diagonals of the tetrahedral structure to give a notable sense of being in a megastructure, almost an Archigram project. But 'Man the Producer' had further exemplary overtones which, because they were accidental, are easier to perceive in retrospect, though they were certainly there to be experienced at the time.

Because the actual exhibits to be contained in the pavilion were barely known at the time of its design, it had to be conceived simply as a system of horizontal platforms in space (**116**), on which 'anything could happen', connected by escalators and stairways. In the end, many of these platforms remained almost empty of discernible exhibits, but were often densely occupied by people – couples, families, schools and colleges from all over the Dominion, visiting architects and designers, all with nothing to do but divert or educate themselves as they felt fit. The result was an accidental but instructive approximation to one of Constant's 'sectors', or even to the Fun Palace, since on one of the smaller spiral staircases a vertical cluster of TV cameras and monitor

117 *'Man the Producer' completed. Clad, and with exhibits in place, the Theme Pavilions lost much of their* ludique *promise, though the seemingly unprovoked eruptions of staircases and platforms between the main tetrahedra still suggested unpredictable goings-on within.*

screens presented the visitor with images of himself discovering that he was playing the role of a visitor seeing images of himself discovering that he was playing the role. . . . Something ludic going on in, literally, Marshall MacLuhan country. Purist Situationists might well decry these unintentional *situations construites*, but as experienced they had a curiously liberating effect, especially on children, and the whole place had an engaging air of mystery. The tetrahedral planning was often confusing, so that minor constructed situations would arise as visitors found themselves on an unpredicted balcony over the canal, in the presence of an unexplained exhibit, confronted by the silhouettes of thousands of other visitors in superimposed layers on bridges against the sky, or at the top of an escalator they were sure they had just descended.

All in all, it was an improvized learning machine for *Homo ludens*, an environmental experience which set the Theme Pavilions apart from all the others at Expo. However sophisticated, however apparently aware of the 'media revolution' they were, the other great showpiece pavilions – the 'Labyrinth', the national pavilions of the United States and Czechoslovakia, even of Cuba – all processed the visitor as the more or less passive consumer of a prescribed linear experience without conspicuous alternative routes. In 'Man the Producer' there were nothing but alternative routes, to be selected at conscious will or simply at random – the Situationists' psycho-geographical drift. This was achieved, of course, through massive redundancies of space-usage beyond what any of the other pavilions could permit themselves, but such redundancies, it often appears, may be of the essence of megastructure. The freedoms demanded by Constant, the control and choice of Archigram, the ability to 'inflate an extra capsule . . . for the arrival of Grandma', in Denise Scott-Brown's neat phrase, all require space to spare.

It was not for these reasons, however, that the Theme Pavilions and other aspects of Expo were occasionally hailed at the time as prototypes of the multi-level city centres of the future. Such salutations depended much less on the surplus supply of space than on the sheer Futurist-revival imagery of super-imposed ground levels mixed with an elaborate layering of different kinds of mechanical transport (**118**). In an age which was beginning to put as much blind faith in high-technology mass-transport systems as in heavy pre-fabrication as solutions to 'the problem of the city', the elaboration of Metro, Expo Express, two different types of monorail, several forms of small rubber-tyred vehicles compatible with pedestrians, canal boats, hovercraft on the St Lawrence River and helicopters almost continuously overhead was a veritable feast of received ideas and approved images.

Those images and ideas are all part of the megastructure package, however; by the end of that year one could almost define a megastructure as a large building with a monorail through it! What was disappointing at Expo was that all these transportation lines were not usefully engaged with the buildings they penetrated or skirted; admittedly there was a station under the edge of 'Man the Producer', but the monorail that actually passed through the Buckminster Fuller dome which formed the cover of the US pavilion could not stop to set down or pick up visitors. It was purely scenic Futurist-revival effect, and to enter the pavilion, however you arrived at it, there was no option but to queue up, under US Marine guard, in the muddy 'refugee compound' outside.

Contrasts like that with the dryshod freedom to come and go at will offered by 'Man the Producer' could only emphasize the improvizatory success of the

118 *The monorails at Expo underlined the megastructure theme less by their physical penetrations of buildings (such as Buck-minster Fuller's US pavilion dome) than by their constant interweaving at different levels, a partial vision of the kind of rich mix of rapid transit desired by most urban planners of the day.*

Theme Pavilions. They were the summit of the megastructure experience offered by Expo, but Expo itself provided a fairly high base-level of experience that was relevant to megastructure as a frame of mind: mechanical movement, multiplicity of levels, emphasis on fun or *ludique* experiences, stylish Archigram-type colours, people in complex artificial environments, visual information saturation. The atmosphere of the times that made megastructures thinkable was in some ways even better manifested at Expo than at the Folkestone conference of the previous year. The times were crucial, however: in defiance of the *Bureau international des expositions*, most of the Expo structures remain on the islands, but the atmosphere has totally departed. The flash vision of an urbanism of the future is irrecoverable.

Downtown Montreal cannot recover it either — if it was ever truly present. Downtown is a fundamentally different proposition that brings forward quite other aspects of megastructure. Almost the only bridge between the two, conceptually and visually, is provided, appropriately enough, by the gigantic grain elevators (**119**) that look across at Habitat as Habitat looks back at the city. The elevators are, like the office towers of downtown, part of the permanent commercial equipment of Montreal as a port; their relevance to megastructure thinking was not really appreciated until Expo year, when they suddenly became some of the most widely commented buildings there.

The reasons are obvious enough. They are enormous, but their impressive size has nothing to do with architecture, its ambitions and visions: their purely

119

120

118

121

functional enormity is another guarantee that megastructures grow naturally in the right time and place. And visitors going to examine them would discover that this indeed 'must be the place', for right behind the largest of them all lies the immensely long and now manifestly multi-functional Marché Bonsecours, which has as good a title as the Königsbau in Stuttgart to be considered a neo-classical megastructure. Further, their element-by-element composition, their extensive command of ground space, their linkages one to another and to sundry outworks by covered elevators and conveyors which draw diagonals across the sky and come together in clearly defined 'nodes' (**120**), and their loose, provisional combination on the scale of large urban design together mean that they would look like megastructures whatever their absolute size.

But mere looks were not enough; the true and contemporary lessons to be learned from them, as Melvin Charney warned in what was effectively the first article to celebrate their presence, must come from more basic considerations:

. . . with the grain elevators we can opt for an understanding of the complexity of organisation rather than a simple appraisal of the design-image; we *can* opt for the telescopic spouts, the mobile towers, the mobile cranes, the moving conveyor belts, the stock of parts that can be inserted into the system when needed, the concrete silos as distended tubes in the conduits of movement rather than the lumpish neo-monuments of yesteryear, but we must opt for them *not* as formal images. It is the process of which they are an image which is important. This process we must study if we believe that architecture is an involvement with human processes rather than designed things.[47]

This particular mode of appraising the grain elevators should prepare us to learn that Charney alone of all the architects who made proposals for pavilions at Osaka Expo '70 seemed to have learned the lessons of 'Man the Producer'. His projected but unbuilt Canadian pavilion, designed with Harry Parnass and (significantly) Janos Baracs, the Theme Pavilion engineer, called for a cluster of self-erecting crane-towers supporting lattice-framed platforms, suspended walkways and travelators, enclosures made from fold-out shipping containers in which the parts would have reached the site, and all the necessary structural and service sub-units for 'the participation of people in the light, sound and movement of an exhibit'. This certainly sounds like an attempt consciously to generalize the particular and accidental qualities of the Theme Pavilions, but the photographs of the model (**121**) strongly suggest that this particular exhibition megastructure was to be realized in a formal aesthetic largely derived from the outworks of the grain elevators.

Charney himself is also part of the bridge to downtown, since he prepared a much-reproduced cross-sectional drawing (**122**) through the central spine of the business area in order to show the extent of the 'pedestrian plumbing . . .

119, 120, 121 *The grain elevators of Montreal came into their own in 1967, partly because they were unavoidable, standing conspicuous and huge at the edge of the water (119), and megastructurally fascinating, their associated outworks (120) exhibiting a loose, aformal connectivity that was the aspiration of many megadesigners of the time. One of the few to achieve anything like these qualities with comparable authority was Melvin Charney in his project (121) for a Canadian pavilion at Osaka Expo '70.*

122 *Cross-section through downtown Montreal (drawn by Melvin Charney, 1967). The network of underground 'pedestrian plumbing' that would ultimately run from the Place Victoria tower (right) under Rue Ste Catherine almost to Sherbrooke Street (far left). The tunnels' connection with almost everything of consequence in downtown, their own shops, parking lots and station concourses, gave rise to the claim that 'Montreal itself is the mega-structure!'*

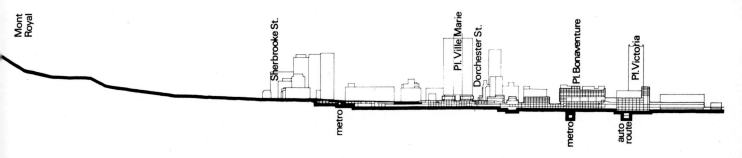

basement architecture on an urban scale' which provides the connective network that encourages the Montréalais to boast that 'La mégastructure, c'est Montréal!' This has occasionally been expressed differently as 'La mégastructure, c'est le Métro!', but these two aphoristic and cheerfully chauvinistic opinions are not necessarily mutually exclusive: they intersect in downtown, and depend largely on the compass-bearing of the speaker's viewpoint.

If one looks north-east, parallel to the river bank, one sees the whole downtown area as a megastructure because of the underground pedestrian plumbing exposed by Charney's section, which is cut across this view. The initiation of this basement urbanism was something of an *ad hoc* brainwave on the part of Vincent Ponte, planning consultant not to the city but to William Zeckendorf, the adventurous US entrepreneur whose Place Ville Marie tower-block (architect I. M. Pei) was one of the keys to the opening up of the new business district. Although the city of Montreal subsequently acquired a planner, Claude Robillard, and a downtown development plan of sorts, the continuity and workability of the underground urbanism has always depended largely on the opportunism of Ponte 'piecing together public and private projects', as Blanche van Ginkel put it.[48] In all this he was greatly aided, as were other downtown opportunists, by the policies and property-holdings of the Canadian National Railway.

For not only are many of the new buildings and complexes carried in CNR air-rights over the tracks, but the physical layout of the tracks themselves has drastically affected the form of downtown: they cross the river well above the level of the lower ground near the water, thus enabling other transportation and services to pass beneath, but then cut a deep gash through the rising ground on which downtown proper stands and are soon deep enough below this first plateau for streets to pass easily above the railway. It was the realization of the problems and promises of these multiple superimposed levels, van Ginkel claimed, that made the downtown axis 'for the first time important in the development of Montreal', and changed the equilibrium of the metropolis.

What equilibrates about this axis is the Metro system. In spite of its long northward branch beyond the Montagne, it is the two lines parallel with the river which have had the most direct effect on downtown, linking together the business, hotel, governmental and university areas that lie between the upstream terminal at Atwater and the main intersection, downstream at Berri-de-Montigny. It is a very consciously 'designed' Metro system, each station the work of a different architectural office and of a markedly, sometimes ludicrously different architectural character. More importantly, the entire system was seen, by Robillard and others, as both the unifying factor in a seemingly disorganized city and the generator of new development in certain selected parts of the urban fabric, with major stations, particularly the interchanges, seen as shopping and business sub-centres into which passengers would be delivered directly as a 'captive audience'.

The point at which the two perspectives on Montreal actually meet at right-angles, where the pedestrian plumbing and the Metro intersect and the whole promise of a subterranean city protected from the elements comes closest to realization, is Place Bonaventure. Located at the first point where the Metro can comfortably squeeze under the CNR, which is also the point where the pedestrian plumbing would naturally break out to the surface, Place Bonaventure is, appropriately if disputably, a megastructure in itself.

Disputably — in spite of its designer's firm conviction that it is truly a megastructure — because of the predominantly vertical emphasis of its exteriors and its very closed look (**123**). The verticality is clearly felt to make nonsense of megastructure's dimension of extensibility which, in spite of the contrary example of Tange's Yamanishi centre, is generally considered to be horizontal. Yet for all its verticality and its untypically closed, box-like exterior (**125**), this is a building which adds greatly to the interest and architectural quality of the exiguous register of completed buildings which might just about qualify for the title of megastructure.

Designed by the Affleck half of Affleck, Desbarats etc., whose Desbarats half designed the Theme Pavilions, it stands above the CNR tracks on a 25-foot column grid whose dimension is derived from the layout of a freight terminal beneath those tracks (**124**). On top of this exemplary complexity of circulation, into which the adjacent Metro must also be bracketed, Place Bonaventure loads an equally exemplary complexity of urban or even metropolitan functions. At Metro/street-entrance level there are three floors of shopping space (**127**), too complex in section and plan to be detailed here, or to be brushed off simply as 'arcades' as is sometimes done. Above them squats Concordia Hall, named after the now legendary property company formed to develop the site, and large enough to house a motor show. Above that again are five floors of the Merchandise Mart (on the model of the famous one in Chicago), and on top of that the single floor of the International Trade Center, which has upward connections with the hotel which tops off the scheme; this is planned like a motel on two/three storeys around a pair of garden courtyards (**126**) whose ornamental waters double as swimming pools and as cooling tanks for the air-conditioning system. Normal office spaces are secreted in various parts of the complex, and there is, of course, ample room for parking around and under its nether parts.

The absence of windows around Concordia Hall, the minimal fenestration of the Mart levels and the remarkably few penetrations of the perimeter, even at the shopping levels, leave Bonaventure with almost unpierced walls of solid vertically ribbed concrete on its three public street façades. The effect is closed, defensive, fortress-like — or, given the small-scale eruptions of the hotel on its cresting, like an ocean liner in its 'definiteness of boundary' and the transience and lack of community among its 'unrelated' inhabitants, to cite only two of the characteristics of liners identified by Paolo Soleri (see p. 22).

If these qualities are megastructural, some of the other defining aspects of the concept are hard to see. It is not easy to read the whole as a system of modular units carried in a massive frame, for instance, in spite of the fact that everything about the design depends, structurally and dimensionally, from that 25-foot grid which originates down below the tracks. On the other hand its functional complexity is undoubtedly in the megastructure range, and, instructively, it is located in the kind of sensitive 'urban frontier' condition which many mega-structuralists saw as the proper deployment of their designs. Place Bonaventure marks the furthest extension of downtown into the lowlands by the water, and has pulled some central business functions in that direction. But they cannot yet, it seems, be pulled much further without losing their downtown credibility. The Place Victoria tower is nearer the harbour, but is visually isolated above ground and half isolated below ground: the Metro stops there, but the pedestrian plumbing is not yet connected to it.

123, 124, 125 (overleaf) *Place Bonaventure, Montreal (Ray Affleck of Affleck, Desbarats, Lebensold and Size, 1967). This great multi-functional urban box (123) was inevitably one of the prize exhibits of Expo year. Its contents, stacked densely on top of one another as the section shows (124), covered a vital range of metropolitan activities, but its stern, almost hermetically closed exterior and lack of obvious extensibility left doubts (not shared by Affleck himself!) as to its qualification as a mega-structure.*

123

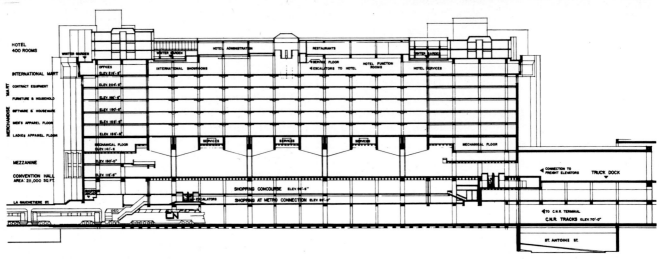

PLACE BONAVENTURE
CROSS SECTION LOOKING EAST
SCALE:

126 *Place Bonaventure: the hotel. Around the perimeter of its highest levels, Place Bonaventure breaks down to the more domestic scale proper to a hotel, and opens up with generous fenestration looking inward into garden courts that seem to have nothing to do with the rest of the building — except that the ornamental waters double as cooling tanks for the air-conditioning system.*

There is also a certain air of pleasure-seeking, however thoroughly commercialized, among the shopping crowds which faintly recalls the *ludique* theme, though there is little enough chance for any individual to arrange his own environments or situations — not without getting arrested for obstruction or wilful damage, that is! Yet in theory, if not in practice until very recently, the idea of ludic/commercial enterprise in megastructures has a history of sorts in Montreal. As early as Expo year François Dallegret, the willingly expatriate French architect who was also responsible for some of the minor fun-and-games architecture at Expo itself, had a commercially sponsored project in hand for *Palais Métro* (128), an indoor megastructure of boutiques, bars, discos etc. to be housed in the cavernous interior of an abandoned drill-hall over the Metro station at Place des Arts. Had it been built, it would have come close to realizing

the kind of fun structures envisaged by Archigram at about the same period (e.g. Herron's 'Oasis'). This was not to happen, however, and although Dallegret later built a modified version for a department store in Kansas City, the nearest realization in Montreal itself was a largely unintentional one – Alexis Nihon Plaza (**129**). The container for this *mégastructure populaire* is a straightforward property speculation by the eponymous Mr Nihon, a not very noteworthy piece of architecture by Harold Ship comprising a large galleried shopping hall with offices and parking on top, squatting over the Atwater Metro terminal but under the shadow of Mies van der Rohe's Westmount Center towers.

The interior shopping galleries as designed had the kind of open-fronted shop units that are also found in Place Bonaventure, but selling activities have spilled out on to the galleries and the central floor of the main plaza. There they

127 *Place Bonaventure: concourse at shopping level. Though seemingly austere in basic conception, these interiors gain immensely from the presence of the human race. Those who found them bleak and 'a bit like 1984', when the building was new, would probably be astonished to see these bustling spaces a decade later.*

have been joined by opportunists and hucksters who are nothing to do with the established retailers in the shop units, but have simply brought in racks of clothes, trestle-tables for selling confectionery, and the like. The result has acquired the vitality and sense of 'place' that many an architect and town planner in the sixties sweated blood to achieve by design, and failed to achieve. At Alexis Nihon Plaza, according to Melvin Charney,

the significance of these new super-buildings is still being resolved on the fringes of cultural practice ... seldom rated among Montreal's architectural achievements, it is always alive with people attracted by its accessible and animated interior. Within, there is a real *place* [a public square]. A wide perspective, vertically and horizontally — six levels from the Metro station to the skylight. The whole is somehow transformed into an urban structure, radical in its function, directly plugged in to surrounding streets and into public transportation, topped by a roof-garden and a platform for the staging of office and apartment towers, replete with up-front *ersatz* styling typical of the Big Sell of much urban architecture of today. . . .[49]

From 'always alive' to 'up-front *ersatz* styling', Charney's encomium on this seemingly unremarkable shopping centre is so complete a register of the urban, social and human ambitions of most of the megastructure movement that one can quite see why he was compelled to add: 'All that is lacking are some boom cranes perched on top of the elevator shafts to complete this home-grown futurist vision.'

Home grown himself, Charney speaks with inside knowledge, a citizen of the one city in the world where megastructures look (or looked for a time) as if they might grow naturally. What happened in Montreal in 1967 happened, one now sees, at the last possible moment, for the times were changing, and there would soon be few enough opportunities for any other wild-growing, free-range megastructures. But while they grew they provided those of us who were lucky enough to be there with a heady vision — no, the pedestrian experience too — of a megastructural future. What had previously been only paper images and verbal speculations could now be discussed in, literally, concrete terms. Urban spaces previously notional could now be walked or traversed by appropriate

128 Palais Métro *project (François Dallegret, with Joseph Baker, 1967). Many astute Montrealers were quick to see a possible and profitable alliance between megastructure, commerce and* la vie ludique. *Dallegret's scheme for an indoor megastructure of boutiques in an old armoury by the Metro station at Place des Arts was first, though still-born.*

129 *Alexis Nihon Plaza (Harold Ship, 1967). Mostly dismissed as architecturally trivial when first opened, Alexis Nihon Plaza has imposed itself on the attention of Montrealers and outsiders as the one place where the promise of a commercial* mégastructure populaire *has come true, especially now that unscheduled retailers persistently invade the empty space of the central plaza with their temporary stalls.*

rapid transit; some sort of full civic life could be seen to be lived in totally artificial environments.

At Montreal, megastructures moved off the visionaries' drawing-boards and momentarily threatened to cover the earth because they had become a building type that Establishments – political, military, academic – now perceived to be buildable. And the most prolific builder among these Establishments was, for half a decade, to be the academic.

Comparative Diagrams

130 Comparative silhouettes of realized mega-structures, all to the same scale: (a) Place Bonaventure, Montreal; (b) Habitat, Montreal; (c) Town Centre, Cumbernauld; (d) Brunswick Centre, London; (e) Centre Pompidou, Paris; (f) Scarborough College, Toronto; (g) Theme Pavilion, Montreal; (h) Yamanishi Centre, Kofu; and (i) the Post Office Tower, London, a multi-functional vertical structure of the same architectural generation.

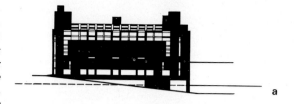

a

b

c

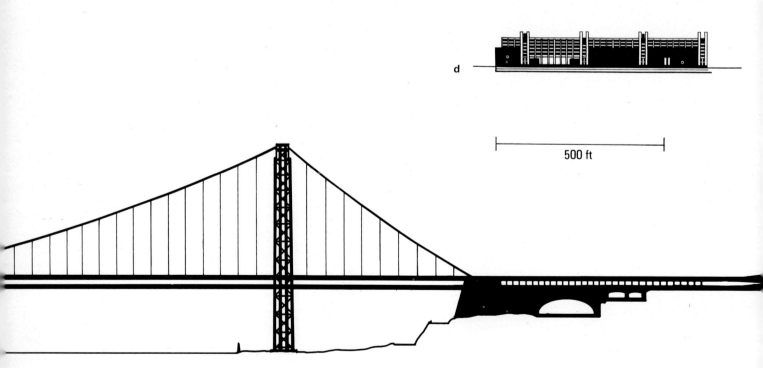

d

500 ft

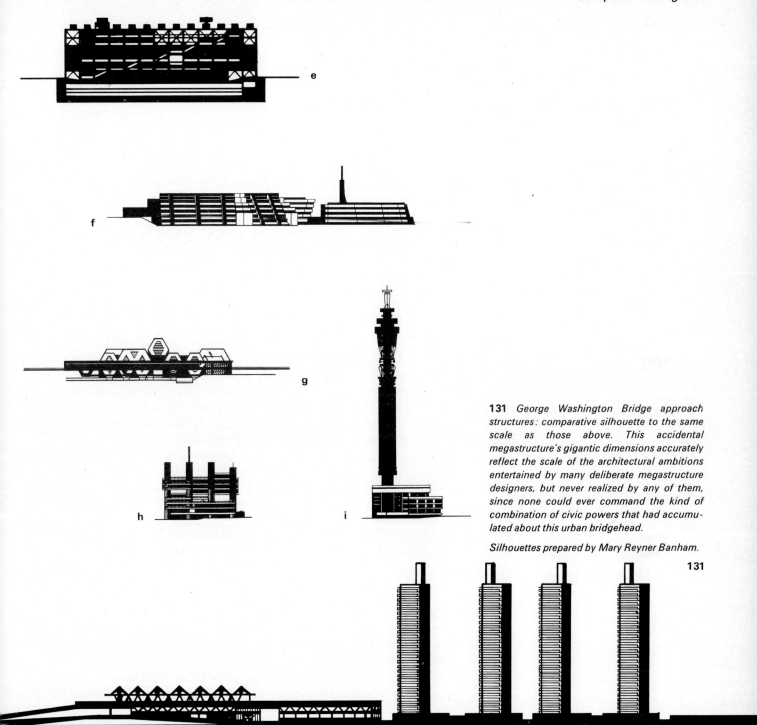

e

f

g

h

i

131 *George Washington Bridge approach structures: comparative silhouette to the same scale as those above. This accidental megastructure's gigantic dimensions accurately reflect the scale of the architectural ambitions entertained by many deliberate megastructure designers, but never realized by any of them, since none could ever command the kind of combination of civic powers that had accumulated about this urban bridgehead.*

Silhouettes prepared by Mary Reyner Banham.

131

7 Megastructure in Academe

The institutionalization of megastructure as an 'idea in good currency' was overwhelmingly the work of the architecture schools and universities. They presided over its birth in Horacio Caminos's project for the new University of Tucumán, defined by Cesar Pelli, Tucumán's most distinguished alumnus, as the first megastructure, and they nurtured its development as a teaching aid in Tange's MIT project for Boston Harbor. For more than a decade after the latter, megastructure was to flourish as the preferred studio exercise in architecture schools throughout the Western world, in Japan and even, briefly, it seems, in the USSR. Universities were also the most consistent clients for megastructural buildings, and saw more of them built than any other single class of patrons. This megamania was at its peak in 1968, and in spite of the fact that academics were among the most vociferous in articulating the hatred of 'the people' for all large urban buildings in the reaction that followed the *événements* of that turbulent year, many architecture schools were to continue to be preoccupied with megastructure for years after that, and many universities were to continue building megastructures deep into the seventies — often with good reason, as will appear before the end of this chapter.

There were many reasons for the grip and persistence of megamania among academics; most of them were common to the architectural profession at large, but even so the schools were instrumental in expounding the attitudes or crystallizing the forms. Many a time, two or more originally unrelated conceptions would run together to create an academic opportunity or reinforce an academic interest. An obvious case in point concerns the rise of 'urban design' itself, megastructure's most important 'constituency' in many contexts. It is clear, though hardly documented in so many words, that many architecture schools perceived the opening up, during the late fifties and early sixties, of a conspicuous interdisciplinary gap between architecture on the one hand and advanced town planning on the other. As planning studies advanced further into a stratosphere of complex mathematics and abstract strategic studies, disdaining the kind of detailed on-the-ground decision-making that had previously been the domain of 'civic design', an unoccupied territory appeared where many people, especially architects, felt that detailed formal decisions were urgently needed. That territory was sometimes defined as 'urban situations about half a mile square'.

Coincidentally the political and financial concept of 'urban renewal', whether commercial or governmental in its funding, entered the scene to give financial muscle and social conviction to these half-mile-square perceptions. Indeed, retrospect suggested to commentators that the relationship was causal; the phrase '. . . the 1960's, when urban renewal spawned urban design'[50] appeared in *Progressive Architecture* in 1973. This is an obvious over-simplification, as any eye-witness of that period in Academe can vouch, but the coincidence was certainly close.

In practice, however, most of the opportunities to work on this scale that came to megastructuralists in the sixties were for the design of new campuses or the reworking of old ones. An intense body of serious study and arrant wishful thinking about urban problems and how to solve them architecturally was brought to bear on a design situation which is not significantly comparable to urban planning, however similar the dimensions of the task and the population-density of the resulting structures may appear. On the other hand, these conditions can be manipulated to make a campus plan resemble an ideal model of an urban plan, and there are some striking instances of frustrated or aborted town-planning schemes reappearing as university layouts: the outstanding example is the Frankfurt scheme of Candilis/Josic/Woods which resurfaced, little altered in its essentials, as their prizewinning entry for the design of the Free University of Berlin.

More commonly, however, one finds that concepts like that of the pure pedestrian street as a good human environment in its own right inform both campus plans and urban-design schemes, associated in both cases with the idea of adaptable linear planning, but that they get built on the campus, not in the city. 'Street campuses' were much discussed and much projected, but some of those that were built contrived, in their final forms, to conceal this urban intention almost entirely. Thus Warwick University in England, which one must now perceive as a number of rectangular buildings strung tidily across a long site, was originally conceived, in a student research project by Michael Cassidy, as a bustling multi-level pedestrian street with subsidiary buildings 'clipped on' along its length as need dictated.

Again, the Metabolist distinction between the permanent and the transient can be sensed in many campus projects such as Warwick, and more explicitly in Denys Lasdun's visually impressive and obviously megastructural University of East Anglia. There the 'permanent' large administrative, teaching and laboratory facilities were conceived as a few substantial blocks at the centre of the scheme (**132**), with the extensible accommodation for the students spreading away

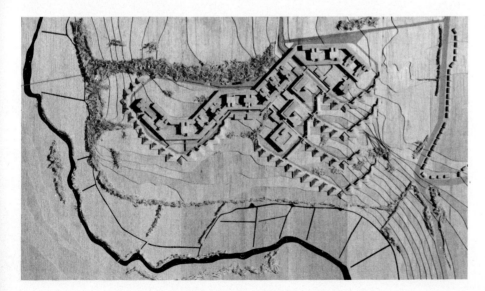

132 *University of East Anglia, Norwich; plan model (Denys Lasdun and Partners, 1966). The basic concept makes the distinction, as did the Japanese Metabolists, between the more permanent structures (faculty and teaching, in the closed square compositions at the heart of the plan), and the more transient, or at least extensible (student housing, in the long zig-zag blocks extending into the countryside).*

from them in zig-zag *Terrassenhäuser* blocks which give most of the megastructural air overall (**133**). It was soon being asked, however, whether the distinction had been correctly made: given the fact that students were not likely to change much in physical form or residential needs, and that their numbers on the site were within the control of the university, were not the residential parts likely to be the more stable and permanent? And given the rapid expansion of the sciences (this proved almost a rapid contraction at East Anglia!) and the violent transformations in information handling, computerization and teaching methods in all disciplines, was it not the heavy teaching plant that was liable to be the more deciduous and variable?

The bulk of university residents were far less likely to raise growing families or to need to 'inflate a spare capsule for Grandma' than the average urban population; their activities were much less varied, whether in timetabling or in spatial needs; their mutual relationships were, both socially and administratively, more structured and less varied; their behaviour, student riots notwithstanding, was more predictable; and the total population could be regulated in a manner that most municipalities could only regard with helpless envy. Socially, and in many other ways, the university campus was too impoverished an example to serve as a useful test-model for real city situations, but the concept of the university as a mini-city or a sample city neighbourhood was remarkably persistent. Paradoxically, it could be productive on occasions.

133 *University of East Anglia: student housing. Stacked in single-slope* Terrassenhäuser *format, these concrete ziggurats have the unmistakable air of megastructure, even though they fulfil few of the structural or adaptive norms thought to be essential to the concept.*

For instance, the comparative isolation of most new campuses, on suburban sites far from central city pressures, deprived them of the opportunity to perform the paradigmatic exercise of straddling over or incorporating mechanical transportation, a task enjoined on modern university buildings ever since Le Corbusier's *Pavillon suisse* was programmatically raised on pilotis to 'leave the ground free for circulations' in 1931. In compensation for this ancestral lack, it seems, the importance attributed to pedestrian circulation increased; the pure pedestrian street was not only seen as a desirable environment, but was also valued as the main generative force in the plan, often, as in the case of Scarborough College (**134**), with the underlying implication that it was still serving as the surrogate for the monorail, or whatever, that really ought to be there.

The close attention and obvious approval given to John Andrews's design for Scarborough College, which played a similar role in building his reputation as did Habitat in Safdie's, shows how well it mirrored, or gave shape to, the architectural ambitions of its time. Executed in strongly ribbed off-the-form (unrendered) concrete for almost all of its exterior surface that is not glass, it has a section that is normally a kind of lop-sided A-frame, with classrooms and auditoria terracing back or corbelling out on one side and large areas of window on the other, leaving a tall, usually triangular space between. The use of the A-frame section (**135**) varies in different parts of the complex. In the science wing it is conventional, with six floors of laboratories and teaching spaces terracing back in regular steps (**136**), but with the exposed 'balconies' closed in by glazed penthouse roofs. In the humanities wing, contrariwise, the section is inverted, the block standing narrow on the ground with the classrooms cragging out in four ever-deeper overhangs on one side and two ranks of superimposed auditoria plugged in to the other. At the heart of the plan, generalized facilities —

134 *Scarborough College, Toronto (John Andrews, with Page and Steel, 1964–5). Spread along the top of a small ridge, with social and administrative spaces in the centre (marked by the chimney-stack) and the science faculty and the humanities spreading to left and right respectively along a covered pedestrian street, Scarborough College was recognized as a megastructure almost as soon as the word became available to describe it.*

135 *Scarborough College: section through humanities wing. Both wings of Scarborough depend on an A-frame section of sorts, but on the humanities side the external aspect of the section is reversed so that the upper floors crag out over those below.*

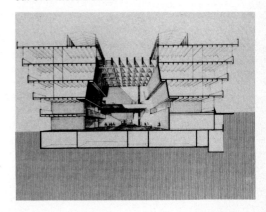

133

136 *Scarborough College: exterior of science wing. Effectively a* Terrassenhäuser *section, but interrupted by large sloping duct-bodies, and with the exposed 'balconies' roofed over in glass to give top-lit laboratory space inside.*

137 *Scarborough College: internal pedestrian street. Whatever social and academic hopes may have been loaded on this echoing space, its most powerful justification is that it provides covered circulation between departments, out of the Canadian climate in the winter.*

administration, refectories and so forth — are housed in a seemingly more regular rectangular structure. Even here, however, there are echoes of the A-frames in the upper parts, while the two pedestrian streets that occupy the space left within the A-frames feed directly into the 'meeting-place', the vast indoor piazza that occupies the whole of the lowest inhabited level of the central block.

This line of pedestrian communication, threading through the college from one end to the other and given form as a tall, well-lit interior street, was clearly meant to be read as the dominant of the design — as indeed it was. By Oscar Newman, for instance: '. . . Scarborough has given its circulation system iconographic significance — making it symbolic of the whole campus and the dominant element of its form'.[51] Newman then goes on to load a whole crop of other megastructural hopes over the building: '. . . on this plateau in the next few years, some new urban design theories (Plug-In Cities, Action Architecture, Service and Traffic grids, etc.) will be given their first practical work out'.[52]

Alas for stereotyped hopes; the human race at large never waits around for their fulfilment. What actually happened was that the great pedestrian street (**137**) began to fill up over the next few years with carrells, bookshelves, tables and chairs, until by 1970 parts of it were difficult to perambulate. In spite of the fact that Scarborough was supposed by its designers to expand accretively by the repetition of its standard units along extensions of the two wings — accretion which its loosely articulated megaform could absorb without distortion of its aesthetic — that was not what had happened. With barely half of its proposed total volume built, increasing student numbers were accommodated by expanding internally, out of the classrooms and into the welcome gift of unoccupied square-footage presented by the monumental but redundant floor-space of the pedestrian street.

Not often was the inherent spare capacity of megastructure, noted by Denise Scott-Brown, so neatly put to work. Normally it was the under-exploited capital investment represented by this inherent redundancy that made megastructures economically unconvincing, and that is why most of them were built outside normal methods of financing; no commonly constituted North American public housing agency, and very few commercial enterprises (except possibly Hyatt Hotels, who later built John Portman's *cité-paquebot* monsters), could afford to deal so wastefully with their expensive enclosed and serviced volumes.

However, there was a species of 'Canadian accountancy', such as handled the economics of the pedestrian plumbing of Montreal, which applies to several campuses north of the forty-ninth parallel, though not to enough of those immediately south of it: unquestionably including the cost of coping with the climate. The contrast between getting around the Scarborough campus in January 1970 and battling through sub-zero blizzards on the Fargo, North Dakota, campus in the same month made the volume of that academic street seem far from redundant; and in a college where much of the teaching volume consists of laboratories which must be artificially ventilated, the extra cost of servicing the atmosphere of the enclosed street is not a major element in the budget.

This special Canadian accountancy also serves to justify, if only symbolically, a number of other 'street' or 'megastructure' campuses such as Scarborough's near neighbour, York University. York, however, manifestly lacks the clarity of organization given by a linear plan. Composed of what are effectively hollow pyramids of classrooms and work-spaces heaped over a linked network of large

138 *Amherst campus (Ellicott complex), State University of New York, Buffalo (Davis, Brody and Associates, 1974). A residential, social and teaching megastructure that fully lives up to the epithet 'complex', Ellicott is also a unique example, on the US side of the border, of a university structure that accepts the 'Canadian accountancy' principle of putting its circulation under cover.*

139 *Simon Fraser University, British Columbia; general sketch (Erickson, Massey, 1966). More frequently described as a megastructure than any other North American university building, its street-like organization is less concerned with protection against an extreme climate than with extensibility and creating space for an almost classical conception of academic discourse.*

140 *University of Alberta, Edmonton (A. J. Diamond and Barton Myers, 1974). Compared inevitably to the Galleria in Milan — a rare comparison in megastructure circles — this 800-foot glazed and air-conditioned student street should more properly be compared to a cité-paquebot (see chapter 3), since the rooms and shops can be opened up to the interior or exterior climate, whichever seems preferable. The importance of the concept of street life — note the sidewalk café! — to the self-imagery of Academe is underlined by the fact that this radical university building nevertheless follows the existing street grid of the district. Contrast the Great High Schools at Pittsburgh (165, 166), which deliberately set out to overthrow the existing pattern of the city.*

square indoor piazzas, it has a layout which is labyrinthine and repetitive in detail to such a degree that, it is alleged, even regular users of the complex are forced to go out into the parking lots and look back at the building to work out where they are and how to get to the next room they are supposed to be at! Similar jests are already and prematurely in circulation about the barely completed Amherst campus of the State University at Buffalo (**138**), on the US side of the line, designed by the New York firm of Davis, Brody and Associates and demonstrably more simple in both its articulation and its use than York.

The culmination of this 'Canadian accountancy megatrend' — apart from the sheer size of Arthur Erickson's enormous Simon Fraser University scheme (**139**) in British Columbia — is best seen in two striking projects in the notoriously draughty prairie states. The more spectacular in purely dimensional terms is the 900-foot glazed gallery for the University of Alberta at Edmonton (**140**). Designed by A. J. Diamond and Barton Myers (with R. L. Wilkin), it is effectively a *cité-paquebot* solution, an air-conditioned street with visible air ducts under its glass roof and underground service-ways beneath, flanked on either side by shops, student apartments and other facilities whose inner ends open on to the volume of conditioned air, their outer ends to the normal atmosphere without. Unusually, in spite of its 'town-breaking' scale, its design and arrangement on

141, 142 *Centennial Hall overbuilding, University of Winnipeg (Moody, Moore, Duncan, 1972). Almost a realization of Friedman's* urbanisme mobile *(see 60, 61), though the fact is largely obscured by the necessity for sealing the perimeter against the climate (141). Much of the interior (142), however, exhibits an air of possessing the freedoms that* architecture mobile *had hoped to offer.*

the ground follows and respects the existing street grid rather than transforming or straddling over it.

Straddling-over is the conspicuous aspect of the other prairie-campus megastructure, the Centennial Hall extension for the University of Winnipeg (**141**). Designed by a team from the appropriately numerous megapartnership of Moody Moore Duncan Rattray Peters Searle and Christie, this is a rare example of a built megastructure which genuinely oversails an existing ground-level environment, as Friedman or Isozaki proposed, while leaving it almost untouched. A deep-trussed frame straddling over older campus buildings on tall four-column legs, it sounds in verbal description remarkably like a realization of Friedman's *urbanisme spatial*, but Canadian accountancy ensures that it does not look like one. The need to exclude a hostile climate requires the exterior to be walled or glazed on all sides, and the openwork structure is not therefore available to outward view: the complex presents a solid, impermeable, almost armoured appearance.

Internally, however, the open disposition of structure, stairways, lights, services and usable floor surfaces (**142**) comes closer to the Friedman concept of the *ville spatiale*, and closer yet to the kind of ludic frameworks envisaged in Dallegret's *Palais Métro*. There is also some feeling here of a more substantial

Canadian ancestry in the tradition of megahospital planning which grew up in the late sixties, of which the monster at Hamilton, Ontario – the McMaster Health Sciences Center by Craig, Zeidler and Strong – is an example. Typical of the whole generation, McMaster consists of a pattern of massive vertical structure/service towers (**143**), with deep-truss floors spanning between, the ward floors standing on the trusses while the spaces in the depth of the trusses act as service floors. Winnipeg, completed in 1972 after nearly a decade of development of this kind of three-dimensional thinking, benefited from being a late megastructure; by comparison, Scarborough was something of a primitive. And even Winnipeg was not the last of the North American academic megastructures; the Knight campus of Rhode Island Junior College, designed by Robert Reilly of Perkins and Will and completed late in 1972, packed three thousand students into a single, sub-Corbusian mass of concrete, and was hailed by *Architectural Forum* as a megastructure. What is baffling, however, is that *Forum*'s headline actually reads 'Return of the Megastructure' . . . *return*? This was one context in which megastructure never went away long enough to notice.

There remains one major academic megastructure that must be discussed here, though it is very difficult to fit it into any of the easily recognized

143 *McMaster University Health Sciences Center, Hamilton, Ontario (Craig, Zeidler and Strong, 1970 onwards). The ultimate medical megastructure, in which ward units are fitted where required into a grid of upright service towers and horizontal service floors as deep as the wards they support and serve.*

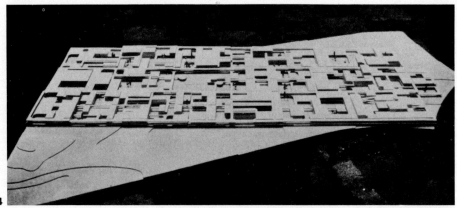

144

megastructure categories: Shadrach Woods's Free University of Berlin (**144**). As mentioned earlier, the basic planning concept is clearly related to the low and extensive, unemphatic 'mat-building' organization proposed by Candilis/Josic/Woods for an inner-city urban-renewal site in Frankfurt am Main, but the university's site at Dahlem is an open suburban one whose unaccented topography would allow the campus to spread gently and unhindered down the very slight slope of the land.

The history of this important building has been a long and slow one. The competition results were announced in 1963; the first small section of the scheme was completed almost a decade later in 1972, not long before Shadrach Woods's untimely death. Inevitably, because of its 'exposed political situation', the long history of the Free University building has been accompanied by a great deal of mostly political commentary. Yet, in spite of all these words, the character of the scheme remains remarkably elusive.

This must be largely due to its refusal to make any large architectural gestures, a rarity in anything reckoned to be a megastructure. In spite of its large total volume, the structure rarely rises more than two storeys above apparent ground level, and in its incomplete form its enormous horizontal dimensions remain difficult to comprehend. Its intricate internal planning – an elaborate pattern of small courtyards and teaching pavilions (**145**) carried in a rectangular grid of access corridors – cannot be seen from outside, and is not rapidly understood from within. Variability and change are provided for, but not by any spectacular methods such as interchangeable capsules or redundancies of frame. Instead there is a technically sophisticated system of cladding and partitioning (**146**), unemphatic but elegant, devised by Jean Prouvé, master-panellist to the Modern movement, and manufactured by Krupp.

Executed all in exposed metals, of which the most conspicuous is the self-oxidizing Corten steel, and glass, without major projections or re-entrants, the exterior presents an almost painfully unrhetorical reticence (**147**). This effect is emphasized by its refusal to do anything emphatic about the changes of level required by the progressive fall of the site; all that happens is that, at intervals along the length of the structure, one bay is deflected down out of the rectangular into a parallelogram shape, with floors and roof sloping enough to take up the necessary difference of levels, after which the frame resumes the even rectangular tenor of its ways until the next downward deflection is required.

144, 145 *Free University of Berlin; model and air view (Candilis/Josic/Woods/Schiedhelm, 1963 onwards). The model and view show the basic conception: a low and extensive mat-building in which teaching spaces and small courtyards are carried in a theoretically extensible rectangular grid of two-storey communications (pedestrians above, services below). In megastructure terms, the communication grid represents the permanent frame within which the transient enclosed volumes can be deployed as necessary.*

146, 147 *Free University of Berlin under construction. In spite of the extreme care and great concentration of talent that went into the design of the structure, the resultant visual image – against the grain of the times – is unsettlingly ineloquent. Few accredited megastructures have been so little interested in cutting a silhouette against the sky; even fewer can have been so submissive to the terrain they traversed that they would accommodate changes in level simply by deflecting their frames downwards, as can be seen at three points in 147.*

140

145

146

147

Because of the general rectangular reticence of the whole conception, this angular device is extraordinarily compelling. But the whole mode of design is alien to what is normally expected of megastructures, especially academic ones. As Günther Feuerstein commented: 'All this might ... be interpreted as a complete denial of the great educational institutions' traditional claims that their image expresses the source of the nation's intellectual strength. ...'[53] Certainly, all the other major academic megastructures reviewed here have presented powerful imagery of one sort or another, even if they have not made massive Teutonic claims to proprietorship of national intellectual muscle.

How, then — or how *far* then — can the Free University of Berlin be called a megastructure? In fact, inspection will show that it answers every point of Wilcoxon's definition: it is modular, large, extensible, and has a more permanent structure (and service infrastructure) carrying less permanent subsidiary structures. Its only serious deficiency 'by definition' is that these subsidiary structures do not come on site as finished capsules that can be moved about, plugged in, clipped on as discrete units, but must be made and remade from standard elements like those of the Fun Palace.

Yet the image-deficiency remains such that it would occur to few observers to call it a megastructure. Feuerstein's point is well made: image-making is normally of great importance to academic megastructures. Cynically, one could say that imagery is all that most academic megastructures were, since for every one actually built for an academic community to inhabit, thousands have been produced on paper by students and staff of academic institutions all over the world. Cynically or otherwise, however, the special relationship obviously existing between Academe and megastructure is one that any study of the subject must acknowledge and attempt to explain.

The earliest example of the relationship that I observed directly was of the same generation as the Tucumán University project of Caminos; this was the 'Zone' project (**148**) produced by three students at the Architectural Association School in London (Andrew Derbyshire, Pat Crook, John Voelcker) in 1952. True to the tradition which was subsequently to emerge, it was allocated — or it claimed — wide terms of territorial reference (the county of Hertfordshire), a national political 'constituency' (the New Towns legislation), and Utopian overtones of a sort: as one of the team notoriously informed the head of the school, 'We haven't actually drawn anything yet, Mr Jordan, but we have pretty well decided how the people should live!' Not all of this high-flying project could be seen as proto-megastructure, since it was largely concerned with agriculture; but a substantial part of the urban portion was contained in a single complex multi-storey residential structure whose parts were linked by internal street-decks which met at 'community spaces' at the junctions of the blocks. Apartment units were to some extent prefabricated and interchangeable, and were suspended from massive box-ducts running the length of each block. Though the component blocks were disposed on a rectangular grid that arranged them to form a sequence of enormous courtyards, the scheme could be extended by single blocks as well as by complete courtyards. And it is now clearly recognizable as a megastructure of sorts by its overweening ambitions and the powerful image-making qualities of the drawings.

It may be that one of the academic fascinations of megastructure lay in its ability to generate something that architectural academics have always admired since the high days of the *Ecole des Beaux-Arts*: splendid drawings. Certainly,

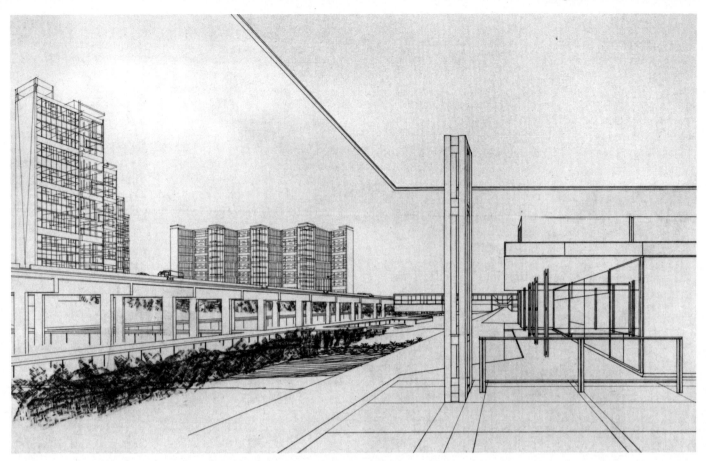

conspicuous draughtsmanship runs right through the English megastructural tradition, and was one of its most admired characteristics elsewhere (in Italy, for example) ; and it runs strongly through the succession of megastructure projects that formed a large part of the significant student output at the Architectural Association for a decade and a half after 'Zone'.

Since the affairs of the Association are more public property than are those of any other architecture school in the world, and since it has published so much of its students' work, the development of this megatrend and its relationship to architectural practice can be followed more easily here than in the work of most other schools. Thus in 1953 Patrick Hodgkinson – later the designer of the first building in London to be acclaimed a megastructure, the Brunswick Centre finished in 1974 – executed a third-year housing project which, though modest and rectangular, also has the 'craggy but directional' qualities supposed to characterize English megastructures, the linearity and the loose linkage by raised pedestrian walks. In the immediately succeeding years one could see stepped *Terrassenhäuser* and Sant'Elian stair-towers, followed by giant frames full of suspended and apparently transient accommodations. In 1956 a famous, aformal, loosely linear and spectacularly well drawn project for high-density housing in Paddington (**149**) was so elaborately worked out (by Dalton, Eardley, Knott and Fraser, all then in their fifth year) that it was virtually buildable as it stood, and seems to have had immediate impact on work being designed

148 *Zone project (Architectural Association students Crook, Derbyshire, Voelcker, 1952). The first manifestation of emerging mega-structure ambitions among British architecture students. The entire population of a mixed agricultural and urban area was to be housed in a cluster of super-blocks like those at the left. In spite of the use of vast framed structures with transient suspended housing within, the visual imagery is too thin and 'pretty' to match the megastructure ambitions of the sixties.*

149 *High Density project, Paddington (Architectural Association students Dalton, Eardley, Knott, Fraser, 1956). The perspectives for this project were a legend in their time, and come a great deal nearer than does 148 to the imagery of fully developed megastructure.*

'for real' in London at the time. In 1959 there was a vast project for Westminster (**150**) which lagged behind Tange's MIT students only in a lack of clarity of overall form, which may even have been deliberate; and the series culminated in Martin Godfrey's Battersea urban-renewal project of 1965, which was unmistakably an urban megastructure as the term is understood today – and was beginning to be understood even then.

In world terms (an interesting phrase to have to use of student designs!) the most influential of these Architectural Association projects was the one produced in 1962 by Jim Hodges, Chris Woodward and Martin Haxworth. The basis of the project was a systematic redesigning and rationalization of the LCC's Hook New Town project (see chapter 4) into a far more compact form than the original 'crumbly' and romantic styling had suggested. The central spine now became a precise but extensible multi-storey slab, with traffic circulation tucked under it and residential spurs running off at tidy right-angles to it (**151**). As has been mentioned, these three students plus Tony Richardson then transferred to the team working on *Traffic in Towns* under Colin Buchanan, to produce, on the

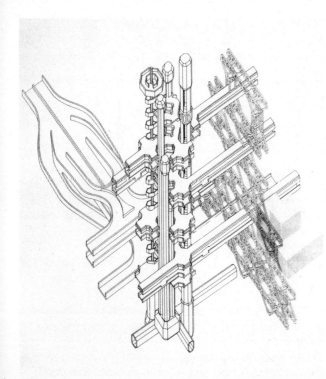

172

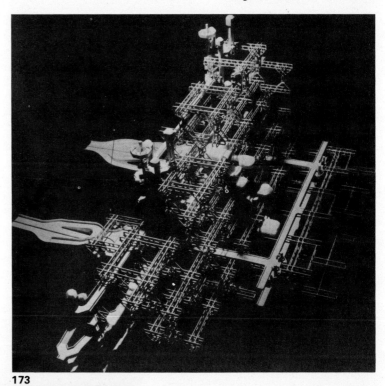

173

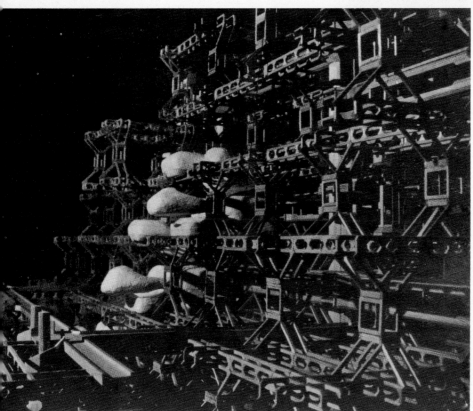

174

172, 173, 174 *Graz-Ragnitz project (Domenig and Huth, 1966–9). The ultimate megastructure model and triumph of the Austrian connection, admired, exhibited and premiated all over Europe until it finally fell to pieces. The basic support system is seen in 172: frame elements at right, roads and ducts on the diagonal of the drawing, connecting with vertical communications and duct-risers. All are seen assembled in 173, and 174 represents the main 'façade' of the model – a scaleless cliff of structure, services and capsules, comprising the most comprehensive and convincing megastructure model ever built.*

labour to it if they were not so convinced? Not that many of those who saw it would necessarily have reasoned thus, nor would they have needed to; that same sheer elaboration simply enhanced the fascination which it was guaranteed to produce anyhow, simply by being a model.

It is difficult not to conclude, looking back on the period from a safe historical distance, that models were accorded a peculiar status in academic megaculture over and above the fascination they have traditionally held in the world of architecture. Or, reversing the proposition, one might submit that the fascination that megastructure held in academic circles was due to the fact that it could be modelled convincingly. The appearance of an intellectual cavity 'half a mile square' between architecture and planning does not, in itself, imply megastructural solutions. The occupation of that cavity by architects probably does imply that the design solutions offered are likely to be unified designs comparable to large buildings, but even this does not of itself require that these large unified designs should necessarily resemble any kind of megastructure, let alone the kind proposed by Domenig and Huth for Ragnitz. Could one suggest, then, at least one reason over and above any general trend of the times toward megastructures: quite simply that, in the form of large models, they made the problems of urban design easier to handle — not intellectually or metaphorically but literally, by grasping with the hand, pushing and pulling with the fingers?

At UCLA, for instance, the rationalization initially offered for architectural models so large that they required the removal of the floor between the basement and the ground-level studio was that in working on that scale it became possible to model the building as a whole, the units of which it was constructed and the equipment with which its parts were furnished *all to the same scale*. Thus it became possible to experiment by cut-and-fit methods simultaneously on both the structure and its contents, and to operate at every level of design organization without having to make, for instance, separate models of a 'typical apartment' — 'operating' in this situation being a manual activity giving instantly readable visual results.

In the same way, direct manual operation of the Archigram or Ragnitz kind of model — that is, a frame containing separate capsules and ducts — was perfectly possible and gave an equally immediate read-out. It is striking, in review, to note how often the models were constructed at scales where individual units such as the capsules were of literally 'handy' size (**175**). Over and above any desire for them to be manipulable, this was also due to the deliberate choice of ready-made components from the shops — 'ready-made' almost in the Marcel Duchamp sense, since plastic soap-dishes, condiment dispensers, photographic developing trays and the like were freely pressed into service to simulate capsules and platforms and servicing units.

Furthermore, there were easily available components from plastic model aircraft and space-vehicle kits which gave a high degree of fine detailing, appropriately high-technology in idiom, but again in easy-to-handle sizes, even if the notional scale of the original were raised or lowered by powers of ten in its new role. Again, the structures could be run up handily from proprietary kits such as Buckminster Fuller's 'D-Sticks', or from erector toys (Lego units were to be appropriated to more unintended uses than one can hope to chronicle here, the most spectacular being Norman Mailer's 'un-fascist' proposals for New York). While we are still in the toy-cupboard, one should also note that molecular ball-and-stick model kits, which were available at that time, have

175 *Megastructure as a 'handy' mode of dealing with urban design problems. Elements of the Archigram cut-out model (see 98) ready for assembly, illustrating the seductive convenience of such models as a manageable way of handling problems that were difficult for students – and their instructors – to manipulate in conventional two-dimensional representations – not to mention their function as educational toys!*

been seriously put forward as a possible source of open-frame megastructures, and this seems quite likely in view of their obvious resemblance to that perenially persuasive foundation of so much modern education, the kindergarten 'gifts' of Friedrich Froebel, especially that direct ancestor of 'D-sticks' which uses toothpicks for the structural members and dried peas (in the absence of any available technological device) as the joiners.

Whatever the combinations in which these influences and suggestive bricolages operated, the results would give urban design simulators that were manageable by hand at desk-top dimensions, but whose parts could be large enough to show a reasonable amount of readable detailing and to be populated by available model-kit figures in scales such as 1:72, 1:48 or even 1:25. It was all very fascinating, and it photographed beautifully. Outside the architecture schools these reasonings and predilections may have carried little weight, but within the shelter of Academe they made megastructures both attractive and instructive as 'teaching machines'; and if in retrospect their actual educational value now seems rather trifling, that may be a more cogent criticism of architecture schools than of megastructures as such.

8 Megadecadence:
Acceptability and Exploitation

If it was the academics who institutionalized megastructure as a concept, its establishment as a buildable proposition could only follow from acceptance by, precisely, the Establishment. Symbolically, therefore, the peak of megastructure's official success can be located with confidence as being in Vienna in October 1969, when the city, together with the Austrian government, promoted a competition for the design of a headquarters complex with conference centre for certain specialized agencies of the United Nations.

Although the regulations did not ask for a megastructure, nobody doubted that a megastructure of some sort was wanted, and that was what Vienna got: the four prizewinning designs were all megastructures of some sort. Above all, the two designs placed first and second (though not necessarily in that order, as far as could be discerned in the diplomatic uproar that followed the announcement of the results) both demonstrated a megastructuralism that contrived to be simultaneously extreme and acceptable. The design by Building Design Partnership of Preston, England, was a thundering great flat-topped A-frame hung with terraced office floors (**176**), bringing out all the off-the-form monumentality that is one major stream in the megastructure tradition; the other, by Cesar Pelli, by then established in the Victor Gruen Organization, was an elegant rank of chamfer-cornered glazed towers (**178**) rising to various heights from a sprawling base of diagonal structure containing auditoria, parking and other ancillaries (**177**).

176 *United Nations complex project, Vienna; competition entry (Building Design Partnership, 1970). Joint winner of the first stage of the competition, sole (but unbuilt) winner of the second: megastructure at the pinnacle of its acceptability, conceivable to international bureaucrats, conceivable by solid architectural professionals rather than wild radicals, and used remarkably intelligently as a format to contain a mixed bag of accommodation.*

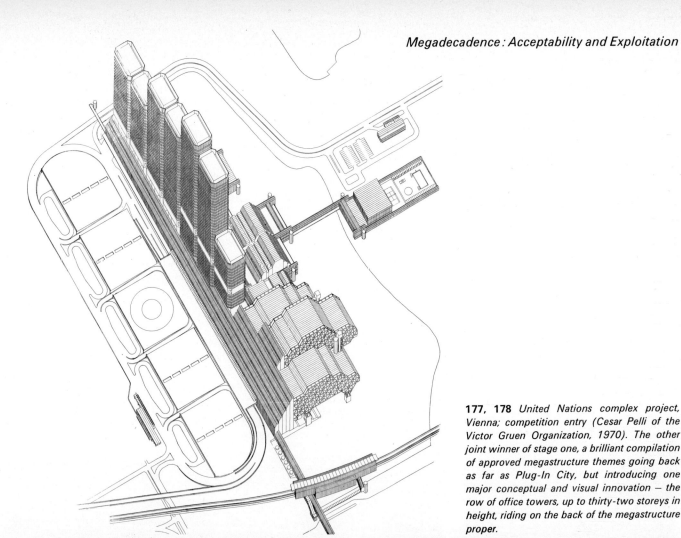

177, 178 *United Nations complex project, Vienna; competition entry (Cesar Pelli of the Victor Gruen Organization, 1970). The other joint winner of stage one, a brilliant compilation of approved megastructure themes going back as far as Plug-In City, but introducing one major conceptual and visual innovation — the row of office towers, up to thirty-two storeys in height, riding on the back of the megastructure proper.*

Partly because of the backstage dramas that were going on, the jury proposed that the four prizewinning teams should take their designs to a second stage, which, naïvely in three cases, they did. 'Naïvely', because anyone who had watched form in Vienna since the Second World War should have known that, whoever gets the prize in Austrian competitions, the building itself is finally awarded to an Austrian! So on the second stage Building Design Partnership went to the top, and Pelli sank to fourth, and what is actually being built is the design of Johan Staber, which had risen from fourth to second place. Staber's design is a series of blocks, each in plan like a concave-faced equilateral triangle, the sides of the triangle being glazed and the angles blunted by massive end-towers in blind reinforced concrete; to say that it looks like a cross between Metabolism and Toronto City Hall is not to insult it. The Austrian Establishment got what it wanted, even if the United Nations did not.

In spite of these disasters of parochial power politics, however, the BDP and Pelli schemes are worth looking at again, if only for the backgrounds and tendencies they represent. Pelli, from Tucumán, with the much-praised Sunset Mountain (**179**) to his credit, as well as a completed megastructure of smallish sorts at the Worldway Postal Center (**180**) near Los Angeles Airport, had been assisted by, among others, some graduate students from the UCLA urban design course to which East Coast, English and Austrian megastructuralists had contributed. It is one of the crowning designs of the whole movement, but in one essential matter it must be judged less remarkable than that of BDP, whose very success showed that it was not only the great international high-flyers who

179 *Sunset Mountain project, Los Angeles (Cesar Pelli and Tony Lumsden of Daniel Mann Johnson and Meldenhall, 1964). The project which launched the so-called 'Los Angeles School' of megastructures, but also one which recalls Horacio Caminos's scheme for the University of Tucumán (see 28, 29) where Pelli had been a student, which likewise used a whole mountain as its base.*

180 *Worldway Postal Center, Los Angeles (Cesar Pelli of DMJM, 1966). Not vast in its dimensions, but seen by Pelli as a megastructure because further bays can be added to the standard frame, which is relatively indifferent to the kind of infilling that is (or is not) inserted into it.*

could produce megastructures that convinced international juries and world-wide bureaucracies. For whatever the personal ambitions of Grenfell Baines, the founder of BDP, the general performance of the office is solidly professional, craftsmanlike and provincial in the most reassuring kind of way, and has hardly ever figured in the international press except at the time of the UN Vienna competition.

Megastructure, then, had become a thinkable and buildable proposition in more widespread and more conservative contexts than would have seemed possible, or desirable, to the front-runners and visionaries of barely five years before. Or would they? It is strange and salutary to be reminded that, since anything as big as a megastructure takes a long time to build, the completed works which began to appear toward the end of the sixties as if in confirmation of the front-runners' visions had, in nearly every case, been conceived and even taken to detail design stage before those visions had been formed. The structures of Montreal Expo '67 were already well advanced on drawing-board and computer by midsummer 1964, while the megastructures of approximately 1966 vintage, like Scarborough College and Cumbernauld Town Centre, had been designed proportionately earlier. In the case of Cumbernauld, *dis*proportionately earlier: its commissioning, let alone designing, goes back to the very late fifties, and means that something like megastructure was conceivable in the minds of established British government officials as early as it was conceivable in the minds of Japanese Metabolists. One needs, therefore, to be very wary of any uncritical acceptance of the idea that megastructure was a radical or

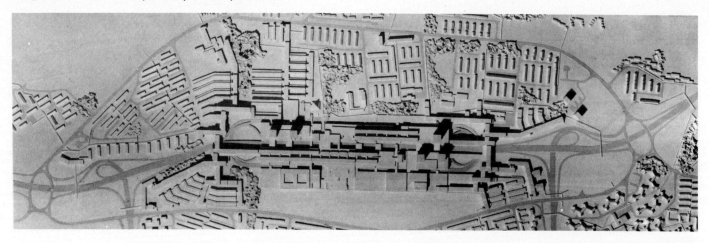

181 *Town Centre, Cumbernauld; model (L. Hugh Wilson, architect–planner for the New Town, and Geoffrey Copcutt, project architect for the Centre, 1960). This earliest plan proposed a double structure stretching the full length of the ridge (from traffic circle to traffic circle on this model). The final version, though barely one-third the size and completed by other hands, remains remarkably faithful to Copcutt's original vision of a gigantic urban machine (not unlike Hollein's aircraft-carriers, 12 and 13) dominating the skyline of the town, as it appears in 183.*

182 *(top and centre) Town Centre, Cumbernauld: section and view from the east, illustrating the fact that the greatest dimension of the whole complex is now at right-angles to the road.*

183 *Town Centre, Cumbernauld, seen over the roofs of the New Town. Note the unbuilt portion under the left-hand end of the superstructure — the symbolic promise of room for change and development.*

ridiculously impractical concept. As a proposition it was always ambivalent; its buildability was its constant undoing as a revolutionary proposal, and the completion of Cumbernauld was simultaneously a triumph and a tragedy for the respective factions among the megastructuralists.

But, for good or evil, its construction had to be a portentous event of some sort. Its very priority would guarantee it an important place in a study like the present one; over and above that it was indeed 'the most complete megastructure ever built', and, since the design (**181**) was well enough published for town planners to speak of 'Cumbernauld-type solutions' as early as 1962/3, it actually helped to shape the megastructure concept and the common Anglo-Saxon understanding of it.

It shaped its times, and was shaped by them, most notably and depressingly in the use of raw, off-the-form concrete, then almost uncontrollably in vogue in architectural circles. It is difficult to think of a more inappropriate material to use on exteriors in that rainy part of Scotland, where the weather seems to keep it permanently a weeping, seeping, drip-stained dirty brown. This single but persistently present aspect of the building seems to have underlain the occasional hostile critical reaction that the design received in 1966–7, though there were already plenty of sociological, architectural and even 'Pop art' rationalizations available to justify these condemnations.

But the condemnations were very few indeed; the general critical response to Cumbernauld Town Centre was conspicuously approving, and culminated in the Reynolds Memorial Award for Community Design, which shows how well it matched the received opinions and 'visions in good currency' of the day. It is worthwhile, therefore, to look at the kind of opinions, images and usages which were, so to speak, legitimized by Cumbernauld.

Firstly, *concentration*: the heaping up in one place of all the social facilities of a city (**182**), and all the commercial ones as well, in a single location. While residence, education, religion and, for some reason, filling the tank of your car were handled distributively elsewhere in the New Town area, all the activities that make urban life urban were packed into the one single building on the crest of the ridge that bisects the town. In a settlement otherwise conceived in terms of exploiting and managing the dispersive effects of a high rate of automobile ownership, this was a defiant gesture in favour of an older type of urbanism, though one perennially popular with architects.

Secondly, *monumentality*: sitting in the middle of a clear green space, Cumbernauld Town Centre comes closer than anything else actually built to the eighth 'point on monumentality' of the Giedion/Sert/Léger essay of 1943, which had called for the creation of 'vast open spaces' in which 'monumental architecture will find its appropriate setting'. Located on the most conspicuous site in the town, the Centre's bulk is seen to almost crushing advantage (**183**), with no other buildings of even remotely comparable size to compete with it for attention. Otherwise it is nothing like the kind of light and mobile monument

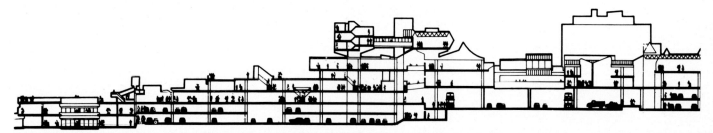

182

183

that Giedion had called for; its monumentality is ponderous and massive, as the taste of the time of its creation required — Le Corbusier's *béton brut* has a lot to answer for! — and it is also of its time in being monumentality for its own sake, a monument to monumentality rather to any person, cause or concept.

Nevertheless, *symbolism* is the third concept legitimized here: the visual aspect of the building symbolizes levels and types of performance it cannot deliver in real life. One of these is indeterminacy — though admittedly much might be added to the existing structure in a society organized only slightly differently from the one the Centre inhabits, and without wrecking its visible aesthetic. More boutiques and hairdressing salons might be tucked into the empty space under the western end of the superstructure; the second superstructure shown on Copcutt's large model could still be added; more bays could be added to the main frame at the western end in particular, fulfilling the promise of extendability inherent in its air of only provisional termination. 'Could', 'might' ... but when one considers how doubly sheltered was the administrative and financial enclave within which it was created, a completely separate operation within the designated area of a legally constituted British New Town, it is hardly surprising to learn that the answer has always been 'won't'. The extensibility of Cumbernauld is a symbolic promise, no more.

Fourthly, a *comprehensive traffic solution* was offered by the Centre, and the offer was widely seen, especially in the USA, as legitimizing the architectural profession's preferred solution to the automobile problem — its burial! From the time of the earliest revisions to the road layout after Hugh Wilson assumed general charge of planning Cumbernauld, the town centre had been seen as lying along a dual carriageway running parallel with the crest of the ridge, so that the basic relationship between centre and traffic was nothing to do with the detailed design of the centre. In Copcutt's design, however, and from his earliest published designs, the town centre structure is made to span over the motorway. In the built version, most of the accommodation is on the downhill side of the road — indeed it terraces some way down the slope — and the spanning-over (**184**) is little more than a ceremonial gesture. However, it is still sufficient to persuade the passing motorist that he is enjoying the Futurist experience of plunging through a vast urban structure, even if all he is really doing is driving down the side of a rather dank loading-dock-cum-bus-station. More importantly, the main shopping-levels of the structure are sufficiently far above road level to make it possible for several levels of parking (not all of them built, though the requisite corbels for the floor slabs are promisingly visible) to be provided in a position where they are well hidden from view and cannot offend the eyes of architecture-lovers. Once more the promise is far from realized, and parking is now well spread round the base of the structure and in full public view. Nevertheless, Cumbernauld was seen as a prime example of 'keeping the motor car in its proper place'.

I could go on. However much its plain conventional surfaces and detailing might depress the radicals, Cumbernauld Town Centre, simply by getting built, established itself as the most convincing paradigm we have of what an urban megastructure should be. It comes close to fulfilling, at least in promise, the four headings of Wilcoxon's definition; it offers at least a simulacrum of the Metabolists' distinction between the permanent tree and the transient leaves; and, by including at least a thin line of penthouse duplexes along the whole length of the superstructure, it houses a far larger range of urban functions than,

say, Habitat, which is purely residential, or Place Bonaventure, which currently houses no civic functions.

It is also, one should remember, the urban heart of a British New Town, one of a dozen or more disputable attempts to give civic focus to the daily life of a newly invented community. This was a function for which megastructure was not elsewhere deemed necessary in the New Towns programme (except for the unbuilt Hook project), so that a comparison between Cumbernauld and other New Towns provides some measure of megastructure's civic success or otherwise. It is not a quantifiable measure, of course, and must depend on impressionistic observation of such conventional indicators as vandalization, unlet shop spaces, and people in the street.

On the count of vandalization, one has always been able to observe rich crops of graffiti and a prevalence of smashed glass in windows on the less regarded outer reaches of the complex, but this should probably be accounted a suburban branch of practices regarded almost as proud local traditions in those parts of Glasgow from which many of the inhabitants have come; and although there has been one echoingly conspicuous department-store volume left unoccupied

184 *Town Centre, Cumbernauld, from the west. In this view it can be seen how little of the road is actually spanned over by the building. As a Futurist-revival experience for the motorist it is therefore rather abbreviated, but for the pedestrian travelling all those ramps, terraces, stairs and passages, Cumbernauld is still the most complete megastructural experience available in the Old World.*

at the eastern end of the structure, there has in fact been a higher rate of letting of commercial floor space than in some of the private-enterprise shopping centres discussed below. Even more conspicuous to any long-term user of the Centre, though, is the remarkable continuity of human presence in the main concourse (**185**). Whereas it is notorious that the centres of most British New Towns are completely depopulated the moment the shops and offices close in the evening, there always seems to be somebody about in Cumbernauld, even at 5 a.m. on the stern Scottish Sabbath! Lest anyone hastily deduce from this that megastructures do in fact generate that 'vital street life' that was so confidently expected of them, let it be said that the deduction needs to be heavily qualified by the state of the local weather. Not only is there nowhere else to go in Cumbernauld, which was deliberately designed with nowhere else to go, but this unique public space is also, unlike the public spaces of all other New Towns, an indoor volume, sheltered from both the frequent rain-squalls and the lively winds that drive them up the slope — the 75-m.p.h. maximum-gust contour crosses the ridge quite near the Centre. There are thus powerful meteorological rather than megastructural reasons for children, teenagers, the unemployed and the aged to hang around whether the shops are open or not.

Something else which seems to have been legitimized, at least stylistically, by Cumbernauld is the kind of high-density downtown shopping centre that has appeared in many English provincial towns. The non-architectural motivations for these centres are usually a combination of private redevelopment money, the less expected by-products of British town-planning legislation, and changes in traffic circulation such as the cutting of new roads or the abandonment of

185 *Town Centre, Cumbernauld: shopping concourse. Only in Montreal will one find other megastructures so used and occupied by the human race, and the basic reason in both cases is climatic — the weather is better inside than out! Whatever the reasons, Cumbernauld enshrines that vision of bustling and populated pedestrian places which was so dear to the hearts of planners in the fifties and sixties, whether megastructuralists or not.*

downtown railway properties. Though the word 'megastructure' must be cautiously applied here, since it refers to little more than a stylistic packaging in some cases, it is hard to find any equally applicable term to describe the format of expediency which has been employed either (*a*) to give organization and form to a largely unpremeditated agglomeration of urban functions, or (*b*) to give maximum visual impact to a predetermined grouping of commercial functions, of which the classic instance is parking over a pedestrian shopping concourse or multi-level arcade.

A textbook example of the former would be Anglia Square in Norwich (**186**), designed by A. D. Cooke and Partners. Initially unrelated decisions about the location of a new office headquarters for a central government agency, and about a new traffic overpass about two hundred yards distant, ran together over a period of about five years with 'normal' commercial redevelopment and the relocation of a major cinema to produce a large, loose complex of stylistically barely unified *design* which can however be experienced as a topographically unified *place*. The result is a less accidental megastructure than, say, the George Washington Bridge complex, but it it is still a largely accidental one.

There seems to be very little that is accidental, however, about the megastructural aspirations of the commercial centres at Portsmouth (**187**) and Gateshead, by R. J. Worthington of the Owen Luder Partnership, or of the original project (if not the final buildings) on the site of the old Victoria Station in Nottingham, by Peter Winchester of Arthur Swift and Partners. If Nottingham Victoria is turning

186 *Anglia Square, Norwich (A. D. Cooke and Partners, 1968 onwards). An initially unrelated grouping of urban renewals, such as the rebuilt cinema (left), the parking garage beyond, the traffic overpass from which this photograph was taken and a large government office block off the picture to the left, now unified ad hoc by pedestrian spaces on two levels, and attempting to come to terms with the two-storey housing in the surrounding medieval street-pattern by means of smaller pavilions round the perimeter of the site.*

187 *Tricorn Centre, Portsmouth (R. J. Worth-*
ington of the Owen Luder Partnership, 1966).
A moderate-sized shopping development on a
central site, with offices and parking above, the
whole deliberately composed into a megastruc-
tural silhouette.

188 *Victoria Centre, Nottingham, first project*
(Peter Winchester of Arthur Swift and Partners,
1964–5). The shopping concourse raised to the
level of Piranesian urban drama — a vision
which came to haunt the megastructure move-
ment in the later sixties but remains to be built.

out vastly tamer than Winchester's heroic and almost Piranesian perspectives (**188**), the Portsmouth and Gateshead schemes as completed have managed to preserve a remarkable amount of their originally intended image-quality. Both are cast — literally — in a concrete idiom which is a shade more sophisticated but no less bloody-minded than that of Cumbernauld, with ramps, lift-towers and Corbusian staircases in rich and picturesque silhouette against the sky above fairly conventionally planned (and, at Portsmouth, notably under-occupied) shopping concourses. Both occupy what are now island sites where they are seen in good contrast to the rest of the urban environment and are thus, no doubt, excellent 'advertisements for themselves'.

Very different is the shopping centre for Runcorn New Town, designed by Roger Harrison, which has been called a megastructure on more than one occasion but enters the category in almost a Berlin sense of the word. Far less interested than any of the foregoing examples in making powerful monumental statements, it is more of a mat-building (**189**) in the extensive sense of the Berlin Free University, with an obsessive geometrical intensity in its planning which may well derive from the common British 'systematic' practice of using tartan planning grids (i.e. with intersecting systems of wide and narrow bays), but which would not look out of place among the insistent rectangular geometries of 'Berlin 1995' — with which, however, it has no discernible connections.

There is one other important trend in apparent megastructure-building in Britain, namely that of mass housing, which has an almost independent tradition and will be discussed later. What is immediately striking, if one looks round

189 *Shopping Centre, Runcorn New Town (Roger Harrison of the New Town Corporation, 1967). A more or less ground-level view which emphasizes the drama of the ranked service towers, but conceals the fact that the plan is a mat-building on the regular British type of 'tartan grid', the towers standing in the narrow stripes of the tartan and the wide spans between forming the larger squares.*

internationally after any kind of review of megastructure practice in Britain, is how little of it there is in other countries. Even at the height of the megastructure mania in American universities, remarkably few were actually put in hand, and this in spite of an apparently propitious economic climate and a body of urban-renewal legislation that could be read as making megastructures almost a mandatory building type.

Rare, indeed, is the office in the USA with a practice that might be said to have been predominantly megastructural for any length of time; the only obvious example, in spite of Paul Rudolph's manifest megastructural ambitions, is the New York firm of Davis, Brody and Associates. Much even of their work consists simply of very large buildings such as massive housing projects or their US pavilion at Osaka Expo '70, which was an enormous artificial crater roofed by a lenticular inflated membrane. However, at Westyard and Waterside in Manhattan, and on the Amherst campus at Buffalo, they have produced buildings which New York opinion, at least, is happy to regard as megastructures.

Westyard as built is the rump of a proposed major multi-functional complex, in which a housing block by Philip Johnson was also supposed to feature, planned for the air-rights over the Penn Central tracks immediately west of Penn Station and the old US Post Office. What Davis, Brody finally built is a massive, high-quality warehouse facility in a single block which spans right across the tracks, give or take a few intermediate columns. Its exterior is mostly good quality concrete work alternating with industrial windows and standard industrial ventilating louvres, the three exposed façades towards the public streets being dramatically battered back, receding some thirty feet from the third to the eleventh story (**190**). At the corners, the angles between the façades make hollow re-entrants only partly filled by blind, square escape-towers — a usage which is strikingly reminiscent of Sant'Elia, especially in the original perspective renderings. Equally Sant'Elian is the imagery of trains plunging under the rear elevation (**191**) below an approach-road for the Holland tunnel which is bracketed off the massive beam at the base of that façade. And even if the accommodations within have not exhibited that variability that might be looked for in a 'strict construction' of the term 'megastructure', they have diversified to include offices, a restaurant, local service shops and surprisingly, on the roof, an ice-skating rink!

190, 191 *Westyard, New York (Davis, Brody and Associates, 1972). Seen in the centre of 190, Westyard spans the point where the Penn Central tracks emerge from their tunnel under the Hudson River. Conceived as high-grade warehousing, it is now used partly as offices; the conception, however, may not be as relaxed as the later uses, since it is difficult to believe that the echoes of Sant'Elia (see chapter 2) at the rear of the block (191) are not just a little calculated.*

191

Waterside, contrariwise, looks at first sight like a modish but otherwise unremarkable New York housing project (**192**) with parking at its feet. In fact, it stands entirely on made-up ground attached to the East River shoreline; the parking-levels make a complicated podium covering almost the entire site, with the towers rising through it and a conventionally handsome plaza with shops and social facilities on its upper surface. The Amherst campus at Buffalo is a design of near enough the same stripe and the same vintage, but far more connective internally, since the local version of Canadian accountancy makes it necessary to be able to circulate through it without becoming weatherbound on external terraces, and also provides a covered bus station somewhere in its lower depths.

Davis, Brody are reported to have megastructures still coming through the pipeline, but once again it must be said that in most of these cases we are dealing with megastructure as, so to speak, a courtesy title or a visual format. By the end of the sixties certain formal usages, groupings of parts, connective devices such as pedestrian bridges etc. were beginning to turn up so persistently in the same connections that they might be called 'the Megastructure Look', without pretending to offer even the simulacra of adaptability or the factual variety of urban functions that could be found at Cumbernauld. In this exploitive phase, when practically no new or radical ideas were going into megastructure, it became one of a number of alternative formats, like the glass tower or the balconied slab, in which conventional building functions could be repackaged. There were, however, one or two functions that would not stay conventional for very long at a time, that could stir new megastructural life even in the work of conventionally successful middle-of-the-road architectural offices.

One such set of functions was those of large hospitals, such as the McMaster Center in Hamilton, Ontario, discussed in the previous chapter. In this context it is interesting to note that one of the pioneer advocates of indeterminate extensibility and variability in hospital design, John Weeks, whose indeterminate design for Northwick Park Hospital near London goes right back to the fifties, cheerfully applies the term 'megastructure' without reservation to the highly-coloured models of interlacing structure, services and special functional volumes that stand about on his desk when hospital designs are under study.

More spectacularly, however, the ever more demanding functions of large-scale airport operation generated radical megastructure-type designs out of unprecedented traffic-movement problems. Not all new airports of the sixties responded to these challenges in this way, though one would think it must be a very dull mind indeed that would not respond to the romance of air travel, the presence of high technology and so forth. Yet there is a group of late-sixties American airports, projected or realized, complete or partial, for which no other term but 'megastructural' will serve. Ironically enough, their extensible and provisional nature means that less rather than more than the first phase has been built in some cases, and with the apparent slowdown in the previously headlong growth of air-travel business some of them look like staying at less than first-stage completion for the rest of their useful lives. Thus few travellers who passed through the usual inexplicable alternations of endless single-storey sheddery and outbreaks of dark-glazed air-conditioned monumentality at Boston's Logan International Airport (**193**) in the early seventies could have guessed that the high and handsome departure lounge was but a small part of the proposed finger of John Carl Warnecke's immense project of 1967.

192 *Waterside, New York (Davis, Brody and Associates, 1972). The four residential towers rising from made-up ground in the East River (the United Nations School in the foreground is not technically part of Waterside) are clearly related to those of the Amherst campus (138), though the function of the podium from which they rise is the provision not of covered circulation, but of parking and services, and residents in the towers normally enter from the plaza on the exposed top of the podium.*

193

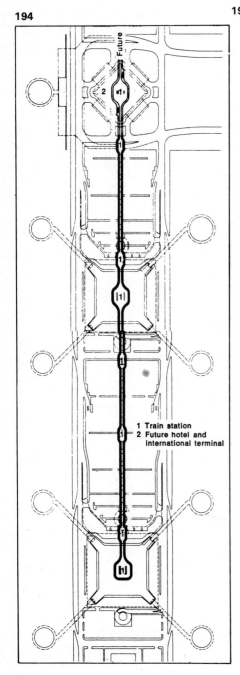

194

1 Train station
2 Future hotel and
  international terminal

180

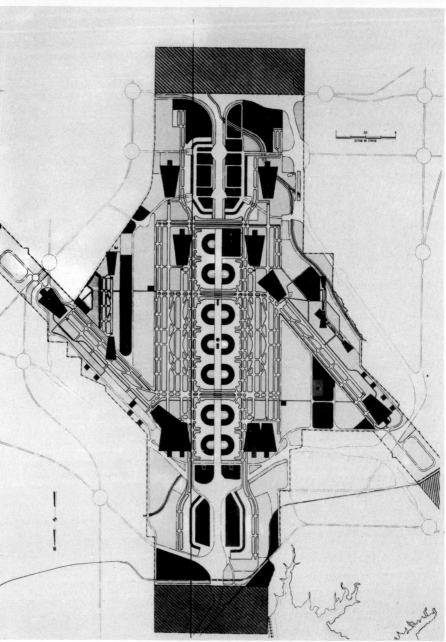

195

Two other schemes which came much nearer to visible megastructural completion, however, both inevitably in Texas, were Houston International and the quite stupendous Dallas/Fort Worth Airport. The proposal for Houston, designed by Pierce and Pierce as early as 1961 but much modified by later successor-partnerships, envisaged two or three (or later four, if needed) large square passenger buildings, each connected by elevated walkways from its corners to four boarding satellites. These separate buildings are arranged in a linear sequence (**194**) between flanking roadways which pass under the pedestrian walkways, rather as if the terminals were located in the wide central reservation of a gigantic freeway. The plan also calls for an elevated mini-train system connecting at least the first three terminals. The extensible linear disposition along a rich array of parallel transportations is what makes the whole ensemble look like a megastructure, especially in perspectives prepared for publicity purposes. On the ground, however, the effect is apt to look more like a conventional airport at the end of an even-longer-than-usual expressway from downtown.

Dallas/Fort Worth could hardly be so misinterpreted: there is nothing conventional about it, and hardly any terminal buildings in any recognizable use of the word. The land-take for the complete airport (**195**) is larger than the island of Manhattan, and on that New York scale of measurement the terminal complex extends from Washington Square to 96th Street! The fundamental conception of this diffuse giant is essentially one of intersecting and interfacing circulation systems, the spine being, once more, a multiple expressway and its junctions. In making these large traffic-works the basic skeleton of their design (**196**), Hellmuth-Obata-Kassabaum (with Brodsky, Hopf and Alder) have clearly come close to the original visions of Maki and Tange in which large-scale civil engineering generates the basic megaform of a metabolist urbanism.

193 *Logan International Airport, Boston (John Carl Warnecke, 1967). Of all the US super-airports, Warnecke's Logan International is the one which will look most recognizably a megastructure if ever completed, though it arrives at its Cumbernauld-like form through a straightforward response to the importance of parking and internal circulation.*

194 *Houston International Airport (Pierce and Pierce, 1961 onwards). Two square terminal blocks with four satellites apiece straddle a super-highway with a (proposed) mini-train down the central reservation; Houston International is recognized as a conceptual breakthrough, where movement-patterns were finally allowed to dominate the whole design concept.*

195, 196 *Dallas/Fort Worth Airport: plan and general view (Hellmuth-Obata-Kassabaum, 1966 onwards). Probably the ultimate in movement-pattern designs, and in a landscape (Texas) where there is room to accept the consequences: the land-take represented by the plan (195) is the size of Manhattan Island, and the immense road pattern with the flanking loops which effectively form the terminals (196) resembles nothing so much as Tange's Tokyo Bay project with the buildings omitted.*

196

But on this megaform they have hung or clipped little more than further transportation facilities: semicircular parking-lots with their access roads looping round them, each loop being then wrapped in a thin crust of effectively single-storey buildings of extremely simple cross-section, seen merely as holding-spaces for passengers and baggage in the unavoidable but, from the traffic engineer's point of view, deplorable pauses in the process of transfer from one form of transportation to another. The architecture of these waiting-volumes is so boxily simple in its square format and off-the-form surfaces that it is all too easy to mistake it for part of the structural megaform, and to read the aircraft themselves, plugged in via their telescopic walkways, as the high-technology capsules of a more elaborate megastructure.

Such local accidents aside, however, what fundamentally makes this a colorable imitation of a megastructure is its sheer linear extent and its modular extensibility, from the present three terminals to an ultimate thirteen if required. There is also one other matter, trivial in bulk but suggestive in its effect, that makes megastructural perceptions of Dallas/Fort Worth possible, perhaps inevitable. Here the mini-train (**197**) actually exists and works, a piece of computerized, automated, advanced-technology mass transit which, except that it is not a monorail, is the very type of the transportation systems that thread through so many megastructure visions. Furthermore, the route of this 'Airtrans' system, now below ground, now above the rooftops as it threads its way through the complex, gives Futurist dimensions to the megastructural experience. It may even give later generations of historians a unique chance of reliving the urban-design sensibilities of the sixties, not unlike visiting Venice by gondola, or Williamsburg on horseback – a twenty-four-minute (maximum journey-time) trip down megamemory lane.

Dallas/Fort Worth, it seems, may prove to be a terminal megastructure in more than the purely airport sense; it is probably the last of its line. At the time of writing, it hardly looks as if it will be necessary for future generations of airport buildings to be predicated on an apparently unlimited growth of air-travel business. Like some other kinds of megastructure, visionary or realistic, that were also conceived in terms of prospects of unlimited growth in their particular businesses, they may now prove to be the embalmed inhabitants of a fossil future. Just as New York City can now be seen to inhabit a fossil future that was laid down about 1910 – the future that was institutionalized by the Futurists themselves – so dinosaur-designs like Dallas/Fort Worth can now be seen to inhabit a fossil future that was laid down in the days of wide-bodied Jumbo-jets, which may themselves prove to be the last of their lines too.

Yet if the growth-future of air travel is now a dwindling one, that of housing is not. Even those well-favoured nations that can claim to have achieved the ecologists' dream of zero population growth are nowhere near zero residential growth. And one of the major constituencies of megastructure-look architecture continues to be in the domain of housing.

The word 'continues' is used with due historical deliberation. The conscious provision of housing for the masses has always, from its earliest beginnings, had deep ideological and operational connections with concepts of large scale and extensive planning. Rare indeed, whether one regards the matter on a global scale or even within Britain alone, has been any very sustained campaign of mass-housing provision in small packets, as in cottage estates. Throughout the history of popular housing, the large or even very large residential block has

dominated to the point where sheer size has become almost a symbolic earnest of good intent in 'giving homes to the people'.

Perhaps it is not surprising, therefore, that even so humane and committed a hater of 'mass housing' as Nicholas Habraken (see pp. 9–10) should have conceived the setting for his proposed do-it-yourself housing in the form of gigantic support-structures far larger than any actual housing blocks he could ever have seen with his own eyes. Or that the members of Team-X, the radical successors to the old Establishment of the *Congrès internationaux d'architecture moderne,* architects like the Smithsons, J. B. Bakema or Candilis/Josic/Woods, should persistently, and in spite of their proclaimed and genuine care for the individual and the family, propose housing complexes the size of Bakema's scheme for Tel Aviv-Yafo, or actually build one the size of Candilis/Josic/Woods's megastructural housing satellite at Toulouse le Mirail. What finally got built at Toulouse may have been spoiled, as is often claimed, by the unimaginative rigidities of the financing organizations, but the point is that unimaginative organizations were prepared to finance it.

The point is important; it means that, insofar as any housing scheme that got built could be called a megastructure – and an increasing number were – then to that extent megastructure was not a radical concept. Davis, Brody's various quasi-megastructures around New York, or the whole Roosevelt Island scheme in the East River as currently being built, were conceivable (at a stretch sometimes) within the available financial procedures established in the Greater New York area, and must have seemed safe propositions – as their appearance generally confirms. The more genuinely radical a megastructure looks in its context, and the nearer it therefore comes to the revolutionary hopes of some

197 *Dallas/Fort Worth's few buildings are modest in scale and detail, following each terminal loop with a shallow layer of accommodation just deep enough to shelter passengers during processing. Threaded through the whole complex is that most refined of megastructure touches, the mini-train that connects all the parts of this far-flung installation.*

183

megastructuralists, the more likely it is to depend on distinctly freakish financing or an unrepeatable political situation, as with the Expos or Cumbernauld.

Defenders and amateurs of megastructure will probably want to make an issue of this point, because it is these financially safe and politically established housing megastructures that have got the type a bad name in radical circles, especially in Britain. The true origins of that bad name are complicated, of course, by the fact that most of these large housing structures were completed after a major upheaval in architectural and sociological taste had given all large buildings a bad name. However, megastructures are not to be excused on the grounds that they were the victims of a historical coincidence; it is in the nature of megastructures that they will take as long to build as any other very large monuments, and much can change in that time. Insofar as megastructures were the children of fashion at the time of their conception, they were doomed, given the normal ten-year cycle of style and taste in the present century, to be newly, and therefore absolutely, out of fashion at the time of their completion.

This has been made very clear by the reception, ranging from the tight-lipped to the intellectually vandalistic (the graffiti on the site fences were all in educated hands), accorded to the crop of housing megastructures in London more or less complete at the time of writing. The Brunswick Centre in Bloomsbury is a classic product of the megayear 1964, since its design, by Sir Leslie Martin and Patrick Hodgkinson, effectively crystallized at that time; but as early as 1970 an educated activist hand had sloganized 'Bloomsbury Prison' on the site fence. Of an even earlier vintage is the enormous Barbican estate in the City of London, which Chamberlin Powell and Bon had designed into virtually its present shape by 1956.

The Barbican (**198**) should probably be regarded as a hard case: its sheer size – just on two thousand apartments – and its multiplicity of function – housing,

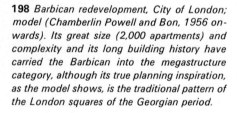

198 *Barbican redevelopment, City of London; model (Chamberlin Powell and Bon, 1956 onwards). Its great size (2,000 apartments) and complexity and its long building history have carried the Barbican into the megastructure category, although its true planning inspiration, as the model shows, is the traditional pattern of the London squares of the Georgian period.*

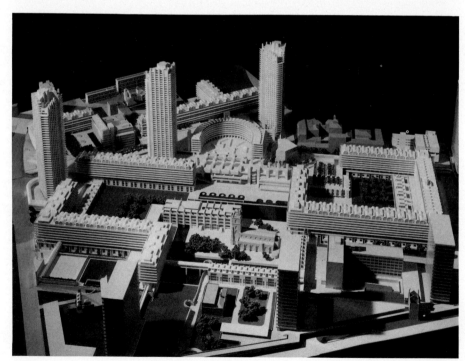

schools, recreation and ultimately an arts centre – put it organizationally in the megastructure class, but the vision that informs its style and conception is considerably less megastructural than that of its pioneering northern contemporary, Park Hill in Sheffield. Its detailing picks up the romantic classicism that lurks in late Le Corbusier, with concrete left *brut* or bush-hammered and a general air of 'architecture is what makes magnificent ruins', and the planning conception is like a pair of very long slabs raised on pilotis above decks of car-parking in the *Unité d'habitation* manner, each of them bent round three sides of a square to evoke memories of the classic Georgian planning procedures of inner London. Only the fact that it was still hanging about uncompleted in the seventies ever earned it the hostile epithet of 'another bloody megastructure'.

The Brunswick Centre (**199**), by contrast, cleaves much closer to what is normally taken to be the megastructure idiom, and was formally acknowledged to be a megastructure by Theo Crosby in the *Architectural Review* in October 1972: '... perhaps the first built example of the idea of the urban megastructure – a building that is a city, rather than being merely a component *in* a city'.[61] And by the purely visual criterion as well, it obviously looks like a megastructure.

The residential accommodation is carried in two back-to-back stepped *Terrassenhäuser* sections (**200**), one down each side of the site, but the A-frames that carry them are asymmetrical; not only is one leg of each frame vertical, but the terracings are asymmetrically disposed, so that those on the outer faces start, and finish, two storeys lower than those on the inner faces. For

199 *Brunswick Centre, London (Patrick Hodgkinson, in succession to Sir Leslie Martin and Patrick Hodgkinson, 1962 onwards). The most pondered, most learned, most acclaimed, most monumental, most bedevilled in its building history of all English megastructures – and seemingly the best-liked by its inhabitants. In spite of numerous vicissitudes, the original concept of two long banks of back-to-back* Terrassenhäuser *facing one another across a handsome public space has survived, and it carries the learning of its patent borrowings from Sant'Elia with ease. It gains from its site, facing a traditional green Georgian square, but suffers the opprobrium of having required the clearance of equally traditional Georgian buildings from that site.*

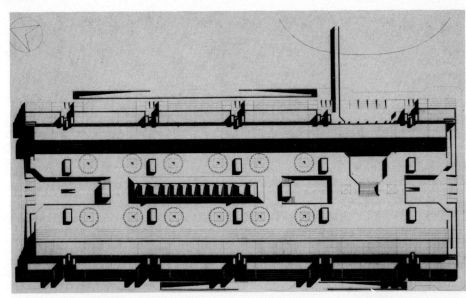

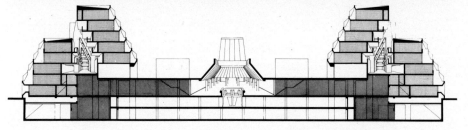

200 *Brunswick Centre: plan and section. Though truncated because the land for the last bay and a half beyond the fourth staircase has not yet been acquired, enough has been built for the intellectual conception to be understood. The plan draws attention to the almost traditional 'civic design' formality of the monumental approaches to the interior spaces; the section reveals the two levels of parking below the lower (shopping) concourse.*

eight bays of the eastern outer face the terracings are omitted altogether, and the vertical columns form a gigantic portico (**201**) through which one passes from the public space of Brunswick Square into the public spaces of the centre itself: a shopping mall at entry level, with a pedestrian piazza above (**202**), parking and a subterranean cinema below. The entrance to the cinema forms a free-standing island block between the columns of the portico, and the grandiose monumental theme of the entrance is sustained by a ceremonial flight of steps which rises, on the axis of the portico, to the pedestrian level above.

Coincidentally megastructural is the fact that the existing building is, by design, extensible – but in the negative sense of the unfinished American airport buildings. Among the miscellaneous accidents that befell the scheme in its long history was the failure to acquire the most northerly block of the intended site, so that what one now sees is truncated, indeed amputated, with a provisional northern elevation from which, if deemed feasible, building could be continued. Another of these historical accidents was a cash-flow crisis within the organization of the commercial development company which had initiated the project; as a result, the residential upper parts were sold off to the local housing authority, while the developers kept the profitable podium with its shops and other commercial facilities. This not only resulted in design changes, but also meant that the financing of the whole project has been freakish even by the eccentric standards current among megastructures!

But what the well-informed architectural visitor (and they have come in their thousands) cannot fail to note is how sustainedly and in what detail the design

201

201, 202 *Brunswick Centre. The civic design ambitions are most clearly shown in the portico (201), which at seven storeys in height must be the most imposing entrance to any public housing anywhere in the world. The sheer size seems less daunting here than on the inner terraces (202), which seem to go on, scalelessly, for ever, in spite of the 'homely' human touches of the glazed living-room extension to each flat.*

202

203

204

203, 204 *Brunswick Centre. The almost traditional sense of monumentality that made the Centre a pilgrimage-place for architecture-fanciers is most starkly seen in the interior spaces under the A-frames that support the apartments. The adverse effects of exposing this kind of architecture to the English weather are all too unpleasantly revealed in 204, where the patterns of rain-streaking make the building dirty without dignifying it with the patina of age.*

pays tribute to one of the ultimate ancestors of megastructure, Antonio Sant'Elia. Not only do the residential sections, with their *case a gradinate* over tall public access-spaces within the A-frames (**203**), proclaim his paternity; so also do the twinned towers (**204**) flanking the entrances and stairs, the modelling and the battering of the surfaces around those entrances, and even the horizontal lines grooved in the exposed flank-walls. Even the profiling and tapering of the vertical columns, as revealed in the open portico, looks unmistakably Futurist, though the source for this, if conscious, would have to be Chiattone rather than Sant'Elia.

In a period and an architectural culture that was distinctly learned, this was a conspicuously erudite building, not only in its more-than-nodding acquaintance with the history of Modern architecture, but also in its confident employment of an almost *Beaux-Arts* grand manner in the axial relationship of portico and ceremonial steps. Such professionalism and almost old-fashioned learning is not, in retrospect, to be despised. This is not the only building of its class that can be said to have been saved by old-time architectural skills in composition and design from the kind of cheerless chaos that infected so

188

205 *Utopian Housing, London (Design Five, 1974). Mini-megastructures as an acceptable format for upper-middle-class housing, with parking for large cars under the A-frames. The traditional brick facings, as much as the class of tenant, show how far megastructure has now advanced toward social acceptability.*

much of the less determined 'megastructure' housing of that period in England. All too often, what seems to have been an unintelligent misreading of the apparently disorderly aformal geometry of, say, the great axonometric of 'Plug-In City', coupled with a belief that practically anything at all can be joined up into a comprehensible 'something-or-other' with a few ramps and pedestrian bridges, led to schemes which, whether in system-built panelling or brown brick terraces, merely exemplify the architecture of indifference.

Practically every British local authority seems to have built some of this adequate but uninspiring megaroutine stuff. And it is not confined to public authorities, for a housing association rejoicing in the appropriate name of the Utopian Voluntary Housing Group built, to the designs of an architectural office cryptically entitled 'Design 5', a cluster of mini-megastructures (**205**) of entirely routine conception – *Terrassenhäuser* A-frames, semi-underground parking, pedestrian bridges – on an extremely valuable centrally located site in London, overlooking Hyde Park and within two hundred yards or so of Marble Arch.

This self-styled Utopian proposition is, to be fair, one of the better examples of megaroutine as practised in Britain. All too often work of this kind takes looseness of composition as an excuse for thoughtless planning, and permissive variability as an excuse for not designing. The line between extensibility as an ideology and just not caring how long the building turns out proves to be an easy one to cross; so does the line between allowing a building to generate its own form and not caring what shape it is. Above all, these megaroutine situations show how different is the architectural performance that can be extracted from a concept when it is new, hot, and in the hands of its inventors, from the same idea when it has died into 'good currency', has ceased to amaze or inspire, and has fallen into the hands of average salaried architects.

Some ideas can survive this kind of devolution and dilution; the 'Megastructure Look', it seems, could not, unless stiffened and regularized by the supposedly permanent values of architecture (i.e. those more than one generation old). On this basis, the ultimate tombstone of the institutionalized and run-down concept of megastructure must be the largest and most terminal monster of them all: Thamesmead. This complete new town located downwind of a sewage works in a remote and inaccessible south-eastern suburb of London was conceived as a single designed entity and, in the model (**206**) prepared by the Greater London Council's Architect's Department, appears as if it could be a single building. It is not, nor was it likely to be, since its overall dimensions are measured in miles; but the first part was sufficiently continuous as a structure and as a circulation system to be read as a model housing megastructure, and not a bad one either at first sight, with its lakeside *Terrassenhäuser*, shops and schools and health centre all safely accessible through its picturesquely varied network of raised pedestrian decks. Yet even before structural and financial alarms had combined to undermine Thamesmead's golden promises, chiefly by ensuring that everything beyond stage one would be built down to the most

206 *Thamesmead New Town; project model (Greater London Council Architects' Department, 1967 onwards). As the model shows, the bulk of the accommodation for the fifty thousand inhabitants of this complete town would be in what is virtually a single, though very complex, building, deliberately planned on the scale of the motorway which traverses the site. Whether the design can be carried through as originally conceived is now economically doubtful, but there have always been doubts in human terms about whether it should be so carried out – even architects originally excited at the idea of a three-mile building from a single hand (or group of hands) now seem to doubt whether the result would be tolerable.*

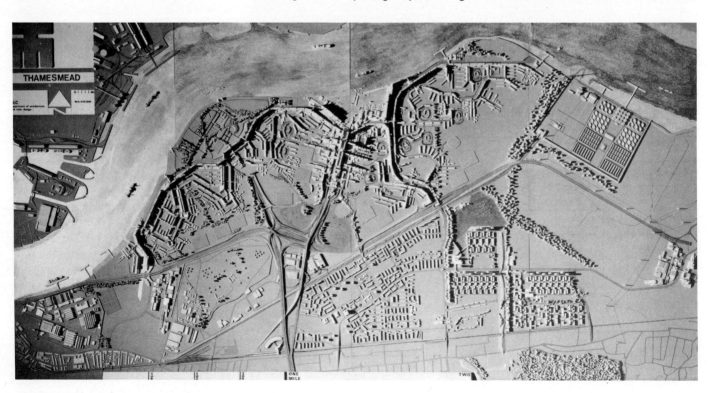

grudging economic standards, the future it promised when fully completed had begun to alarm rather than inspire. The unmitigable sameness of the domestic environment generated by its very restricted range of constructional panels (**207**) seemed to be emphasized rather than relieved by the routinized attempts to introduce variety in the facings of walls towards public walkways.

It was not merely a matter of taste having changed since the design was first conceived, but more a question of routinized design being unable to cope with two major problems: variation and scale. The variation problem had been lurking ever since architects moved into mass housing, though megastructure had highlighted it. The dilemma here is one that architects do not often care to confront, since it invites them to get out of the public housing business, but Alan Colquhoun did once air it in an unpublished lecture at University College, London, on 'The Superblock':

... I mean the distinction between the public and the private realms. The public realm was representative. It not only housed activities of a public and collective nature, but it symbolised those activities.... In traditional cities the living units did not constitute a part of the public realm. It was only in the ideal cities of the nineteenth century, and then with gathering momentum in real cities, that the unit of living became subject to conscious and overall design.... Housing, in contrast to public buildings, has traditionally formed part of the unconscious infrastructure. This is precisely its appeal to us; it is 'architecture without architects'. The laws of its organisation are seen as being beyond the threshold of conscious manipulation.[62]

207 *Thamesmead: residential terrace. Part of the concern over tolerability comes from the monotony caused by the very limited kit of parts from which the housing is assembled — about two-thirds of the total repertoire of elements is seen in each house-front here — and their lack of adaptability to variant house-forms. In the first and much published phase the layout at least of the housing was diversified, but as economic stringency and the logic of the system began to grip, more and more was done in straight parallel terraces like the one seen here.*

So when architects, practising a profession which is based historically on the designing of representative public buildings, set out on a course of conscious manipulation of the organization of the private realm of housing, must they fail? Many would claim that to be too defeatist a conclusion, yet Thamesmead certainly makes it look as if it might be true. The system is too rigid, the overall conception too cut-and-dried, the parts too much at the mercy of the representative whole, and much too tight a fit on their legislatively defined housing functions, for there to be anything like the kind of variability that vernacular practice had unconsciously built into the housing of the past. Previous housing schemes, however vast and regular, had usually had undesigned urban environments around them on to which non-conforming uses could be offloaded; Thamesmead had only marshland which was subject to flooding.

Measured against these inadequacies and against thoughts like those of Colquhoun, the 'let-em-all-come' approach implicit in supposedly visionary propositions like, for instance, Plug-In City looks less like romantic wishful thinking than like a sane appreciation of what a city is all about. Indeed, the frame-and-capsule concept makes a proper and comprehensible distinction between public and private realms. That distinction was fundamental to megastructure from the beginning; it is basic to Le Corbusier's Fort l'Empereur project, for a start. The absence of a separate frame at Thamesmead makes the distinction impossible within that system, and also leads directly to its problems of scale, for there are no components bigger than storey-high or room-wide. The result is not only monotonous, but becomes unreadable without a larger visual frame against which it can be measured. The idiom will barely stretch over what has been built so far; extended over a whole city it becomes inconceivable.

Admittedly, these are only the 'architectural' worries about Thamesmead; there is also a large body of sociological concern about the nature of the design and its location. Partly this is merely a modish change in radical chic tastes, cynically exploited by the use of Thamesmead as the setting of a key sequence in the film *A Clockwork Orange*, but more than that it is the result of extensive field experience of genuine social distress among the earliest inhabitants. Such discontents rarely have single causes, and it is less easy than is sometimes supposed to know how accountable the architecture may be in this case. Such historical perspective as we have on the social performance of very large housing schemes suggests that it is not always as automatically disastrous as is often supposed, though it is certainly very variable. Against an alleged social disaster area like the notorious Pruitt-Igoe development in St Louis must be set the seemingly comfortable social situation in Sheffield's Park Hill, designed according to almost exactly the same architectural precepts, street-decks and all, as Pruitt-Igoe.

Even if the architecture is finally absolved from responsibility for all these sundry social ills, there still remains one major concern that will not go away: is it humanly credible that one man, or one design team, can genuinely conceive a single unified architectural system that can serve all the needs of a growing city for the first half-century or so of its life? It is a problem that lurks in all megastructure propositions, and was confronted by those like the Metabolists or Habraken who were prepared to let small matters look after themselves on a vernacular basis while a large megaform of some sort held the ensemble together and gave professional permanency where it was socially needed. In a

208 *Alexandra Road housing, London, under construction (Neave Brown, for Camden Council, 1968 onwards). Unvaried* Terrassenhäuser *need not be visually boring. The long regular curve of Alexandra Road gives a unity and form to its repetitions that the eye can just about perceive and comprehend.*

system like that at Thamesmead, this cannot happen: there are no gross megaform elements, the structure being built up from the walls and floors of the housing units, and these cannot be varied without completely altering the system and destroying the economies of scale which can only come from sustained repetition without modification of the moulds and machinery of the panel-producing plant — which is itself locked up into the design of the whole, and physically located on part of the Thamesmead site! In spite of its apparent looseness of organization, Thamesmead is conceptually and urbanistically rigid to the point of paralysis.

Against this one may try to measure also the apparently total rigidity, in the one case, and the seemingly uncontrolled free-form conception, in the other, of two further British municipal housing megastructures still under construction at the time of writing. One is the Alexandra Road scheme designed for Camden Borough Council (proprietors of the upper parts of the Brunswick Centre) by Neave Brown, a member of an Anglo-American connection, involving also Peter Eisenman and the Institute for Architecture and Urban Studies in New York, who are prone to use the word 'megastructure' in a fairly restricted and frankly hermetic sense. With the main structure of Alexandra Road now all in place (**208**), it reveals itself as the epitome of geometrical simplicity among megastructures. It uses a standard — perhaps one should say *the* standard — *Terrassenhäuser* section, backed up against a main-line railway but with its open terraces facing south away from the tracks. The section, seven storeys high, is repeated without variation for the full thousand feet of the block, the only relief coming from a slight but measurably precise curvature over its whole length. This curvature, and the perfect clarity of the invariable section, should just, though only just, raise the design above the accusations of inhuman tedium levelled at such products of the so-called 'Cool School' as the Clipstone Street development in London by Mike Gold of the Armstrong and McManus office. Alexandra Road is a very 'minimal' design, but such aesthetic signals as it emits

193

209, 210 *Byker redevelopment, Newcastle-upon-Tyne (Ralph Erskine, 1968 onwards). If this must be classed as a megastructure, then the class is the richer for it, yet it is unlike any other that has been built, and owes nothing visible to the visionary fervours of the sixties. On one side (209) it is a seemingly endless, almost unpierced serpentining wall of brick-work patterned with patches of colour that are, in some cases, longer or higher than some accredited megastructures. On the other side (210), away from the threat of motorway noise, it opens out in a festival of highly coloured wooden balconies, canopies and plant-boxes, all of cottage scale. If there can be a 'rustic megastructure', Byker is it.*

are, once again, witness to the value of traditional architectural skills when megastructure is deprived of its original promises of adaptability and extensibility.

Utterly different, but equally obsessive in its way, is the 'Byker Wall' on a ridge above the central valleys of Newcastle-upon-Tyne (**209**). Designed with at least nominal 'local citizen participation' by the Anglo-Swedish architect Ralph Erskine, its protective 'wall' format derives ultimately from Erskine's studies of sub-arctic housing done almost two decades earlier (his semi-subterranean shopping centre for the northerly Swedish mining town of Lulea has had an underground reputation among the megastructure connection since pictures of it were first published in the late fifties). At Byker the defensive wall serpentines for over a mile (when completed, just over 1,000 yards when last visited), richly decorated with areas of coloured brickwork on a scale commensurate with the height of this outer façade, which is over seven storeys high at points, and almost blind, pierced only by minute kitchen or bathroom windows and highly coloured ventilators, the better to exclude traffic noise. On the other side the block is opened up with large windows commanding views over the city, and hung with wooden balconies and access-galleries stained in various bold colours (**210**). Visually, this often rather improvised-looking woodwork is meant to pick up the idiom of the fences and sheds of the smaller terraces that Erskine has placed at the foot of the wall, in order to give a homogeneous sense of place to the whole development; but it thereby leaves the present study in the grotesque situation of concluding with a sort of 'rustic' or even 'gardenesque' megastructure.

Does this mean that megastructure as a concept could now absorb almost anything that could be stuffed into it — a grab-bag category containing anything that came to hand, so long as it was large? Or simply that megastructure was now a decadent architectural typology and running out of useful meaning? Or does it mean that Byker is not a megastructure at all? There are many ways in which even Byker aligns with the high-technology ambitions of the pioneer megastructuralists (the external wooden elements could be unplugged, and probably will be in time); but if the word has to mean Byker at one extreme and, say, Plug-In City at the other, does it mean anything useful at all?

9 Epilogue: The Meaning of Megastructure

The purely lexical meaning of megastructure, when it is finally committed to the standard dictionaries, will probably be as wrong-headedly correct and boringly true as that offered by Cook and Klotz, viz.:

megastructure; An over-scaled, colossal, multi-unit architectural mass.[63]

The concept clearly has more layers of 'meaning' than this, even in the purely technical sense current in linguistic studies. But what in coarser human terms is the meaning of megastructure? What does it tell us about the state of the world and of architecture when a distinguished magazine like *Domus* of Milan could publish, in 1969, a project by two apparently sane young British architects, Mike Mitchell and Dave Boutwell, for a single-building city (**211**) stretching in a straight line from New York to San Francisco — and call it 'Comprehensive City'?

One thing we can reliably deduce is that the designers, like most of the megastructure generation, had their eyes on North America as the part of the world that had problems vast enough to require 'visionary' solutions and the biggest technological resources for dealing with them, and that sheer dimensional bigness was an essential part of the solution to these continent-sized problems.

The first essential is planning on a national scale. Leaving parochially minded regional administrators to envisage the future is disastrous. An overall definition of conveyance systems by speed-zoning and superimposed loading, and the raising of compacted cities and towns above these systems as rafts will allow their separate but interdependent functions to develop. . . .[64]

Such language comes so close to parody that there is no need to parody it, as Peter Hall points out in a cutting non-parody which is quoted later in this chapter. In this fantasy megaworld where a whole region can be dismissed as 'parochial', Mitchell and Boutwell insist that they are reasonable and practical men, in touch with the realities of the hour: 'This is our city, we have not sensationalised. All that we have described is feasible today. . . .'

This, of course, was exactly the line that Le Corbusier had taken forty-seven years before in introducing his *Ville contemporaine pour trois millions d'habitants* in 1922, insisting that it was indeed a contemporary city that could be built at once, mistaking purely technical feasibility (though even that may be doubted) for political and fiscal possibility. So in this, as in a curious number of other matters, Mitchell and Boutwell, far from being as *outré* as might at first appear, were almost conventional traditionalists, standing firm in a Modern movement tradition which was already most of half a century old, going back to the very beginnings of modern town planning itself.

Megastructure, then, contains some elements of atavism, a harking back to the 'heroic age of Modern architecture', and a constant preoccupation with the

original Italian Futurist movement and with the sketches of Sant'Elia. There was undoubtedly a nostalgia for a past (and a hypothesized future) in which Modern architecture had been (and could become once more) a matter of large clear-cut gestures, without the compromises and dilutions and scalings-down that had corrupted the purity and radicalism of the original intentions.

Yet there is a very important change here, at least in expressed attitudes to the applicability of these ideas. Le Corbusier's *système préconise*, as he modestly termed it in language which endows it with the infallibility of a Papal pronouncement, was a 'solution-type': an idea or platonic model created in the abstract on a site as pure as a sheet of tracing paper, a perfect paradigm from which all actual solutions for real sites (e.g. the *Plan voisin de Paris*) should be derived. Mitchell and Boutwell are much more modest — 'We are not saying that this is the city of the future, but rather one of the possibilities deserving serious consideration' — and this sentiment is clearly much more in line with the mega-period's professed belief in the permissive and the open-ended, in a future with 'alternative scenarios'.

These libertarian sentiments, however, do not alter the fact that Comprehensive City, as drawn and as published, must be construed as a closed system. Its width is the same from coast to coast, and when its transcontinental length reaches either of its terminal metropolises it shows no ambition to continue and

211 *Comprehensive City project (Mike Mitchell and Dave Boutwell, 1969). If the idea of a single building stretching right across North America now looks ludicrous or — worse — old-fashioned, it is the more important to remember that this kind of proposition was in fashion and credible less than a decade ago, at least as a 'vision'. Nor was it alone: by that date the Austrian Raimund Abraham had already proposed a structure covering the entire surface of the globe!*

197

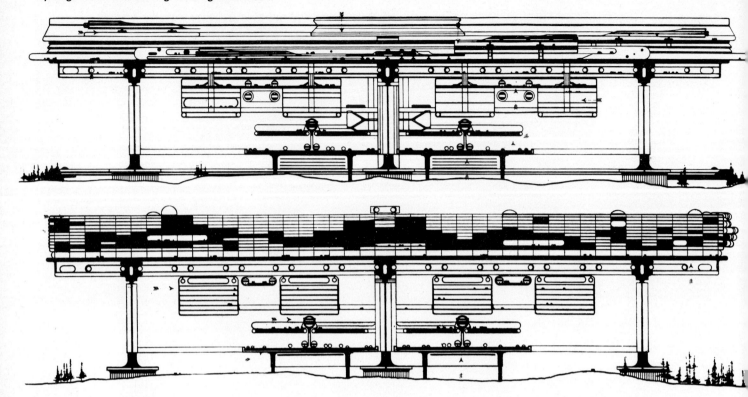

212 *Comprehensive City's sectional organization reveals the underlying sense that made it credible: it is really a monumental version of a great transcontinental highway like Route 66, or an updated version of the Great Arterial Way (39), with its associated warehousing and industry, that traversed Frank Lloyd Wright's Broadacre City.*

paddle its substructure in the ocean beyond. Furthermore, the scheme as drawn treats the map of North America as exactly the same kind of ideal surface as Le Corbusier had employed for his ideal *Ville contemporaine*, whose topographical accidents have no effect on the design, in spite of the fact that the sections of Comprehensive City (**212**) that are provided by the architects show that it nowhere stands on legs tall enough to stride over the Rockies or the Appalachians as if they were not there. If the concept was seriously intended to be adaptable to changes in the terrain, this was not acknowledged in the drawings, which present a simple image of a single unvaried system.

If it be objected that this was little more than a student fantasy, and does not deserve such massive exegesis, one can counter-argue that *Domus* was sufficiently impressed by it to give it five pages, two of them with colour overlays, and that in any case the whole design is full of matter that sheds light on the mind and meanings of the time. For instance, the use of the word 'comprehensive'; to most common understandings a city of one *billion* inhabitants would be comprehensive in little more than the purely statistical sense that any object so vast would probably contain everything anyhow. It is certainly not comprehensive in the sense that every single thing has a specific place designed for it; as the word 'megastructure' so often was in conversational use, this too is little more than a grab-bag concept into which everything can be stuffed, somewhere, somehow, some time. However, the word seems also to have intentional overtones of 'comprehensible': that when absolutely everything had been lined up in a straight run from sea to shining sea, you would at least know where everything was; above all, that it would not be distributed at random all over the landscape.

This, one may suspect, was one of the most persistent meanings or motivations for megastructure: that in spite of its extensibility and uncertain outline, its sheer concentration of activities would bring an end to the situation where 'the huge, uncontrolled and sprawling chaos that we now call City is choking our civilisation. . . .' Thus Mitchell and Boutwell; but the sentiment was omnipresent and powerful. It goes back to Le Corbusier and beyond, this urge to impose a simple and architectonic order on the layout of human society and its equipment. In spite of their hang-loose, libertarian words, most megastructuralists wanted cities to have an order that they could understand as architects, not the kind of order that might be generated by business, transportation or whatever. At its most direct, this desire to impose could be seen in a programme in the school at UCLA to redesign Wilshire Boulevard as a megastructure. Neither the functions nor the length nor the overall width including the present parking lots would be changed, but the result would be a visible work of architecture rather than an *ad hoc* commercial strip.

The most persistent and persuasive voice among megastructuralists calling for this kind of order was undoubtedly that of Paolo Soleri, who represented most forcefully in words and designs (**213**) the desire to stop the persistent tendency of the human race to spread:

The natural landscape is thus not the most apt frame for the complex life of society. Man must make the metropolitan landscape in his own image: a physically compact, dense, three-dimensional energetic bundle, not a tenuous film of organic matter. The man-made landscape has to be a multi-level landscape, a solid of three congruous dimensions. The only realistic direction towards a physically free community of man is toward the

213 *Mesa City project (Paolo Soleri, 1959). The first of Soleri's heroic urban visions, born out of his experiences with Frank Lloyd Wright in the American south-west, but already exhibiting that predilection for vaults and apses that pervades his works of the sixties, as well as his desire to concentrate the human race at enormous densities in order to disencumber the earth's crust from suburban sprawl.*

214 *Babelnoah Arcology project (Paolo Soleri, after 1964). The characteristic hollow spool-shaped towers of Soleri's mid-sixties Arcology style are often accompanied by more 'conventional' megastructures such as the one which forms the rear wall of this drawing. As can be seen from the labelling of the parts — 'factories', 'residential', 'cultural centre' — Soleri's conception of urban zoning and functions was still remarkably 'un-liberated' at this period, however imaginative the structures in which the functions were zoned.*

construction of truly three-dimensional cities. Physical freedom — that is to say, true reaching power — is wrapped around vertical vectors.[65]

Soleri emerges as a kind of maniac for compactness; even his vastest projects are claimed to be 'about miniaturization', and his ideal vernacular model is less the Mediterranean village, piled up over its hill, than cliff-dwellings like those at Mesa Verde, because they are 'non-acreage' land — they occupy no horizontal land-surface at all. Consistently with this view that men should live on contour lines rather than between them, most of Soleri's Arcologies wear their habitable apartments in the vertical or near-vertical skin of the structure (**214**), looking out over horizontal Nature with the dense vertical services of the core behind them.

Yet in spite of the fact that Soleri places great importance on these services and insists that his cities would be 'like an efficient plumbing system for modern society', many commentators have noted that his projects are weak in clear delineations of the services required (or even romantic delineations of them, such as might be found in Archigram projects). His preoccupation with the purely structural aspects of his Arcologies (**215**) would be strange if he were not an architect, and therefore a member of a sub-culture which prefers structural design and finds mechanical design embarrassing; to anyone who is not a member of the architectural sub-culture, it must be clear that at the densities of population that Soleri is proposing the design of mechanical life-support systems is likely to be more important and more critical than that of structure. Even some of Soleri's supposed admirers have felt forced to comment on this manifest weakness, and on other inadequacies:

Man is conceived as a supersocialized vector requiring complete macro-architectural definition. Planning as a discipline of economic, communication, social or even mechanical systems is hardly outlined. Most surprising, Soleri's idealized cities display a rather rigid packaging of function — an Athens Charter belief in zoning compartmentation — that seems out of place with both present city-planning theory and the post-Beatles generation. . . .[66]

The author of these strictures was Jeffrey Cook, one of the leading academic explainers of Soleri. Other critics may have been more derisive about Soleri's deficiencies, but none was so perceptive as Cook in noting the survival of Athens Charter thinking from the early thirties. He is right in finding such rigidity of planning surprising among the post-Beatles generation, and one certainly does not find it in most Archigram proposals. But, confusingly enough, most of the members of Archigram were at least as old as the Beatles. The Archigram break-away from the separately zoned categories established, with the authority of Le Corbusier, by the Athens Charter — the city seen as composed of distinct areas devoted to work, leisure, housing and transportation — was unique, if only in its thoroughness. For most of their generation, as for those preceding and, to a slightly lesser extent, those following who had been through architecture school, the Four Functions of the Athens Charter had almost Mosaic authority and were graven on the consciousness of the profession with a permanence made greater by the fact that they were believed (with some justification) to be the pronouncements of Le Corbusier himself.

So the Swiss Justus Dahinden, in *Urban Structures for the Future*, the first academic compendium of megastructuralism to appear after the movement had

215 *Veladiga Arcology project (Paolo Soleri, after 1964). For many commentators the most convincing of Soleri's Arcologies, and one to which he has recently returned, Veladiga uses a mighty dam as the support for a skin of human habitations. The main structure would then be a work of conspicuous ecological usefulness, while the inhabitants would efficiently occupy 'non-acreage land' — exactly the kind of mating of ecology and architecture that an Arcology is supposed to be.*

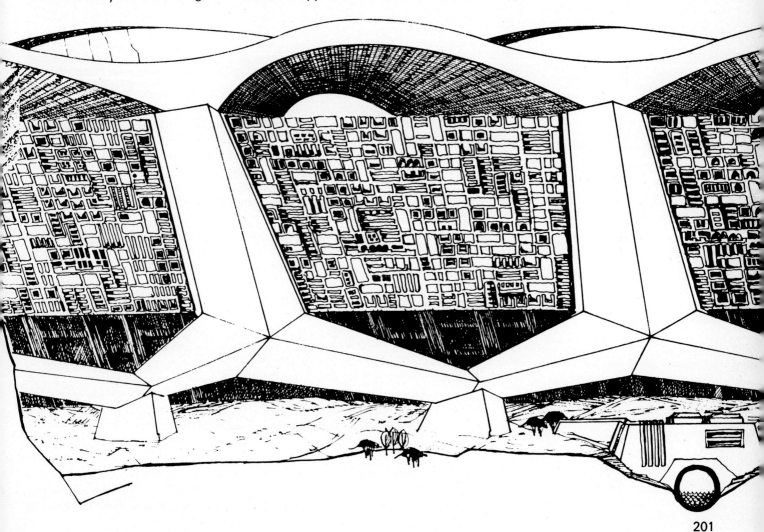

216 *Radio City project (Justus Dahinden, 1968–70). Dahinden, together with his researcher Walter Stahl, was the first encyclopaedic scholar of megastructure: his book on the subject came out in 1971, just as the movement was expiring, and his projects seem to sum up the dying movement just as encyclopaedically, as in this dashing perspective with its echoes of Fuller, Soleri, and even Archigram's early science-fiction fantasies.*

ceased to move (**216**), almost automatically cites the Charter before going on to insist that it should now be replaced by

a new development which will reintegrate our social and urban structures and reunite the different social groups and activities. Consequently, future town-planning must be synthetic. . . . For this reason, contemporary town-planners are recommending that megastructures of enormous compactness should be built: instead of being spread out over a wide area, the different social spheres will be 'packed' one on top of the other.[67]

This is a very revealing passage indeed. On careful scrutiny it shows that what Dahinden is talking about is not synthesis at all: the social spheres remain different, but instead of lying on flat ground edge to edge they are to be piled on top of one another at the same map reference. No other mechanism for synthesizing them is offered; simplification of architectural image, rather than any integration of life, is all that is at stake.

In spite of his Athens Charter rigidities, however, Soleri did indeed survive to become one of the heroes of the genuinely post-Beatles generation. Whereas, after about 1968, the execration of high technology by eco-activists virtually destroyed the constituency of megastructure among the young (who had always been its main supporters), Soleri's following grew. For this, some obvious reasons can be advanced: his very lack of interest in the energy-consuming mechanical aspects of his Arcologies has bred a myth that they would consume no energy, and this myth apparently is seen as being confirmed by the fact that the built parts of the first of his megastructures that actually exists, Arcosanti, have been constructed by hand by his students using only the most primitive of technical aids. Such manual performance, which few other architectural educators have been able to command, is clearly a response to Soleri's status as a natural guru-figure, and one whose operating style has matched the anti-urban, back-to-the-bush sentiments of the early seventies.

Yet one still has to wonder if it is not the sheer physical exhaustion brought on by all that hand-labour that prevents his loyal students asking themselves what they are doing working for such a thoroughly old-fashioned and Establishment figure. For not only does his planning depend on an Athens Charter conception that elsewhere produced *la Ville Radieuse* of Le Corbusier which, Jane Jacobs had taught the Beatle generation and those following, had led to all the urban housing projects they despised and to the disaster at Pruitt-Igoe; but also his overall conception of an immensely dense Arcology has the support of the academic/capitalist Establishment of professional futurologists whose high-technology dreams the young have also taught themselves to despise.

Yet as early as 1961 a special issue of *Daedalus*, the official organ of the American Academy of Sciences, edited by Lloyd Rodwin of MIT, contained, among other matters, Kevin Lynch's 'scenario' for 'Core City', which

might even become 'solid' with a continuous occupation of space and a cubical grid of transportation lines. . . . Accessibility would be very high, both to special activities and to open country at the edges of the city. . . . Such a metropolis would indeed produce a vivid image and would contribute to a strong sense of the community as a whole . . . a three-mile cube [could hold] twenty million people with generous spacing. . . .[68]

Phrased thus, and in this particular political and academic context, a vision startlingly close to Soleri's Arcologies becomes 'thinkable' in the sense in which Herman Kahn had made thermonuclear war 'thinkable'. Abstract futures of barely discernible human dimensions are offered as 'alternative' scenarios (and Lynch has a variety of other 'cities' in stock to cover all eventualities) in which the fate of large sections of the human race is discussed in studiedly value-free language. Assumed rhetorics aside, however, the only real difference between Arcology and Core City is that the latter genuinely is only one of a number of very different cities offered by Lynch, whereas in Soleri's book there are no real alternative scenarios, only different packagings of Arcology.

To the megastructural generations, and notwithstanding the mild disclaimers of Mitchell and Boutwell, there were no alternative scenarios ever; they predicated a 'standard urban future' far more narrowly determined than any of Herman Kahn's standard futures, and megastructure must ultimately be seen as being, in a more general sense admittedly, as much a *système préconise* as, more literally, had been Le Corbusier's *Ville contemporaine.* There is a sense, which may have been understood from the preceding chapters, in which megastructure was one of the inevitable destinations of the Modern movement.

Even if it was not consciously so envisaged until a fairly late date, the concept of megastructure, once formulated, was immediately acceptable to those who had consciously set that movement in motion. The most striking case of this concerns Walter Gropius, who was consciously written into the history of megastructure, either by himself or by his followers. There is a curious project, dating from 1928, for a *Wohnberg* — a giant A-frame of considerable length, with terraced housing without and several layers of transportation at scattered levels within (**217**) — which had been kicking around in fringe periodicals for some years after the Second World War and surfaced officially, as it were, in the 'Visionary Architecture' exhibition of the Museum of Modern Art, New York, in 1961. In the catalogue it is correctly dated, but ascribed to 'German. Architect unknown.' The same pictures appeared in the Gropius exhibition of 1973 in London, and here they were attributed to the late master, and described as a 'megastructure' in the captions and the catalogue. Furthermore, Mrs Gropius specifically drew attention to the design as a megastructure in her speech opening the exhibition, supplementing this later with conversational references to Archigram and other 'young men who think they invented everything'.

In just over a decade, therefore, a project that presumably had been disowned by Gropius because it was too 'visionary' for the father of serious and socially responsible Modern architecture to acknowledge had come into such good currency that it was a desirable property for inclusion in his portfolio. There were

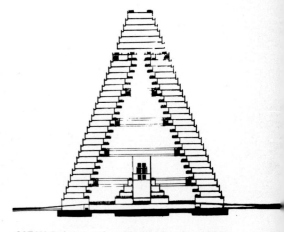

217 Wohnberg *project (Walter Gropius, 1928). A megastructure reclaimed: after years in the limbo of attribution to 'architect unknown', this vast 32-storey A-frame project was proudly re-admitted to the canon of Gropius's works after his death.*

certainly intellectual and psychological pressures to include it; within the established but by now beleaguered rationale of the orthodox Modern movement, megastructure must increasingly have come to look like architecture's last best hope of retaining a foothold in the design and development of cities. But what is interesting is that at this point in time, when the rationality of megastructure became something that could be accepted by serious architects (having apparently been underwritten by the likes of futurologists on the one hand and guardians of the urban environment like Colin Buchanan of *Traffic in Towns* on the other), it began to be beleaguered by precisely some of those who might have been expected to endorse it.

Here one must distinguish between internal and external critics. When, in 1964, for instance, Peter Smithson objected to Tange's MIT Boston Harbor scheme, it was on the relatively technical grounds that its tight physical integration of transportation and structure left no room for the subsequent 'inevitable' growth and change of transportation systems. This must be accounted an internal criticism, and so must much of what was to appear in the professional magazines from 1968 onwards. External criticism came from a widely scattered set of voices, as might be expected, and some of it went unnoticed at first precisely because it was so expected.

Thus any objections to megastructure that came from, say, Lewis Mumford and his bio-technic theories, or from committed proponents of the Garden City movement like Frederick Osborn, could be brushed aside as 'old men doing their usual dreary old numbers', and was ignored because it was so totally surprise-free a response. But when Peter Hall published his very damaging article 'Monumental Follies' in 1968, the case was significantly and historically different; the relative silence which greeted its publication must have come partly from sheer disbelief. Hall, a geographer and the academic jet-set wonder-boy of British planning, pursuer of novelty, author of a Los-Angelised future for south-east England (*London 2000*) and other swinging goodies, was often abused by student activists as 'the friend of large-scale developers'. Yet in 'Monumental Follies' he pulled the flush on megastructure when it was still, for most of the world of architecture, the newest and most promising novelty around.

Hall's critique had two cutting edges: one was the destruction of existing urban fabrics. The article began with a 'documentary image' that was to become familiar to the point of tedium four or five years later on British television: a bewildered old-age pensioner wandering lost across the brick-dust tundra that had replaced a familiar downtown area destroyed to clear the site for the kind of 'comprehensive redevelopment' that made so many British pseudo-megastructures possible. However, his thrust was not yet against megastructures, merely against the kind of 'clearance mentality' that was uprooting so many ancient urban areas without caring what would replace them.

He then went on to explain what the replacement was likely to be, and now megastructure felt the other cutting edge directly, being attacked not only for what it was, but also for the intellectual pretensions of its exponents:

. . . the next generation of architect-planners have got something better in store. They have gone to colleges in the mid-Sixties which were decorated with Captain Marvel and Superman and enormous blow-ups of space-ships. They now write the prevalent architectural criticism in England in an amazing mixture of arid technical jargon and hip culture language which would have provided an object lesson for George Orwell. A pastiche, not a parody of the style, would read something like this — 'Parametric shifts in technologic possibilities, released as fall-out from defence-oriented goals, create forms appropriate to space-age desires and raise potentialities for hallucinogenic light-and-sound cultures which ultimately blow the mind.'

If anyone thinks this is a joke, he should start reading the architectural magazines to find out what's in store for him. The new generation are devoted to preparing megastructures. Megastructures are difficult to describe, they have to be seen, but basically they are like everything at Montreal's Expo 67 rolled into one and built about a mile high. They are autodestructive (important word that) and auto-renewing, through the agency of giant machines which perpetually roll up and down within them, ultimately controlled by giant computers.[69]

After a demolition job as accurate and as well observed as that, Hall hardly needed to invoke the standard British gibe against all modern architects — 'Their designers, of course, will still be in the few remaining bits of Victorian London . . .' — though this too is very well informed, since all of those whose prose style is identifiably mimicked above (including myself, who coined the phrase 'light-and-sound culture') were indeed living at that time in property built before 1910. But he could have acknowledged that our boredom with the inadequacies of that property, which we inhabited out of only a very limited range of choice, and with the Victorian infrastructure of malfunctioning services below it, was a powerful motive behind the demand for technological amelioration that powered so much megastructural thinking.

At first blush, one might have expected a critique of the kind mounted by Peter Hall to have come from the committed Left, but it was a very long time coming, and the reasons for the tardiness of this response are to be sought in the traditions and inner contradictions of left-wing thought itself. In spite of some toying with small-scale cottage housing by card-carrying members of the Communist Party of Great Britain in the early fifties, the traditions of the Left had become increasingly preoccupied with building on the very largest scale possible.

In the USA, for instance, the post-McCarthy survivors of the Old Left, their liberal sympathizers, and above all the great liberal-style political builders like Robert Moses in New York or Clark Kerr at Berkeley, seem to have been effectively committed to urban giantism and interstate planning. They took the Tennessee Valley Authority as their *beau idéal*, and studied, in 'multiversities', the problems of 'megalopolis', for which they proposed legislation that led to the urban-renewal programmes and mass-transit schemes which were to be the legal and financial constituency of the urban designers' megastructures.

In Britain, the Labour Party was not only the 'party of the masses', but it had also committed itself in the mid-sixties to the 'white heat of technology'. It had an even longer commitment in practice to large-scale urban renewal, going back to the slum-clearance agitations of the twenties and thirties, and practically every megastructure-type building in Britain depended on powers to purchase, requisition, condemn, build, rebuild, finance or plan that went back to originally socialist-inspired legislation.

In Europe, particularly France, paranoia about *la politique pavilionaire* (owner-occupation) kept most of the Left so solidly against single-family dwellings in their own plots of land that they were almost automatically in favour of very large mass-housing projects. Even without the examples of such housing schemes in the socialist countries of eastern Europe to emulate, their belief that the working classes should live in compact and central settlements where they could conveniently be rallied and deployed as a political army when the Revolution finally dawned ensured that they had no difficulty in remaining true to their Fourrierist traditions of the gigantic *phalanstère* as the proper abode of the working man.

When the Left finally began to mount cogent criticism of megastructure, it was with arguments that probably derive from the neo-Marxism of Herbert Marcuse, maintaining that the permissive freedoms offered by megastructure's adaptability and internal transiences were illusory, since all they involved were choices between fixed alternatives prescribed by the designers of the mega-system, and were thus as meaningless as the consumers' supposed choices between different products offered by the capitalist system's supermarkets. This critique did not come, to the best of my knowledge, from anywhere in the established and organized Left, but was put to me, appropriately enough, by dissident Parisian students on the second night of the *événements de Mai* in 1968. What is even more striking is that they were not students of sociology or politics, but of architecture. It was, in fact, internal criticism, coming — like all internal criticism — from architects who wanted to do a different kind of architecture.

For where Hall — to double back briefly — can be faulted is in having failed to observe that many of those on whose prose styles he had exercised his satirical wit had themselves begun to question megastructure and its exponents. He would have needed to be a quick reader to observe this as early as October 1968, but a close scrutiny of the pages of *Architectural Design,* for an outstanding example, would have shown him that the tide had just begun to turn. Thus he could have found a very sceptical view (the first in print) of Cumbernauld in the September issue, and an attack on Tange's Shizuoka office tower as early as May. It was not only the month that was significant here, but the author as well, since he was Günther Nitschke, whom many had hitherto regarded as the official apostle of Metabolism to the Europeans. Yet here was Nitschke attacking Tange for just those monumental image-making characteristics that had hitherto recommended his work to so many megastructuralists:

The single core not only acts as the main structural support for the building, but incorporates the services; thus that part of the architecture — *the services* — which is generally assumed to be the most likely to require early change, is integrated with that part — *the structure* — which is most likely to remain in position until the building is demolished. The whole is a cumbersome fantasia on an unsound premise. . . .[70]

Further suggestions that the Japanese had in some way failed appeared in the same magazine in December of that year from the (undeclared) hand of its assistant editor, Robin Middleton:

Arato Isozaki's sketch for a spatial city more than any other project might be said to have launched the Japanese Metabolists on their way to fame. . . . Since then students throughout the world have so effectively adjusted, transformed and contorted these prototypes that the hideous nature of the proposals is at last becoming apparent.
Yet for all its visionary quality, Isozaki's sketch seemed to have a new realism that made it more applicable than earlier Utopian notions. The slender concrete support and service towers were linked by lattice-work bridges that sailed lightly and loftily over tumbled Doric columns. The columns represented the old towns, the concrete pylons the new cities. It seemed that the wondrous new Megacities could be created high above the old towns, avoiding all the disagreeable complexities of usage, land-ownership and bureaucracy. Vested interests could be elegantly by-passed. . . .[71]

The sense of loss and disappointment signalled here also draws attention to one of the radical, anti-Establishment meanings of megastructure, one that had been promised not only by the Metabolists but also by Yona Friedman: that the ancient disorders and discontents of the cities could be overpassed, and a new world created in the sky, purified of the *membra disjecta* of past and exhausted civilizations on the ground below. That had been the promise; the performance was less exciting:

But like many seminal ideas, the Megacity has proved inelegant in practice. The first Japanese interpretations are of a most lumbering awkwardness. . . . Similarly Masato Ohtaki's much-lauded 'artificial land platform' at Sakaide is no more a megacity model than any other housing scheme built on a first floor slab. . . .

It is worth noting here that the grumbles so far are largely aesthetic ones about inelegance and lumbering awkwardness, plus a rather marginal one to the effect that Metabolism apparently could not deliver what it promised which does not really explain why not. However, the reasons why it could not so deliver were already being sketched elsewhere in this same issue of *Architectural Design*. Chris Abel, in an article that makes an early pitch for the advantages of ultra-low density and the 'lessons of dispersion', advances the following critique of megastructure:

. . . Berlin Free University has the distinction of being the nearest thing to the megastructure concept that is actually under construction. It is widely regarded as a model of the 'flexible city of the future' . . . . Any changes the system does permit must, however, be severely limited by the overlapping of such a mixture of activities, all of which are disciplined by the same constraints. It is difficult to see how the system can renew itself without serious disruption of its cohesive organisation.
The ideal underlying such proposals may be highlighted by a comparison between Archigram's Plug-In City and Scarborough College at Toronto (also merited [*sic*] as a prototype city structure) by John Andrews. In spite of the obvious differences in technology they make remarkably similar impressions. *Both are characterised by a closely integrated or cohesive ordering of multifarious activities. In both cases the image is a highly coherent one.*
It is this desire for coherence that negates the planners' efforts to come to terms with adaptive systems. A living system by the very nature of its self-organising properties will defeat any such imposition of rules. The necessity to compromise the system as circumstances change means that the urban system can never attain the controlled form that is the planner's ideal.[72]

These criticisms of Plug-In City and Scarborough are demonstrably valid; and as they wrote up the results of their academic safari through Nevada in *Learning from Las Vegas*, Robert Venturi and Denise Scott-Brown were being driven toward similarly anti-megastructural conclusions that were to become explicit and systematic when they rewrote the original article in book form.[73] However, it should be remembered apropos Plug-In City that Archigram, by the time of the Cushicle and Suitaloon of 1968, had come to the same conclusions themselves – that the permissive and adaptive qualities of the transient accommodations were of more interest to them than was the ordering coherence of the great frame of the megastructure. Six months before Chris Abel's strictures were printed, Archigram's various 'Popular Paks' at the aborted *Triennale di Milano* had served notice that the greatest practitioners of megastructure were phasing themselves right out of the concept, which had ceased to be innovative ('everybody can do megastructure now') and could no longer deliver the performance they sought from 'responsive environments'.

However, if megastructure had failed to deliver its apparent promise of 'the flexible city of the future', the sense of loss at its failure is at least a negative measure of the importance of that promise for a whole generation. For another of the meanings of megastructure was that it symbolized the libertarian aspirations of a whole post-Beatles generation. Cities, as found in real life or envisaged in conventional town-planning wisdom, were perceived to be too lumberingly unmanageable to satisfy the demands of what was described as 'the Now generation'. What they wanted was 'instant city', and although megastructure proved incapable of delivering it fast enough, it had seemed – as of 1964 – that it might. At Montreal Expo '67 it probably came as close as it ever would to realizing that promise in physical reality, but that physical reality could be examined and inhabited at Expo, and the gaps between vision and reality could be studied at first hand. The gaps were to become so clear that the former megaradicals could only maintain their radical posture by getting out of megastructure as fast as possible.

And as fast as they got out, the Establishment got in, enjoying for the moment an illusory afterglow of assumed radicalism. It took a little time for established conservatives and radical activists to separate out completely, and some desperate would-be radicals from the wrong side of the generation gap were to be seen striking megastructural attitudes years later, with effects as grotesque and depressing as those produced by a reading of Charles Reich's *The Greening of America* (New York, 1970). With hindsight it is clear, anyhow, that an increasingly compelling reason for the radicals to get out of megastructure was the press of Establishment figures trying to get in at the back, as architectural tradition began inexorably to reclaim megastructure's inherent monumentalism for its own.

Thus in July of 1968 the magazine *Progressive Architecture* (not notably radical ever, in spite of its title and some injudicious dabblings in hallucinogenic design) published a special issue under the title 'Omnibuilding'. Its contents proved to be, with rare exceptions, monumental megastyle buildings with all the permissive variability left out (in spite of claims to the contrary) and excessive 'coherence', and those undesirable 'imposed rules' castigated by Chris Abel, cemented firmly in:

. . . large-scale complex buildings made necessary by the growing congestion of metropolitan areas . . . we call them omnibuildings rather than megastructures because it is not their *mega* (great, mighty) quality which is important, but rather their *omni* (all) aspect that is of interest. These buildings represent a beginning attempt at a synthesis of all man's extensions. . . .[74]

Note the drastically narrowed sense in which the word 'megastructure' is used here; indeed by this date it is difficult not to call it an ignorant use of the word. Note also the close association of the words 'synthesis . . . all', which signals that we are back in the world of 'total architecture' from which most of the megastructuralists had been trying to break out. In any case, the gaff had already been blown by Philip Johnson at the very beginning of the issue: omnibuilding, he implied, is megastructure recalled to the ancient monumental traditions of architecture, thus:

The megacity requires megastructure. The problems are out of scale. The megastructure does not yet exist, but it must, and it will. It will if management is ready. It will if the public is ready. Above all, it will when our civilization is ready to create architecture. . . .[75]

'When our civilization is ready to create architecture. . . .' That takes us even further back than Gropius and his 'total architecture'; it is the true voice of Hermann Muthesius calling the Prussian state back to architectonic order in 1911. And after such statements it is hardly surprising that, in spite of introductory lip-service to flexibility and extensibility, there is little that is radical in the rest of the issue. Many old friends from the established roster of historical megaprototypes are trotted out again, but now supplemented by some non-adaptable or totally closed systems as well, like medieval fortresses or a plan of the Escorial.

However, if *Progressive Architecture* was backing up into a more traditional view of urban structure, it was far from backing winners. It illustrated or described some forty-six designs for omnibuildings: of these, ten had already been built (Cumbernauld, for instance), and of the other thirty-six only three were built in anything like the published form, and thirty were not built at all. Thus even the shrunken and conventionalized understanding of megastructure represented by omnibuilding was far from acceptable in the market-place of buildable concepts. Even the traditionalist aspects of megastructures were likely to remain as 'visionary' as the radical ones, in the sense that neither stood much chance of actually getting built. Both were, in their differing ways, part of the ancient architectural dream of imposing a grand order on a disorderly world; 'the only reason for megastructures', said Cesar Pelli, 'is the ambition of architects'.

However, what survived of the megastructure dream after 1968 was what remained in the hands of the traditionalists and the organs of establised power. The radicals had deserted the concept for one reason already given, namely that it could not deliver its permissive promises, but their overwhelming reason was increasingly that, if they were abandoning the conceptual basis of the high-technology bourgeois capitalist system, then they must abandon megastructure as well, since it shared the same conceptual basis.

Note how, once again, Philip Johnson had blown the gaff by saying that there would be megastructure when *management* was ready, before he said a thing about the *people* being ready. Megastructure was, obviously, close kin to Big Management; those to whom conglomerates and multi-nationals were unacceptable would find megastructure unacceptable too. Megastructures that could come anywhere near delivering even the limited permissiveness of Plug-In City would represent very massive investments in very high technology; neo-Marxists and neo-Luddites would therefore unite in finding megastructure unacceptable. Megastructure, almost by definition, would mean the destruction or overshadowing of small-scale urban environments; those who had just rediscovered 'community' in the slums would fear megastructure as much as any other kind of large-scale renewal programme, and would see to it that the people were never ready. For the flower-children, the dropouts of the desert communes, the urban guerrillas, the community activists, the politicized squatters, the Black Panthers, the middle-class amenitarians and the historical conservationists, the Marcusians, the art-school radicals and the participants in the street democracies of the *événements de Mai,* megastructure was an almost perfect symbol of liberal-capitalist oppression. It was condemned almost before it had a chance to happen.

As has been said, Paolo Soleri and his Arcologies alone survived this mass desertion — or almost alone: there remained residual constituencies of an exiguous kind for Moshe Safdie's Habitats and for Rudolf Doernach's much less

218 *Biomorphic Biosphere project (Glen Small, 1968 onwards). Almost unknown outside Los Angeles, Small's endlessly elaborated 'superstructure' is one of the few developed projects that exceeds the work of Soleri in scale – it is seen here branching across the full width of the Los Angeles basin – while being detailed in considerable depth, at least in sketch form. A system of organic-looking spicules supports streets and gardens 5,000 feet up in the air, with an occupancy of 250,000 souls per linear mile. The aim, more succinctly put than by the authors of other ecological megastructures, is to 'minimize taxation of natural resources . . . collects water . . . grows food . . . traps pollutants . . . phase out existing urban areas . . . return land to natural state'.*

buildable 'Biotectures', and Glen Small's romantic visions of garden-girt spicules branching habitably above Greater Los Angeles (**218**) continued to be loved locally. But when Justus Dahinden published *Stadtstrukturen für Morgen* ('urban structures for the future') in 1971, that *morgen* was already a fossil future, the book an unintended memorial to a dead movement, and the more affecting in that the sad demise of the beloved appeared not to have been noticed. With Dahinden, megastructure retires into the visionary tradition from which it had emerged, and is at one with the great still-born designs like Inigo Jones's Whitehall or Boullée's cenotaph for Isaac Newton. . . .

Within architectural circles, that is; elsewhere, megastructure could still show occasional belated stirrings of life. One such area was that part of Academe where Big Management was still thinkable. Rather like the mad inventor in the basement who has been working on something that will probably prove, in 1980, to be black-and-white television, two American systems-specialist professors – George B. Dantzig and Thomas L. Saaty, authors respectively of *Linear Programming and Extensions* and *Optimization in Integers and Related Extremal Functions* – popped up in 1973 with a book called *Compact City, a plan for a livable environment.* Exactly what 'livable' means in this context may come as a surprise to many readers:

In order to conserve and maximise the effective use of space and to lead to a less encumbered life, man needs to free himself from the syndrome of day-night cycles by utilising the facilities of the city more evenly throughout the twenty-four hour day. . . .[76]

An accompanying diagram shows how restaurant capacity could be reduced to a twenty-fourth of present levels by having the population take lunch on an even spread throughout the twenty-four hour cycle instead of all at midday! No architect's megastructural city in a single building went to such dictatorial extremes as this, but then Dantzig and Saaty appear to have conceived their mile-diameter, terrace-edged circular city-building in almost total innocence of what had been going on in architecture for the previous ten or fifteen years: one architect is credited for help with drawings, and there are references to Soleri, Fuller and Kikutake, but that is all.

Where *Compact City* fascinates while it repels is in revealing what a vast body of academic and managerial *idées reçues* of a megastructure-inducing kind had been in the air in the sixties. If Dantzig and Saaty could arrive at their Compact City almost entirely without architectural assistance, does this mean that megastructure was in some sense inevitable, that the internal logic of a managerial-capitalist society made megastructure historically necessary? Or did this body of established opinion simply make the idea of megastructure easier to formulate if one was determined to do so?

The factor of determination seems to be critical. However much architects of the sixties may have seemed to desire evidence that megastructures 'grew naturally out of the cities of the times', it can be historically observed that no megastructure consciously designed as such was ever built without some architectural monomaniac scheming and pushing, wheeling and dealing to make it come about. This was true from the beginning at Cumbernauld, where the Town Centre stands as it does and in the shape it does almost entirely because of the determination of Geoffrey Copcutt to make it so, however much other hands may have contributed to its detail design and execution. And personal determination remains critical right up to the ultimate end, which must in every sense, for the purposes of this study, be the Centre Pompidou — formerly known as the Centre Beaubourg — in Paris.

The commissioning and execution of this project, in fact, constitute a monument to the determination of more than one man, and it is unlikely that this, in some ways most extreme, of all built megastructures, would have been carried through at all without very influential supporters. One was indeed the most influential man in France, since the availability of the site and the initiation of the scheme both derive directly from a series of those 'presidential interventions' which have marked the recent town-planning history of Paris. The name of the Centre records this intervention for posterity, but, since it is closely linked to the virtual destruction of the whole of the area of Les Halles, will probably do no good at all to President Pompidou's posthumous reputation. Add to this the determination of the architects, Renzo Piano and Richard Rogers, who won the competition for the design in 1970; and the even greater determination of the engineer, Edmund Happold of Arup and Partners; and the less public but far longer sustained managerial determination of the *programmaticien* (so much more than a mere 'manager'!) François Lombard, whose connection with the scheme goes back to the writing of the competition brief; the result is the kind of 'body of will' required to create what will surely be, when completed, the most comprehensive standing memorial to the aspirations and style of the megastructure age.

The project is not, in fact, of overweening size; dimensionally it is average for megastructures that got built: a shade longer than Cumbernauld, not so tall as Place Bonaventure, for examples. Conceptually it is a shade less adventurous than the Fun Palace of Cedric Price and Joan Littlewood, because it does have permanent fixed floor levels. Everything on these floors is movable, however, so that, mechanically at least, it comes close to the *ludique* character of Constant's *Neo-Babylone.* However, it is far less free-form or participatory in its proposed uses than Constant's Situationist programme would have demanded; it is best regarded as an extreme case of the conventional category of *édifice polyvalente* serving as a cultural centre in more or less the currently established sense in France, only far more flexible and well serviced in use.

211

219 *Centre Pompidou, Paris: first model of competition project (Piano, Rogers and Franchini, 1970). This early and now slightly mystifying model, with its rounded Archigram-style corners, already exhibits the rudiments of the fully developed structural frame and the deep floor-trusses of the final versions.*

What adds to its comprehensiveness as a monument to the movement it terminates is that its visual aspect remains Archigrammatic. In some ways it has become more so: the competition-winning first version (**219**), with large-radiussed corners to its glass-house roof line, is superficially of the style of some of Archigram's 'Instant City' drawings, but the drastically revised second version that is being built (**220**) comes closer to Plug-In City in its visibly open frames, with communications etc. threaded through them, and even more so in the graphic detailing and the *ad hoc* transient-function implications of the very large presentation drawings that were made for it. These show a world of bright colours, keen shapes, inflatables, clip-on gadgetry, giant projection screens and all the rest of the good old imagery of fun and flexibility, stylishly drawn and photocollaged (**221**) by members of the Archigram-trained 'Crysalis' group who had come over from Los Angeles specifically to work on the project in the Paris office.

What is clear already, in its state of construction at the time of writing, is that the finished building should look remarkably like those sketches; indeed, it should look more like a megastructure even than the sketches do, because of the way the outer layers of the building-frame are handled. The vast clear floors are carried on trusses hung at the outer ends from the short arms of heroically sculptural cast-steel levers, which balance about the vertical columns with their long arms projecting well beyond into surrounding space. The extremities of the

220 *Centre Pompidou: model of the final design. The frame has here been regularized, with all its bays occupied to the same height, and braced by the external sub-frame which secures the outer ends of the levers supporting the floor-trusses (see 221). Across this face of the structure are draped the external escalators in their transparent tubes — a final buildable version of an idea that had haunted megastructure since the early sixties.*

221 *Centre Pompidou: part-section, presentation drawing. At the left is seen the system of levers which carries the outer ends of the trusses that support the clear and uninterrupted floors, and contain the services and mechanisms needed to make those floors freely and adaptably useful. More important, in some ways, is the drawing itself, a kind of grand summary, by members of the Archigram-trained Crysalis group, of the whole tradition of imagery of 'fun' and* la vie ludique *that had been accumulating for a decade.*

213

222 *Centre Pompidou: final model, street side. The 'wall of services' that almost brings together the two ends of the megastructure epoch, from the exposed and highly coloured service ducts of Mike Webb's Sin Centre to the defensive wall that Ralph Erskine's Byker turns against external disturbances of its internal life. Even the bright primary colours with which the ducts and pipes and power-packs are painted seem to recall the gaieties of the merry megastructural middle sixties. Whatever further megastructures may be built, Centre Pompidou seems likely to remain for a long time the most complete monument to the decade when the concept was born.*

long arms are then stabilized and linked together by an outer frame of lightweight horizontal and vertical struts, diagonally braced by tension-rods.

This not only gives the elevations a richer structural imagery, but also creates a servicing zone, outside the main floors, running the length and height of both sides of the building. Within and upon this frame and the zone it creates are hung, almost like sacred relics of the dreams of the sixties, such familiar devices as transparent tubular pedestrian walkways and escalators (**222**), coloured ducts and service-runs and equally highly-coloured capsules full of servicing machinery. The visual effect of these two image-rich elevations will ensure that what is seen standing on the Plateau Beaubourg in the name of Georges Pompidou will be perceived to be a megastructure: it answers the ultimate acid-test of looking like one.

This argument *ad visibilia*, though it deals with superficial externals, nevertheless touches the heart of the matter of the meaning of megastructure. Whatever

the social or anti-social, mechanical or functional, civic or environmental, professional, radical or conservative meanings that have been demonstrated by or imputed to megastructures, they are also a body of imagery, carrying the kind of imprecise but intensely emotive significations that visual images always do. These significations are not the same for all percipients; they abound in ambiguities and redundancies, and communicate with different effects even to different individuals in the same general class of observers, be they urban designers, community activists, the parka-hooded parties of schoolchildren on the open decks of Montreal Expo '67 or the floral-shirted and badge-bedecked experimental architects at the Folkestone conference the year before.

This study has throughout dealt mainly with architectural perceptions of megastructure, and rightly so, I submit, since it was architects who presented the concept and the word to the world, and they who first rejected it. One of the lessons of the architecture of the mid-twentieth century is that building types

215

come and go chiefly at the behest of the architectural consensus. The abandonment of high-rise dwellings, for example, did not begin because sociologists found them socially inadequate or because fearful accidents proved them structurally dangerous; bright-eyed young architects had already opted for low-rise high density even before Pruitt-Igoe had to be destroyed or Ronan Point had collapsed. Events like those merely served to confirm what had already become accepted wisdom among the front-runners of the profession.

So too with megastructure; its worst significations, ultimately, were in the eyes of architects, in some cases the same architects who had most loudly proclaimed its virtues when the concept was still new. In its end, as in its beginning, its most potent meaning is the architectural one, visually perceived by men at drawing-boards and modelling benches. As a way of imposing a form of order on 'the chaos of our cities' it was an invention of architects, whatever other tides of opinion appeared to support it; and it was finally abandoned by them because it offered to generate a form of order that they themselves could not manage.

That order threatened to become unmanageable whenever and wherever it strove to embrace other perceptions of the state of the cities. Architects strove to impose an architectural order because they found the cities architecturally incomprehensible; other orders of society found it incomprehensible in other ways, or, more often, found it not incomprehensible at all, and even preferred it the way it was — or found the way it was preferable to the way that the megastructuralists might want to make it! In this situation, megastructures were only likely to be taken seriously in culturally or economically sheltered environments where the words of architects would be heeded. By the end of the sixties the supply of such priviliged environments was about exhausted, and Plateau Beaubourg may well prove to be the last.

But it is also clear that, by then, the concept itself was about exhausted as well. Why? Why did that tide of opinion recede so quickly and leave the dozen or so built megastructures worthy of the name stranded like dinosaurs in a desert of distrust and misapprehensions? Possibly because the concept was faulted right through by an inner contradiction that could not be resolved. Some time around 1968 it seems to have been perceived that a city or a large part of a city designed by one man, or by any group unified enough to produce a comprehensible design, would be a parlously thin, starved and impoverished environment, both visually and in larger, less precise cultural terms; Thamesmead remains the extreme case, but the problem was manifestly present at Habitat in Montreal. It was also — I suspect — perceived, though not clearly articulated anywhere, that the logical solution to the problem was to leave so much liberty for the self-housing and self-determining intentions of the inhabitants that they had liberty also to destroy the megastructure itself. Peter Hall was obliquely right; 'autodestructive' was a prophetic as well as an important word, and since no architect who considers himself worthy of his craft can bear to stand by and see his designs destroyed, especially grand designs on the scale of the city, megastructure proved to be a self-cancelling concept.

Appendix: Maki on Megastructure

from Investigations in Collective Form (Washington University, St Louis, 1964), pp. 8–13.

The megastructure is a large frame in which all the functions of a city or part of a city are housed. It has been made possible by present day technology. In a sense, it is a man-made feature of the landscape. It is like the great hill on which Italian towns were built.

Inherent in the megastructure concept, along with a certain static nature, is the suggestion that many and diverse functions may beneficially be concentrated in one place. A large frame implies some utility in combination and concentration of function.

Urban designers are attracted to the megastructure concept because it offers a legitimate way to order massive grouped functions. One need only look at work in the recent Museum of Modern Art show of 'Visionary Architecture', to sense the excitement generated among designers by megaform. While some of the ideas displayed in the show demonstrate structural virtuosity at the expense of human scale and human functional needs, others have a quality which suggests no divergence between compacted, economic function and human use.

That utility is sometimes only apparent. We frequently confuse the potential that technology offers with a kind of compulsion to 'use it fully.' Technological possibility can be sanguinely useful only when it is a tool of civilized persons. Inhuman use of technological advance is all too frequently our curse. Optimum productivity does not even depend on mere concentration of activities and workers.

Paul Goodman says in *Communitas* (p. 13):

We could centralize or decentralize, concentrate population or scatter it. . . . If we want to continue the trend away from the country, we can do it; but if we want to combine town and country values in an agri-industrial way of life, we can do that. . . . It is just this relaxing of necessity, this extraordinary flexibility and freedom of choice in our techniques, that is baffling and frightening to people. . . . Technology is a sacred cow left strictly to (unknown) experts, as if the form of the industrial machine did not profoundly affect every person. . . . They think that it is more efficient to centralize, whereas it is usually more inefficient.

Technology must not dictate choices to us in our cities. We must learn to select modes of action from among the possibilities technology presents in physical planning.

One of the most interesting developments of the megaform has been done by Professor Kenzo Tange with MIT graduate students when he was a visiting professor there. In a series of three articles in the October issue of *Japan Architect*, Professor Tange presents a proposal for a mass-human scale form which includes a megaform and discrete, rapidly changeable functional units which fit within the larger framework.

Professor Tange says:

Short-lived items are becoming more and more short-lived, and the cycle of change is shrinking at a corresponding rate. On the other hand, the accumulation of capital has made it possible to build in large-scale operations. Reformations of natural topography, dams, harbors, and highways are of a size and scope that involve long cycles of time, and these are the man-made works that tend to divide the overall system of the age. The two

217

tendencies – toward shorter cycles and toward longer cycles – are both necessary to modern life and to humanity itself. (*Japan Architect*)

Tange's megaform concept depends largely on the idea that change will occur less rapidly in some realms than it will in others, and that the designer will be able to ascertain which of the functions he is dealing with fall in the long cycle of change, and which in the shorter. The question is, can the designer successfully base his concept on the idea that, to give an example, transportation methods will change less rapidly than the idea of a desirable residence or retail outlet? Sometimes, the impact and momentum of technology become so great that a change occurs in the basic skeleton of social and physical structure. It is difficult to predict to which part of a pond a stone will be thrown and which way the ripples will spread. If the megaform becomes rapidly obsolete, as well it might, especially in those schemes which do not allow for two kinds of change cycle, it will be a great weight about the neck of urban society.

The ideal is not a system, on the other hand, in which the physical structure of the city is at the mercy of unpredictable change. The ideal is a kind of master form which can move into ever new states of equilibrium and yet maintain visual consistency and a sense of continuing order in the long run.

This suggests that the megastructure which is composed of several independent systems that can expand or contract with the least disturbance to others would be more preferable to the one of a rigid hierarchical system.

In other words, each system which makes the whole, maintains its identity and longevity without being affected by others while at the same time engaged in dynamic contact with others. When optimum relationship has been formed, an environmental control system can be made. The system that permits the greatest efficiency and flexibility with the smallest organizational structure is ideal.

Two basic operations are necessary to establish this optimum control mechanism. One is to select proper independent functional systems and to give them optimum interdependency through the provision of physical joints at critical points. . . .

Although the megastructure concept presents the problems outlined above, it also has great promise for:

1 Environmental Engineering: Megastructure development necessitates collaboration between the structural and civil engineer. Possibilities in large spans, space-frames, light skin structures, prestressed concrete, highway aesthetics, and earth forming will be developed far beyond their present level. Large scale climatic control will be studied further. A new type of physical structure, environmental building, will emerge.

2 Multi-functional structures: We have, thus far, taken it for granted that buildings should be designed to fulfill one specific purpose. In spite of the fact that the concept of multi-functionalism must be approached with caution, it offers useful possibilities. We can within the megaform structure, realize combinations such as those in Kurokawa's 'Agricultural City'.

3 Infra-structure as public investment: substantial public investment can be made in infra-structures (the skeleton of megastructures) in order to guide and stimulate public structures around them. This strategy can be further extended to a new three-dimensional concept of land use where public offices will maintain the ownership and upkeep for both horizontal and vertical circulation systems.

References

1 Fumihiko Maki, *Investigations in Collective Form* (St Louis, 1964), p. 8.

2 Ralph Wilcoxon, *Council of Planning Librarians Exchange Bibliography* (Monticello, Ill.), 66, 1968, p. 2.

3 See the catalogue of the exhibition, published by the Museum of Modern Art, New York, 1964, and later editions under various imprints.

4 N. J. Habraken, *De Dragers en de Mensen* (Amsterdam, 1961); English version: *Supports, an alternative to mass housing* (London, 1971).

5 John W. Cook and Heinrich Klotz, *Conversations with Architects* (New York, 1973), p. 109.

6 J. M. Fitch, *American Building: the environmental forces that shape it* (Boston, 1972), caption on p. 263.

7 Scully used the phrase in his Annual Discourse at the Royal Institute of British Architects in April 1969, but it does not appear in the published transcripts.

8 *Casabella* (Milan), December 1961, p. 1.

9 *Architectural Forum* (New York), August/September 1964, p. 114.

10 *Journal of the American Institute of Planners* (Washington D.C.), July 1968, p. 230.

11 Antonio Sant'Elia, *Messaggio sull'Architettura* (Milan, 1914); English version (transl. Reyner Banham): *Theory and Design in the First Machine Age* (London, 1960; New York, 1961), p. 129.

12 Paolo Soleri, *The City in the Image of Man* (Boston, 1970), p. 14.

13 This resounding phrase comes from a note on the future of the pier in the monthly *Bulletin* of the *Institut de l'environnement*, Paris, for July 1975.

14 *Architectural Forum* (New York), August/September 1964, p. 75.

15 *Architectural Forum* (New York), March 1967, p. 72.

16 Sigfried Giedion, *Architektur und Gemeinschaft* (Hamburg, 1956); English version: *Architecture, You and Me* (Cambridge, Mass., 1958), p. 60.

17 See *Bauen + Wohnen* (Munich) VII, 1959, p. 235 ff.

18 *Cahiers du Centre scientifique et technique du bâtiment* (Paris), *livraison 31, cahier 204*, p. 21 ff.; also in a separately bound offprint publication from the Centre: *Comment construire au Sahara* (July 1958), p. 56 ff.

19 *Architectural Design* (London), December 1968, p. 565.

20 In Oscar Newman (ed.), *CIAM '59 in Otterloo* (London, 1961), p. 186.

21 *Japan Architect* (Tokyo), May 1959, p. 3.

22 Manfredo Tafuri, *l'Architettura Moderna in Giappone* (Rocca San Casciano, 1966), p. 155.

23 *Architecture d'aujourd'hui* (Paris), June/July 1962, p. 2.

24 Johan Huizinga, *Homo Ludens* (London, 1949).

25 Yona Friedman, *l'Architecture mobile* (Paris, 1970), p. 11.

26 *Architecture d'aujourd'hui* (Paris), September/November 1964, p. XLIII.

27 *Casabella* (Milan), December 1962, pp. 18 and 22 (incorrectly numbered in magazine); see also *Casabella,* July 1964, p. 50 ff. for a review of the book *La Città-Territorio* (Bari, 1964) and the various student projects.

28 *Casabella* (Milan), January 1962, p. 42 ff.

29 *Casabella* (Milan), August 1963, p. 3. This was a special issue devoted entirely to the Turin *quartiere direzionale* competition, and gives very full illustration of all the prizewinning entries.

30 Fumihiko Maki, *Investigations in Collective Form* (St Louis, 1964), pp. 4–13.

31 *Architectural Forum* (New York) 122, 1965, pp. 58–62 (April) and 58–61 (May).

32 *Architects' Journal* (London), 19 February 1969, p. 505.

33 *Architectural Forum* (New York), August/September 1964, p. 75.

34 Ulrich Conrads and H. G. Sperlich, *Fantastic Architecture* (London, 1962), pp. 25–6.

35 Tomás Maldonado, *La Speranza Progettuale* (Turin, 1970); English version: *Design, Nature and Revolution* (New York, 1972), pp. 27 and 101n.

36 Mechthild Schumpp, *Stadtbau-Utopien und Gesellschaft* (Gütersloh, 1972), p. 121.

37 *Journal of the American Institute of Planners* (Washington D.C.), July 1968, p. 230.

38 *Architectural Design* (London), June 1964, p. 304.

39 Notes on 'Marine City' in the catalogue *Visionary Architecture* (Museum of Modern Art, New York, 1961).

40 *Architects' Journal* (London), 29 July 1964, p. 253.

41 *New Scientist* (London), 14 May 1964, p. 433.

42 In Peter Cook (ed.), *Archigram* (London, 1972), p. 7.

43 Ibid., pp. 36 and 38.

44 *Japan Architect* (Tokyo), January 1967, p. 26 ff.; for the second competition, see *Japan Architect*, December 1967, p. 17 ff.

45 Moshe Safdie, *Beyond Habitat* (Cambridge, Mass., 1970), pp. 52–3.

46 See Guntis Plesums, 'Architecture and Structure as a System' in *Architecture Canada* (Toronto), April 1969, p. 23 ff.

47 *Architectural Design* (London), July 1967, p. 331.

48 Ibid., p. 332.

49 In Pierre Beaupré and Annabel Slaight (eds.), *Exploring Montreal* (Toronto, 1974), p. 22.

50 *Progressive Architecture* (New York), March 1973, p. 71.

51 *Architectural Forum* (New York), May 1966, p. 53.

52 Ibid., p. 30.

53 Günther Feuerstein, *New Directions in German Architecture* (New York, 1968), p. 50.

54 Paola Navone and Bruno Orlandoni, *architettura 'radicale'* (Milan, 1974), p. 20.

55 *Architectural Review* (London), February 1972, p. 80.

56 *Architectural Forum* (New York), March 1967, p. 40.

57 *World Architecture* (London) IV, 1967, p. 12.

58 *Architectural Forum* (New York), June 1967, p. 50.

59 Costantino Dardi, *Il Gioco Sapiente* (Padua, 1971), p. 153 ff.

References

60 O. M. Ungers and others, *Berlin 1995* (Berlin, 1969), p. 90.

61 *Architectural Review* (London), October 1972, p. 195.

62 Alan Colquhoun, unpublished lecture delivered as Bannister Fletcher Visiting Professor at University College, London, May 1972.

63 John W. Cook and Heinrich Klotz, *Conversations with Architects* (New York, 1973), p. 267.

64 *Domus* (Milan), January 1969 (no page number).

65 Paolo Soleri, *The City in the Image of Man* (Boston, 1970), p. 14.

66 *Architectural Association Quarterly* (London), April/July 1971, p. 63.

67 Justus Dahinden, *Stadtstrukturen für Morgen* (Stuttgart, 1971); English version: *Urban Structures for the Future* (London, 1972), p. 11.

68 In Lloyd Rodwin (ed.), *The Future Metropolis* (London, 1962), pp. 112–13.

69 *New Society* (London), 24 October 1968, pp. 602–3.

70 *Architectural Design* (London), May 1968, p. 201.

71 *Architectural Design* (London), December 1968, p. 565.

72 Ibid., p. 564.

73 Denise Scott-Brown and Robert Venturi, *Learning from Las Vegas* (London and Cambridge, Mass., 1972).

74 *Progressive Architecture* (New York), July 1968, p. 91.

75 Ibid., p. 89.

76 George B. Dantzig and Thomas L. Saaty, *Compact City, a plan for a livable urban environment* (San Francisco, 1973), p. 32.

Sources of Illustrations

Archigram Architects 10, 22, 82–4, 89–97, 99–102; The Architectural Association 148–51; *The Architectural Review* 37, 59, 107, 182a, 209; *Architecture Canada* 113, 114; courtesy Arcop Associates 124; Mary Reyner Banham 130, 131; Reyner Banham 7, 19, 27, 98, 121, 175, 186, 201–5, 208, 210; Bauhaus-Archiv, Berlin 217; Bazzechi-Foto, Florence 104; Brecht-Einzig Ltd 199; The British Petroleum Co. Ltd 23; courtesy Building Design Partnership 176; courtesy Candilis, Josic, Woods, Schiedhelm 145; Cement and Concrete Association 108–12, 184; courtesy Chamberlin Powell & Bon 32, 198; courtesy Melvin Charney 120, 122; Courtauld Institure of Art, London 5; Cumbernauld Development Corporation 181, 182b, 183, 185; courtesy François Dallegret 128; courtesy Davis, Brody & Associates 139; Michael Drummond, courtesy Arcop Associates 117, 123, 125, 126; Stephen Dunham, Kiku Obata 197; courtesy Yona Friedman 60–62, 64; John Fulker 140; courtesy Fuller & Sadao Inc. 169; GLC Photographic Unit 206, 207; by permission of the Greater London Council 76; courtesy of Gregotti Associati 154–6; Habegger Ltd, Thun 118; Hans-Sa, courtesy Arcop Associates 115; Hans-Sa, courtesy Harold Ship 129; Etienne Hubert, courtesy of Paul Maymont 65, 66; Martin Hürlimann 4; courtesy Arato Isozaki 57; courtesy François Jamagne 33; Kawasumi, courtesy Kenzo Tange 48, 50, 52; The Kobal Collection, London 103; Sam Lambert 187; Landesbildstelle Württemberg, Stuttgart 6; courtesy Denys Lasdun & Partners 132, 133; courtesy Fumihiko Maki 75; Mann Brothers, courtesy Patrick Hodgkinson 200; Barbara Martin 196; Marshall D. Meyers 36; Donald Mill, courtesy Denys Lasdun & Partners 159; John Mills Photography Ltd, courtesy of Runcorn Development Corporation 189; Osamu Murai, courtesy Kenzo Tange 51, 54; Museum of Modern Art, New York, courtesy Hans Hollein 12; Jon Naar, courtesy of Davis, Brody & Associates 191, 192; National Aeronautics and Space Administration, Washington 16; National Film Board of Canada, courtesy Melvin Charney 119; Netherlands National Tourist Office, London, 21; Richard Nickle, courtesy of Reginald Malcolmson 41; Collection Claes Oldenburg, courtesy Hans Hollein 13; courtesy John C. Parkin 63; Chris F. Payne, courtesy Arcop Associates 116; courtesy Cesar Pelli, Gruen Associates 40, 77, 177–80; courtesy Piano & Rogers 219, 220, 222; The Port Authority of New York and New Jersey 25; courtesy Cedric Price 85–8; John Reeves 134; Royal Town Planning Institute, Journal 78; Scarborough College, Toronto 135–7; courtesy Colin St John Wilson 171; Shokokusha Publishing Co. Inc., Tokyo 45; courtesy Glen Small 218; courtesy Alison and Peter Smithson 30, 81; courtesy James Stirling 31, 157, 158; courtesy Kenzo Tange 46, 47, 53, 55; courtesy Stanley Tigerman 168; Eitaro Torihata, courtesy of Kisho N. Kurokawa 74; United States Information Service, London 1; United States Navy 17; University of Winnipeg 141, 142; courtesy Peter Winchester 188; *World Architecture* 144.

Illustrations have been reproduced from the following publications:
Le Corbusier, *The Radiant City* (Faber & Faber, London) 2; Justus Dahinden, *Stadtstrukturen für Morgen* (Verlag Gerd Hatje, Stuttgart) 11, 216; Museum of Modern Art, *The New City: Architecture and Urban Renewal* 160–64; Vincent Scully Jr, *Louis I. Kahn* (George Braziller, New York) 34, 35, 38; Paolo Soleri, *The City in the Image of Man* (MIT Press, Cambridge, Mass.) 15, 214; Donald Wall, *Visionary Cities: the Arcology of Paolo Soleri* (Praeger, New York) 213.

Select Bibliography

For the specialist reader, there is no doubt at all about what he should read next: Ralph Wilcoxon, *Council of Planning Librarians Exchange Bibliography* (Monticello, Ill.) No. 66, 1968, which, though rendered marginally incomplete by later publications, is still so full (especially if taken together with other bibliographies on, for example, Soleri, to which Wilcoxon refers) and wide-ranging that it must remain for a long time the true foundation of all megastructure studies.

For the general reader, there is no equally obvious place from which to set out; the most general chart of the territory is Justus Dahinden, *Urban Structures for the Future* (London and New York, 1972) — with the important proviso that 'the future' simply means 'not today' and the book is entirely innocent of any completed structures.

For general illumination, it is necessary to read the passages on megastructure in Fumihiko Maki, *Investigations in Collective Form* (St Louis, 1964), but since this book is now very difficult to find, the relevant pages have been appended to the present work. In the same way, the book version of *Archigram*, edited by Peter Cook (London, 1972; New York, 1973) is also to be rated as basic reading, though it is no substitute for the original 'comics' themselves.

For a detached, amused and blessedly common-sense view of the whole phenomenon of megastructure in full flower, read Denise Scott-Brown, 'Little magazines in architecture and urbanism' in *Journal of the American Institute of Planners (*Washington D.C.), July 1968. Another short coverage which is often cited together with Scott-Brown is the present author's 'A Clip-On Architecture', a special issue of *Design Quarterly* (Minneapolis), No. 63, 1965. More 'flavour of the times' can be gained from the catalogue of the Museum of Modern Art show *The New City: architecture and urban renewal* (New York, 1967), and those who want to wallow in a full year of unbridled megastructure optimism — 1967 again — should address themselves to *Architectural Forum* (New York) vols. 127 and 128, which cover that year.

On more specific topics, Soleri covers himself well and at very full spread in the giant MIT Press volume Paolo Soleri, *The City in the Image of Man* (Boston, 1970); Habraken is rather elusive in the pioneering book N. J. Habraken, *Supports, an alternative to mass housing* (London, 1971; New York, 1972). The French Connection are given effective summary treatment in Michel Ragon, *Où vivrons-nous demain?* (Paris, 1963), with Friedman explaining himself in considerable detail in Yona Friedman, *l'Architecture mobile* (Paris, 1970) and *Pour une architecture scientifique* (Paris, 1971). Safdie is to be found at some (combative) autobiographical length in Moshe Safdie, *Beyond Habitat* (Cambridge, Mass. and London, 1970).

Beyond that again one should point to the series *New Directions in* (e.g.) *Japanese Architecture,* published by Studio Vista (London) and Braziller (New York) in 1968–9, which were commissioned and written at the height of the period of megastructure enthusiasm, and reflect in some detail, country by country, the state of play within the general architectural ideas prevalent at the time.

Index

223